COMPLETE CONDITIONING FOR BASKETBALL

National Basketball Strength & Conditioning Association

Bill Foran

Editor

HUMAN KINETICS

Library of Congress Cataloging-in-Publication Data

Names: National Basketball Strength & Conditioning Association author. |
  Foran, Bill, editor.
Title: Complete conditioning for basketball / National Basketball Strength
  & Conditioning Association ; Bill Foran, editor.
Description: Champaign, IL : Human Kinetics, 2026. | Includes
  bibliographical references and index.
Identifiers: LCCN 2024024022 (print) | LCCN 2024024023 (ebook) | ISBN
  9781718216600 (paperback) | ISBN 9781718216617 (epub) | ISBN
  9781718216624 (pdf)
Subjects: LCSH: Basketball--Training. | Basketball--Physiological aspects.
  | Physical fitness.
Classification: LCC GV885.35 .N39 2026 (print) | LCC GV885.35 (ebook) |
  DDC 796.32307/7--dc23/eng/20240703
LC record available at https://lccn.loc.gov/2024024022
LC ebook record available at https://lccn.loc.gov/2024024023

ISBN: 978-1-7182-1660-0 (print)

This publication is written and published to provide accurate and authoritative information relevant to the subject matter presented. It is published and sold with the understanding that the author and publisher are not engaged in rendering legal, medical, or other professional services by reason of their authorship or publication of this work. If medical or other expert assistance is required, the services of a competent professional person should be sought.

The web addresses cited in this text were current as of May 2024, unless otherwise noted.

Developmental Editor: Julie Marx Goodreau; **Managing Editor:** Hannah Werner; **Copyeditor:** Laura B. Magzis; **Proofreader:** Alan Bellinger; **Indexer:** Andrea J. Hepner; **Senior Graphic Designer:** Sean Roosevelt; **Cover Designer:** Keri Evans; **Cover Design Specialist:** Susan Rothermel Allen; **Photograph (cover):** Sam Hodde/Getty Images; **Photographs (interior):** Terek Pierce/© Human Kinetics, unless otherwise noted; **Photo Asset Manager:** Laura Fitch; **Photo Production Manager:** Jason Allen; **Senior Art Manager:** Kelly Hendren; **Illustrations:** © Human Kinetics; **Printer:** Sheridan Books

We thank the Miami Heat for assistance in providing the location for the photo shoot for this book.

Human Kinetics books are available at special discounts for bulk purchase. Special editions or book excerpts can also be created to specification. For details, contact the Special Sales Manager at Human Kinetics.

Printed in the United States of America   10 9 8 7 6 5 4 3 2 1

The paper in this book is certified under a sustainable forestry program.

Human Kinetics
1607 N. Market Street
Champaign, IL 61820
USA

United States and International
Website: **US.HumanKinetics.com**
Email: info@hkusa.com
Phone: 1-800-747-4457

Canada
Website: **Canada.HumanKinetics.com**
Email: info@hkcanada.com

E8853

COMPLETE CONDITIONING FOR BASKETBALL

Contents

Foreword

Since Micky Arison and Pat Riley took the reins of the Miami Heat organization in 1995, it has been all about building a world-class organization that would compete for championships. One of the key factors in performing at such a high level was ensuring that our players were in optimal shape. Fortunately, we had a Hall of Fame strength and conditioning coach, Bill Foran, to make that happen.

Bill designed off-season programs that pushed our players to get faster, stronger, leaner, and more functional in their movements so that they were ready to go full speed into training camp. He also developed programs to help our players continue to build strength and endurance so that they would maintain their high performance levels throughout the long grind of the season schedule and into the playoffs.

The best training programs are self-motivating. It is a challenge for players to continuously work to improve their bodies. But they love it when they see the results—getting to a loose ball quicker than the opposition, using a strong body base to box out and hold position for a rebound, eluding a more fatigued opponent and still having the bounce to rise high and drill a game-deciding jumper. Those kinds of things make the big investment in conditioning all worth it.

Bill's work and guidance were always grounded in the latest science, and his methods were among the best in the field of player performance training. His son Eric is now the Heat's head strength and conditioning coach, and he, like his peers who have worked with other NBA teams for years, has followed Bill's path, incorporating the latest information, technology, equipment, and protocols to enable his team's players to perform at their peak.

The National Basketball Strength & Conditioning Association experts assembled by Bill to create this book present an opportunity for players and coaches to learn and apply the best and most comprehensive basketball conditioning information available. From basic training principles to exercises, drills, and sample workout plans to develop movement skills, strength, power, flexibility, agility, and endurance, as well as to nutrition, rest, and return-to-activity advice, and finally to a year-round conditioning program, *Complete Conditioning for Basketball* is a must-have manual for serious players and an essential guide for coaches who want to have the best-conditioned team in every game throughout the season and in postseason competition.

Those who ultimately excel on the court don't do so simply because of their genetic gifts. Even the most talented athletes must have a growth mindset and the drive necessary to train and develop their bodies and minds to become champions.

Erik Spoelstra
Head Coach, Miami Heat

Preface

The original version of this book was published in 2007. When we decided to do an update, we quickly realized that so much has changed in how the game of basketball is played (and therefore what we prioritize in our strength and conditioning programs) that a simple revision was not possible. For example, in the 2006-2007 season NBA teams took an average of 6,536 shots from the field, 1,389 of which were three-pointers. In the 2023-2024 season, teams took an average of 7,290 shots from the field, 2,879 of which were three-pointers. In just these shooting stats alone, we can see that the game is being played at a faster tempo with more than double the emphasis on perimeter shooting—both of which have significant player training implications. Similar changes have occurred at the college and high school levels, where more than half of the states in the U.S. now use a shot clock.

With these and many other changes to the game in mind, we went about constructing an entirely new book to present the current and most effective training information and protocols for elite basketball performance. So, whereas the 2007 publication contained only 8 chapters, this book totals 12 to provide more detail and training activities for each basketball performance factor. Another reason for expanding the book was to adequately address players' and coaches' growing interest in the "Why?" behind the recommended methods, activities, and programs. You will find those explanations here. Also, since the first edition was published, the sport has gained a greater appreciation for the holistic development of athletes and the healthy behaviors that contribute to conditioning and performance, so in this edition we emphasize nutrition, sleep/rest and recovery, and postinjury guidelines, among other vital components, for the dual purposes of promoting players' well-being and fine-tuning their bodies' ability to respond optimally to the training methods set forth in this book.

Sport science knowledge has advanced significantly in the past 17 years, contributing to many new and improved protocols and programs used at the top levels of basketball. Chapter 1, The Pillars and Science of Basketball Conditioning, provides a brief background on the scientific disciplines and the expertise that has had the greatest impact. You will learn how the thinking and protocols in those science specialties have evolved, including the development of the cutting-edge technology used today that helps coaches and athletes to make informed decisions and implement the best training methods in the weight room and on the court.

Chapter 2, Player Assessment, explains the critical role of relevant, accurate evaluations. Essential for a successful basketball strength and conditioning program, such information is necessary to both determine players' current physical status and design the most beneficial training plan. We know what physical attributes and capabilities are associated with elite basketball performance. A better understanding of those physical qualities, how to measure them, and how to use that data to customize training that addresses deficiencies and enhances current strengths is invaluable in helping coaches and players make the best possible decisions when developing a training program. We present a plethora of useful assessment options, explain how to employ them, and then provide examples of how to use that information most beneficially.

Proper flexibility exercises and warm-up activities remain among the most overlooked aspects of training by players and coaches, despite the obvious consequences of doing so. That is why we chose to emphasize these topics in this book and tried to offer inspiring options that would more likely be used than the old, boring, static stretching exercises that everyone has grown to hate since elementary-school physical education classes. In chapter 3, Movement Preparation, we cover a part of training and performance that has only recently been properly appreciated. Basketball is a multiplanar game that requires athletes to perform dynamic movements such as running, cutting, and jumping proficiently. A well-designed and engaging movement preparation routine increases the athlete's readiness to accelerate, decelerate, jump, and change direction before beginning workout drills and tip-offs. In chapter 4, Mobility and Flexibility Training, we explain the significance of flexibility and mobility in basketball performance and explain how to best train players to achieve proper muscle elasticity and joint range of motion.

Strength is the quality underpinning all actions on the basketball court and is an essential base required to increase athletic performance and reduce injury risk. Strength development and the best training methods for this physical attribute are covered in detail in chapter 5, Strength Training, and chapter 6, Core Training. These two chapters provide a wealth of information and several dozen exercise options. Fundamentals of strength training and basic strength science are included, as well as sets, reps, and step-by-step technique descriptions. We'll show how players from middle school to the pros can build their strength to get to the basket through traffic, set a stonewall pick, establish and hold their position in the lane, and generally compete to their highest potential.

Power is the combination of strength and speed. Explosiveness is the name of the game these days, and it can be developed in the weight room with the plyometric exercises covered in chapter 7, Power Training. Increased power boosts speed, strength, agility, and jumping. Players who succeed in the sport as it is played now all have a good amount of power at their disposal, and more often than not the winning team is the one with the most powerful athletes on the floor.

Speed and agility, in combination, may be the purest expression of athleticism. When sprinting and changing direction, several aspects of physical performance merge into a single event. Strength, power, mobility, flexibility, balance, and coordination all play vital roles in how quickly an athlete can get from point A to point B. Chapter 8, Speed and Agility Training, covers the most important concepts and drills that will maximize the athlete's ability to cover ground, create space, and close angles on the court.

Playing basketball at a high level requires that the athletes be in great overall condition. That means they need sufficient strength and stamina to compete effectively on the court. And, since games are often decided in the last few minutes, the players and teams that are most resistant to fatigue and the lapses in play resulting from it have a huge advantage over the lesser-conditioned opponents. Chapter 9, On-Court Conditioning, explains how to establish a solid conditioning base that will allow you to come out on top in crunch time.

The body—even the most highly conditioned one—can take only so much stress over a period of time. Chapter 10, Recovering and Resting, addresses what strength and conditioning experts have come to appreciate: the need for recovery and rest for athletes to perform at their best. Starting with sleep and nutrition, the two most important components of recovery, chapter 10 presents the latest and best active and passive recovery protocols that coaches and players can use to safeguard health, ensure readiness for training, and obtain proper freshness of the body for competition.

Injuries happen in all sports, and high-performance basketball programs should be ready to deal with them. It is pivotal that the rehabilitation and the return to sport process is conducted properly to minimize risk of reinjury while maximizing performance upon return. Chapter 11, Reconditioning and Returning to Play, explains the proper steps to take after a player has successfully rehabbed from an injury or had an extended time away from competition for other reasons to get the athlete retrained to return to full participation on the court. This process must be very deliberate, with checkpoints along the way to ensure the proper pace of reconditioning, with the ultimate goal of getting the athlete to a point of being even better prepared than previously to perform.

In chapter 12, Complete Conditioning Program, we pull everything together. We saved it until the last because all the information preceding it is important to fully appreciate why the program components were included and how they complement one another. This plan of action shows you how to organize all the key aspects of high-performance conditioning for basketball, be it at the youth, high school, college, or NBA level.

Let's get started training!

Chapter 1

The Pillars and Science of Basketball Conditioning

Nick Cammett/Getty Images

A basketball player's success on the court is dependent on the status of four pillars of performance (see figure 1.1).

1. **Physical:** attributes and abilities of the player's body
2. **Technical:** demonstrated skills applied in competition
3. **Tactical:** knowledge and execution of game tactics
4. **Psychological:** mental makeup, focus, and toughness

Players who are consistently proficient in applying their athleticism, skills, knowledge of the game, and mental approach will achieve success.

These basketball performance pillars are dependent on each other. For example, increasing athletic ability through training supports greater skill development. Jumping higher and accelerating faster allow a player to practice shooting from a greater distance, to be stronger with the ball, and to dribble at higher speeds. Physical fitness also sharpens the execution of game tactics and decision making. In the fourth quarter, as fatigue mounts in the body and brain, the player with a fitter and more resilient body is more likely to make the smart play. To improve in the four basketball performance pillars, a basketball player needs a complete performance plan that addresses each area.

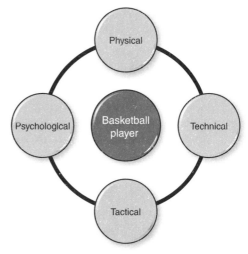

Figure 1.1   Four pillars of basketball performance.

Training the physical pillar—what is commonly referred to as strength and conditioning—focuses on three interrelated factors (see figure 1.2):

1. Body structure
2. Movement
3. Athleticism

Body structure is the dimensions, composition, and form of the human body. This includes height, wingspan, body weight, and body fat percentage. It also includes how those dimensions, and their composition of bone, lean tissue (i.e., muscle and organ tissue), and fat, are put together in a human form—in other words, an athlete's body type and posture. Within a

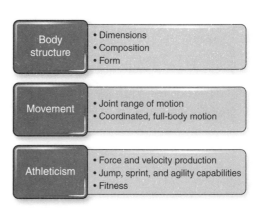

Figure 1.2   Components of the physical pillar.

performance plan, body structure affects exercise selection and an athlete's movement potential. On the court, body structure may dictate playing position (i.e., taller players tend to play frontcourt positions) or strengthen defensive prowess (i.e., longer wingspans cover more area of a passing lane).

Movement involves the range of motion of joints (ankle, hip, shoulder, etc.) and the coordinated motion of the human body structure in controlled body weight tasks like walking, squatting, and lunging (as opposed to athletic tasks described next). Within a performance plan, movement gives insight into limitations or excesses of range of motion that may lead to compensation. On the court, this may take the form of a defender who cannot extend the arms overhead when trying to achieve "verticality" or a player who chooses to defend in a high stance, rather than a low stance.

Athleticism is the expression of movement with force and velocity, often repeatedly. Jumping, sprinting, and agility form the foundation of explosive movement in basketball. The ability to perform these explosive movements repeatedly, and recover from them, throughout the course of a game or training session represents an athlete's fitness. While athletic expression is the pinnacle of the physical pillar—and the most seen on highlight reels—body structure and movement certainly have an influence on athleticism. Within a performance plan, training can help improve a player's athleticism. A weaker athlete may need time in the weight room, focusing on strength and power. An athlete who needs six weeks to recover from an ankle injury may need to focus on his fitness with treadmill training sessions. On the court, athleticism is demonstrated every time a player explodes to the rim, changes direction on defense, and sprints in transition.

THE SCIENCE BEHIND THE TRAINING

Training today's basketball players to achieve their potential involves applying a mixture of physiological, biomechanical, psychological, and neurological knowledge, along with technology and analytics to design a customized program. A single metric should never drive a decision regarding a team's or individual athlete's training. But when metrics spanning a spectrum of key factors are evaluated in aggregate, informed decisions can be made as to where deficiencies remain and what training modifications should be instituted to address them.

To help understand how these scientific and technical factors come into play, here is how they might apply to an important performance area in the game: rebounding. First, we would look at the key on-court performance indicators of a good rebounder. While results-based data like total rebounds, rebounds per minute played, or percentage of rebounds claimed from available opportunities (missed shots) on the court are certainly useful, what is of more interest when it comes to training a player to rebound better are the factors that make a good rebounder that can then be tested, trained, and improved. Therefore, we would want to focus on lower-body strength, power, footwork, flexibility, and body weight.

FUNCTIONAL MOVEMENT SCREEN

In the 1990s physical therapist Gary Gray presented a new way of thinking about and evaluating muscle function. Rather than concentrating on muscle flexion, extension, adduction, and abduction, Gray's approach centered on the operation of kinetic chains and the science of functional anatomy. Whereas muscle activity involved in moving a single joint had previously been the anatomical interest in sports training, Gray got the sports training community to consider how muscles act to move interrelated groups of joints and muscles work together to perform movements.

Recognizing the significant implications of Gray's thesis, another physical therapist, Gray Cook, then created a tool for practitioners such as strength and conditioning coaches to evaluate the functionality of people's movement patterns. Cook's 2003 book *Athletic Body in Balance* was a breakthrough in the field. In it, Cook demonstrates how functional movement screening can be used to identify deficiencies and inform training to improve athletes' movement proficiency.

The Functional Movement Screen involves the assessment of several movements by athletes, including such things as a deep squat, hurdle step, in-line lunge, active straight-leg raise, and push-up. By evaluating athletes' performance of these movements, one can gauge imbalances and deficiencies in their mobility and stability. This information, in turn, can dictate specific training prescriptions to address the problem areas and develop the athletes' movement patterns.

Now, let's break down the movement skills that make for a good rebounder. One is proper ranges of motion because proper joint mechanics reduce the risk of injury and allow the athlete to absorb and produce force. Key ranges of motion involved in rebounding are ankle dorsiflexion, thoracic extension and rotation, and shoulder flexion. Each of these can be evaluated in various ways, including normal goniometer methods and dynamic testing. The Functional Movement Screen (FMS), explained in the sidebar, is a simple and effective way to assess dynamic movement.

The next step in evaluating the ability to rebound is strength testing, since strength is necessary to maintain position on the floor when space is heavily contested. Traditional weight-room tests such as the squat, deadlift, mid-thigh isometric pull, single-leg squat derivatives, or any other exercise that is relevant to strength and rebounding can be inserted here. With a large enough data set, other considerations like strength to body weight ratio or positional norms may be included.

Next, we would evaluate speed of movement or power. A traditional countermovement jump is an easy way to measure vertical power by simply measuring jump height or total height reached. This test works well for post players who are traditionally two-legged jumpers, but for wings and guards who may be crashing the lane from the perimeter for rebounds, a max vertical jump with approach may be a more appropriate evaluation. Since the athlete's height and wingspan play an important part, the total height reached with the fingertips might be a better choice than the actual height jumped. A player who has a standing reach of 8 feet, 4 inches (2.5 m) and a vertical jump of 30 inches (76 cm) (touches 10 feet, 10 inches [3.3 m]) is still at a disadvantage compared to a player with a standing reach of 9 feet (2 m) and a vertical jump of 27 inches (69 cm) (touches 11 feet, 3 inches [3.4 m]).

Rebounding is but one of the many performance-related abilities that can be strengthened by a science-based approach. The following chapters discuss assessing, training, and programming—the scientific knowledge that can be applied to improve basketball players in every aspect of the game.

SPECIFIC SCIENCES APPLIED IN A BASKETBALL PLAYER'S PHYSICAL TRAINING

Before we get immersed in the assessments, exercises and drills, workouts, and programs involved in developing the most physically prepared player, we should take note of the specific sciences that have contributed to our understanding of what training needs to be done and how it should be done.

Anatomy and Biology

Body structure and makeup, the first of the three interrelated factors comprising the physical pillar, significantly affects a player's athleticism. This includes height, wingspan, body weight, and body fat.

Height plays a significant role in basketball. Taller players have an advantage when it comes to rebounding, blocking shots, interior defense protecting the rim, and passing and shooting over defenders simply due to their height. However, shorter players can excel at basketball with exceptional skills, quickness, and a high basketball IQ. Muggsy Bogues was a star in college and the NBA at 5 feet, 3 inches (1.6 m), and many other players short in stature have played major college and professional basketball by working hard on their bodies and skill set to compensate for what they lack in height.

These days a body measure of even more interest to coaches and scouts than height is a player's wingspan, the distance from the tip of the athlete's middle finger on one hand to the tip of the middle finger on the other hand with the arms extended fully to the sides. Wingspan is perhaps the most significant factor in what is referred to as a player's "length" and is very advantageous when it comes to guarding an opponent, cutting off the passing lanes, rebounding, shot blocking, and even passing and shooting in traffic. Though it is a factor, height alone does not dictate a player's wingspan or length. Players of the same height can have very different wingspans. An athlete with a long wingspan can play much bigger than

FAST-TWITCH AND SLOW-TWITCH MUSCLE FIBERS

Body composition entails more than just the percentage of body fat. It also involves the bundles of individual muscle fibers that comprise skeletal muscles. At a very basic level, these fibers are usually categorized as fast twitch or slow twitch. This distinction is based on how those muscle fibers respond to training and physical activity. While every human has both fast- and slow-twitch fibers, rarely does anyone have the same number of each.

Basketball players who have a predominance of fast-twitch fibers are often quicker and more explosive athletes and are commonly referred to as being "twitchy" or "bouncy." That is because fast-twitch musculature is advantageous in performing sudden bursts of movement like sprinting, jumping, and quick changes of direction, all particularly important in basketball. Fast-twitch muscle speed can be improved with proper training. Power exercises in the weight room, intense agility drills, sprints, and max jumps will improve the speed of fast-twitch muscle activity.

Slow-twitch musculature contracts more slowly and contributes most in performing endurance activities. While elite basketball players typically have more fast-twitch than slow-twitch fibers and fast-twitch is a factor in a player's potential, muscle fiber makeup is hardly the sole determinant of success in the sport.

a similarly tall athlete with a short wingspan. That is why, from the high school level to the NBA draft combine, wingspan, not just height, is of such interest.

Body weight and body fat are two factors comprising body structure and makeup that an athlete can control. Proper weight and body fat are crucial for basketball players to be at their best. Weight and body fat affect conditioning, speed, agility, jumping ability, and even injury risk.

A key to proper weight and body fat is nutrition. No athlete can out-train a poor diet. Male basketball players are at their best when they have less than 10 percent body fat. Most NBA players have 6 to 10 percent body fat. An effective training program along with proper nutrition can help players achieve and maintain a healthy and athletic body composition.

Biomechanics

Biomechanics is important to the physical pillar of performance because it provides a systematic, scientific way to analyze and improve players' movements when they are training, practicing, and competing. Biomechanical analysis can detect and correct wasted movements that diminish efficiency and misaligned body parts that can lead to injuries when running, cutting, jumping, and so forth. The goal is to help the athletes achieve movement proficiency to perform skills as quickly, powerfully, and adeptly as possible, to fine-tune their training technique, and to prevent injury.

Technology in biomechanical analysis of athletic performance has advanced significantly in recent years. Wearable devices, 3D cameras, and force plates gather movement information and images that are fed into computer programs to help us understand things that are not apparent to the human eye. Speed, power, vertical jump, landing mechanics, asymmetries, and workload can all be monitored with this technology. With detailed movement assessments gained through this technology we can spot movement deficiencies and help players work to achieve optimal movement patterns for performance and training and to avoid potential injuries.

Coaches and athletes who do not have access to this technology should still be diligent in trying to monitor and improve biomechanics. Most basketball coaches have a good mental representation of what proper technique or form is in executing the fundamental movement skills that are important to successful performance in the sport. If what they see in their players' movements fails to match their well-developed mental picture of correct running form, jumping mechanics, change of direction, and first-step mechanics, they can point out the flaws, demonstrate and (re)teach the proper mechanics, observe the players practicing the proper form, and then see the players demonstrate their improved movement patterns in competition.

A biomechanical analysis is also important for athletes returning to activity after injury. With a baseline biomechanical assessment of the player pre-injury, the goal is to ensure the athlete at least gets back to those baseline levels of movement proficiency and continues to improve to help prevent future injuries.

Physiology

The third factor in the physical pillar is physiology, the study of how the human body works. Of more specific interest in basketball conditioning is exercise physiology, the study of how the body responds to physical activity.

Since basketball is a game of short, intense, and repeated bouts of activity, players' bodies must be trained to perform in such bursts of action throughout a game, game after game. So, there are both anaerobic and aerobic components to the conditioning process, with the anaerobic component being the primary energy system.

Researchers have for many years studied the physiological demands on basketball players' performance while strength and conditioning coaches have attempted to ensure that their training programs effectively address those demands. In their review of various types of efforts to monitor and then match players' training loads with their physical exertion required in game performance, Fox, Scanlan, and Stanton (2017) note that the intermittent nature of basketball and variations in demands imposed between playing positions and level of anaerobic and aerobic fitness mean that some players may reach a higher volume of work for the entire session, whereas others may do less work overall but consistently reach higher intensities. Therefore, it is important that both volume and intensity be considered when planning the physical training players need to excel in competition.

Strength, power, agility, and coordination are the premium physiological attributes for basketball players and therefore what our training focuses on most in this book. Enhanced, balanced strength throughout an athlete's body can also help to prevent injuries. Greater explosive power allows players to run faster, jump higher, and move quicker. Improved agility makes an athlete's movements more efficient and easier. Combined, these attributes constitute much of what we refer to as a player's athleticism.

Furthermore, players who see and feel their bodies developing realize what this improved athleticism can mean on the court and gain a great deal of confidence in their game. Without getting into detail about the neurophysiology involved in the mind-body connection, suffice it to say that the development of physical attributes that translates directly to raising players' performance potential will also boost what they believe their bodies can do in competition.

Athletes whose bodies are unprepared to compete physically will never achieve their playing potential. Conversely, matching training with the demands of the sport and elevating players' athleticism can help those athletes get very near, if not actually reach, their physiological performance ceiling.

CONCLUSION

Each component of the physical pillar covered in this chapter and the scientific research findings and applications associated with them form the foundation for all the training methods, exercises, drills, and programs that are presented in the pages ahead. In the forthcoming chapters, we have distilled the basketball training knowledge gained from science and many years of experience to make the information understandable and useful for both coaches and players.

Developing all the components of the physical pillar of performance gives an athlete a much better chance of reaching their potential. Our expertly designed training protocols and programs lead to better basketball conditioning that will translate directly to improvements on the court.

Player Assessment

Proper basketball performance training plans are based on recurrent assessments and well-executed programming. This chapter explores assessments used to develop a physical profile for a basketball athlete. It covers in detail why coaches should assess, what makes a good assessment, and which tests can be used to assess body structure, movement, and athleticism.

For each test, a protocol is provided, as well as the reason for its inclusion from a basketball performance perspective. By the end of the chapter, coaches and players should be equipped, confident, and successful in conducting the assessments and interpreting the results of a battery of tests that both serve to create a physical profile and inform and direct an athlete's performance conditioning program.

NEED FOR PHYSICAL ASSESSMENT

Assessment of players' body structure, movement, and athleticism provides not only a current snapshot of their physical readiness to perform on the court but also the basis from which to map out a correctly directed training plan.

Analysis of the assessment results allows the athlete and coach to set physical performance goals that provide direction for the performance plan. The performance plan should be carefully designed to help the coach and player progress from the starting point or point of the most recent assessment to the player's desired physical performance goals.

In athletic development, one constant is that nothing stays the same. As athletes execute their performance plans, gain experience, and compete, their bodies change—for better or worse. Over the course of a season, an athlete's body composition, strength level, fitness, and injury status will change. In this case, assessments function as a compass, allowing for course correction and involving an update of the player profile and needed adjustments in the performance plan to better fit the player's status (see figure 2.1).

In other words, assessments provide feedback to coaches and athletes so they can create better performance plans or alter misguided goals. This feedback loop is critical to successful coaching. Knowing if an athlete is not improving may be just as important as knowing if they are getting better, simply because now a coach can make a change to either the plan or the goals of the athlete. Each performance plan can be seen as a miniature scientific experiment with one subject—the athlete. Finding the right combination of training methods and execution will help players reach their physical goals if the program is constructed, monitored, and fine-tuned along the way.

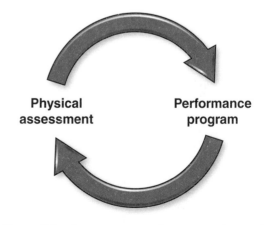

Physical assessment

Performance program

Figure 2.1   Assessment and programming cycle.

KEY FEATURES OF AN ASSESSMENT

A good assessment needs to be sport-specific, valid, reliable, and practical, and provides the information necessary to create a performance plan.

Sport-Specific

Physical assessments should reflect basketball. They must consider the technical and tactical demands of the game. For example, because the rules set a basketball hoop at 10 feet (3 m) high, this gives an advantage to players who possess greater height and display greater lower-body muscular power to dunk. Additionally, time-motion analysis has shown basketball to be a sport with low-intensity movement interspersed with bursts of explosive movements, including jumping, sprinting, and changing direction. Therefore, physical assessments need to reflect the physical qualities necessary to be successful in basketball. The physical components of basketball laid out in chapter 1 (body structure, movement, and athleticism) provide a robust framework for sport-specific assessment.

Valid and Reliable

Validity is the ability of a test to measure the physical quality it is intended to measure. For example, the U.S. Centers for Disease Control recommends using body mass index (BMI) as a screening tool to indicate levels of body fat, which is indirectly determined by using a person's height and weight. However, for athletes, including basketball players, who tend to be more muscular, and therefore heavier despite their leanness, it is not a valid measure of body fat. Tests of body fat percentage, such as skinfold measurements or DEXA scans, are more valid for evaluating body composition in athletic populations, and, of course, validity is foundational in providing the correct interpretation to an assessment.

Reliability is the ability of a test protocol to produce the same result if it is done repeatedly. For example, if an athlete's height is measured with a tape measure using a specific protocol, a reliable test would provide the exact same or very similar result if performed within minutes. Measuring a basketball player's height is simple and reliability is high, but other physical assessments, like body composition, jumping ability, and change of direction tests, inject far more variation and error into test results. Error can arise from instruments used, different coaches performing the tests, and changes in the athlete during testing (i.e., effort or fatigue). While error is inevitable in some cases, adhering to strict protocols allows error to be minimized, which improves reliability and thus increases the value of the test.

Reliability supports the validity of tests, because inconsistent results from a particular assessment will threaten its value. In discussing the assessment procedures later in this chapter, best practices are highlighted to preserve the reliability of each test. Additionally, we consider the validity of the assessments in their relation to the four pillars of basketball performance. The goal in all measurement is to determine the true value of important physical qualities. Minimizing measurement error and picking valid tests will provide a coach with the ability to confidently interpret changes in their data over time.

Practical

Practicality refers to the ability to perform a test in the setting where a coach operates. Coaches and athletes typically have limited time, space, budget, and personnel to test and analyze assessment data. Coaches need to consider their environment, the number of athletes who need to be tested, and, especially, their own skills and scope of practice to determine what testing procedures are appropriate for their team. For example, vertical jump testing can be performed on a force place, but if a coach does not know how to interpret force-time curves, this is not a worthwhile investment of time and money for the coach or athlete. It is critical that coaches perform testing they feel comfortable executing. For example, it is recommended that joint range of motion testing be performed only by coaches with a background in kinesiology. Take these factors into consideration when deciding what assessments are chosen for a team or athlete. It is best practice to start with a small battery of tests that can be executed with high proficiency. Then add more tests later if more information is needed.

PHYSICAL TESTS

This book is designed to offer insights to coaches at all levels of basketball, from high school to the NBA and WNBA. We have attempted to make as many of the assessments that follow as applicable as possible to all levels of the sport, but when testing procedures are likely to be too advanced or costly for the high school level, we will point that out and attempt to offer an alternative for testing that particular attribute.

Tests of Body Structure

Tests of body structure measure body dimensions and body composition. Posture is another area of body structure that can be assessed at higher levels of basketball, but the nuance required to address it is outside the scope of this chapter. Therefore, we focus on anthropometric measures of body structure: height without shoes, wingspan, and standing reach, as well as measures of body composition: body weight, body fat percentage, and muscle mass (or lean mass) percentage (see figure 2.2).

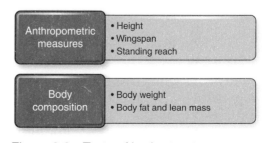

Figure 2.2   Tests of body structure.

Height

Importance to Basketball

There are many advantages to being taller in basketball, such as seeing over defenders and being closer to the rim to score and rebound, to name only two. In the NBA and WNBA, height provides a clear advantage at nearly every position. Height can be used for talent identification at higher levels with more mature athletes since it is genetically determined and not trainable. However, in youth basketball, it may be beneficial to track height over time because research has shown that rapid changes in growth can affect physical performance. For a coach, knowing an athlete is going through a growth spurt may influence their performance plan and provide context to performance changes an athlete may be experiencing.

Test Protocol

This test is performed using a tape measure aligned in the vertical plane on a wall. The athlete stands with the back to the wall, feet hip-width apart, heels touching the wall, feet rotated out 45 degrees, arms at the side, and head positioned so that the ear canal is lined up directly below the level of the eyes from the side view (see figure 2.3). To ensure the heels stay on the ground, the athlete can slightly raise their toes off the floor. Measure to the tallest point of an athlete's skull. Measuring with a right-angle ruler improves accuracy. At the NBA combine, this test is performed twice, once with no shoes and a second time with shoes on. These tests are almost perfectly correlated, so there is no need to perform both. Height without shoes will provide a more accurate measure of an athlete's height, since the heel of a shoe adds to the vertical measure. However, athletes play basketball in shoes, so a validity

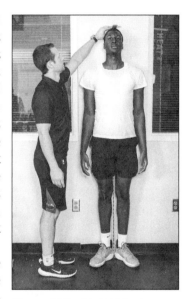

Figure 2.3　Height test.

argument can be made supporting an athlete's "playing height." In most cases, an increase of 0.75 to 1.25 inches (1.9-3.7 cm) occurs when the athlete is in shoes. See table 2.1 for height average and ranges by position from the NBA combine.

Table 2.1　Height Average and Range: NBA Combine (2001-2020)

	Average	Range*
Point guard	6 ft 2.25 in.	6 ft 1 in. to 6 ft 3.25 in.
Shooting guard	6 ft 4 in.	6 ft 3 in. to 6 ft 4.5 in.
Small forward	6 ft 6.25 in.	6 ft 5.5 in. to 6 ft 7.25 in.
Power forward	6 ft 8 in.	6 ft 7 in. to 6 ft 8.75 in.
Center	6 ft 10.25 in.	6 ft 9.25 in. to 6 ft 11.5 in.

*Range is between the 25th and 75th percentiles of the NBA combine data.

Wingspan

Importance to Basketball

Wingspan is the first measure of arm length. Long arms can be a significant advantage for basketball players, particularly in defending passing lanes and attempting steals. Also, a longer wingspan allows guards to dribble the ball farther away from an opposing defender. Wingspan is a measure for talent identification because it is not a trainable quality due to being genetically predetermined.

Test Protocol

This test is performed using a tape measure aligned with the horizontal plane. The athlete faces a wall, with their chest and toes in contact with the wall. Their head should be turned to one side (see figure 2.4). When the arms are raised for measurement, they should be at shoulder level, aligned with the horizontal plane, to maximize wingspan. This is important because the tape measure may not be placed at the exact height of the shoulders and athletes tend to keep their arms on the tape measure, instead of maximizing their wingspan at shoulder level. The tip of one middle finger should be placed on the zero mark of the tape measure. Using a straight edge, measure the distance to the tip of the opposite middle finger. See table 2.2 for wingspan average and ranges by position from the NBA combine.

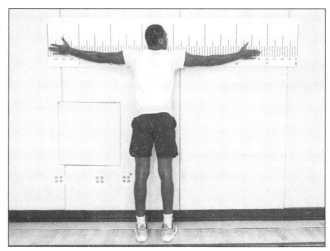

Figure 2.4   Wingspan test.

Table 2.2   Wingspan Average and Range: NBA Combine (2001-2020)

	Average	Range*
Point guard	6 ft 5.5 in.	6 ft 3 in. to 6 ft 7 in.
Shooting guard	6 ft 8.5 in.	6 ft 7 in. to 6 ft 9.75 in.
Small forward	6 ft 11 in.	6 ft 9.5 in. to 7 ft 0.25 in.
Power forward	7 ft 1.25 in.	6 ft 11.5 in. to 7 ft 2.5 in.
Center	7 ft 2.75 in.	7 ft 2.25 in. to 7 ft 5.25 in.

*Range is between the 25th and 75th percentiles of the NBA combine data.

Standing Reach

Importance to Basketball

Standing reach is the second measure of arm length and is important for blocking shots and rebounding. Also, having a higher standing reach may allow an athlete's shot to be released higher. Similar to wingspan, standing reach is a measure for talent identification, since it is genetically predetermined. However, if using a Vertec device for vertical jump testing, this measure is required to calculate jump height.

Test Protocol

This test is best performed using a Vertec device, but it could be performed using a tape measure aligned with the vertical plane. If using a Vertec for standing reach in conjunction with vertical jump testing, athletes should perform it with shoes on since they will jump with shoes on. The athlete stands with heels hip-width apart, directly underneath the Vertec flags, with ankles in line with the vertical stand of the Vertec device. The athlete reaches vertically as high as possible, fully extending the elbow, fully flexing the shoulder, and fully elevating the scapula, with minimal trunk side bend, spine extension, or head tilt (see figure 2.5). Coaches must ensure an athlete's heels remain on the ground and that the reach is performed slowly, under control. Standing reach is subtracted from the total reach height of a vertical jump if using a Vertec to measure vertical jump. If using a vertical tape measure, the athlete faces the wall, with the toes touching the wall and the tape measure centered between the feet. The athlete reaches as high as they can vertically, fully extending the elbow, fully flexing the shoulder, and fully elevating the scapula, with minimal trunk side bend, spine extension, or head tilt. See table 2.3 for standing reach average and ranges by position from the NBA combine.

Figure 2.5   Standing reach test.

Table 2.3   Standing Reach Average and Range: NBA Combine (2001-2020)

	Average	Range*
Point guard	8 ft 1 in.	7 ft 10.5 in. to 8 ft 2.5 in.
Shooting guard	8 ft 5 in.	8 ft 3.5 in. to 8 ft 6 in.
Small forward	8 ft 8.25 in.	8 ft 7 in. to 8 ft 9.5 in.
Power forward	8 ft 11 in.	8 ft 9.5 in. to 9 ft 0 in.
Center	9 ft 1.5 in.	9 ft 1 in. to 9 ft 4 in.

*Range is between the 25th and 75th percentiles of the NBA combine data.

Body Weight

Importance to Basketball

There are advantages and disadvantages to increasing or decreasing body weight. Increased weight is typically associated with more strength and greater momentum. This may be advantageous for physical play. Decreased body weight may help improve quickness and change of direction because less change in momentum is required to move the body. This may be advantageous for athletes who play away from the rim and depend on the ability to create separation from an opponent. Body weight should be a personal choice for the athlete. Coaches must respect that not all body types can gain or lose significant body weight. As always, coaches need to know their scope of practice, and they should consult medical professionals if there are physical or psychological issues associated with body weight.

Test Protocol

Body weight is measured using a calibrated scale. The athlete steps on the scale and the weight is recorded. At elite levels, it may be appropriate for athletes to wear only compression shorts or underwear and socks (or go barefoot) to get the most accurate measure of body weight. However, discretion is highly encouraged when testing body weight on children and adolescents, particularly females. Asking nonadults to be measured in minimal clothing is unwarranted and potentially scandalous. Coaches must be mindful of their situation and respectful of human dignity. Obtaining accurate data is important, but never at the expense of the dignity of the athletes being tested.

HYDRATION: SPECIAL APPLICATION OF BODY WEIGHT

Dehydration has been shown to decrease physical performance. Therefore, monitoring hydration status is beneficial from a performance perspective, as well as a general health perspective. Using this approach allows the coach to recommend how much fluid needs to be consumed following training. Daily monitoring of hydration status with the scale also identifies athletes who sweat heavily, which allows for an optimized preparticipation and in-competition fueling strategy.

Hydration assessments can be performed with advanced methods in a lab or with simple methods that coaches can use. A simple approach to monitoring hydration is to coordinate sensations of thirst, pre- and postactivity body weight (see section on protocol), and checking urine color. If any of these markers—significant desire to drink liquids, a low body weight, or deep yellow urine—are present, it is likely the athlete is dehydrated and needs to consume liquids. Coordinating the markers ensures greater accuracy.

Body Fat Percentage: Skinfolds

Importance to Basketball

There is a common phrase used among many in the performance community: "Fat don't fly." While it is certainly true that lowering excess body fat is helpful in improving jump and sprint performance, an essential level of body fat is required for the human body to maintain healthy function. Dipping below essential levels can be disastrous. There is also a genetic component to body fat and leanness that must be considered. Coaches need to use body fat assessments with extreme caution, particularly with adolescent athletes. While striving for optimal levels of body fat is a noble goal, creating undue psychological stress can be harmful. Coaches should consult medical or nutrition professionals if necessary.

Test Protocol

Body composition using skinfolds requires skin calipers. There are many options for skin calipers, including manual and electronic versions. At the NBA combine, electronic calipers immediately provide an estimated body composition after testing. Regardless of the device used, skinfold measures are applied to an equation to provide an estimation of body fat percentage, which can then be used in conjunction with body weight to estimate an athlete's lean mass.

Different equations require skinfold measurements at different sites. The three-site Jackson-Pollack equation has historically been used at the NBA combine. For men, the three sites measured are at the chest, abdomen, and thigh, all on the right side of the body. For women, the three sites measured are the tricep, suprailiac, and thigh. Men and women have different equations, so be sure to use the correct one. Skinfolds are taken with moderate pressure between the thumb and forefinger, with only fat tissue being considered. Caliper tips should be placed 0.39 to 0.78 inches (1-2 cm) away from the thumb and forefinger, and perpendicular to the skinfold.

For men: The chest is measured at a 45-degree angle halfway between the lateral border of the pectoralis major and the armpit. The abdomen is measured vertically, one inch lateral to the umbilicus. The thigh is measured vertically on the anterior side, halfway between the patella and anterior superior iliac spine. It is recommended to take at least two measurements. If a difference of greater than 0.01 inch (0.50 mm) is recorded between the measures, then an additional measurement should be performed. Use the average of the two closest measures. See table 2.4 for body fat percentage average and ranges by position from the NBA combine using the three-site Jackson-Pollack equation.

For women: Skinfolds are measured at the tricep, suprailiac, and thigh. The tricep is measured vertically on the back of the arm, halfway between the acromion process (top of the shoulder) and the olecranon of the elbow (point of the elbow). The suprailiac is measured horizontally, just above the iliac crest, at the most lateral part of the body. The thigh is measured vertically on the anterior side, halfway between the patella and anterior superior iliac spine.

The Jackson-Pollack equation for a three-site skinfold assessment is not the only estimation equation for body fat percentage. There are equations that include more skinfolds from other regions of the body, as well as other equations for different populations. Further depth on this topic is outside the scope of this chapter, so please see outside resources for additional information.

Table 2.4   Body Fat Percentage Average and Range: NBA Combine (2001-2020)

	Average	Range*
Point guard	6.5%	5.0%-7.3%
Shooting guard	6.6%	5.2%-7.7%
Small forward	7.1%	5.4%-8.0%
Power forward	8.6%	6.1%-10.5%
Center	9.5%	6.5%-12.2%

*Range is between the 25th and 75th percentiles of the NBA combine data.

Body Fat Percentage: Other Technologies

Methods and devices other than the skinfold test can be used to estimate body fat and lean mass, including devices that use water displacement, air displacement, or X-ray technology to scan the body. Each device has limitations. Dual energy X-ray absorptiometry (DEXA) is considered the gold standard of estimating body composition from a research perspective. However, even DEXA scans are prone to some measurement error due to glycogen status, hydration status, and certain assumptions presumed by the devices. Regardless of the technology used, it is important to consider potential error involved with any measurement, particularly when using results to determine positive or negative change. Also, it is advised to not compare the body composition results of different technologies. In basketball populations, three-site skinfold measures typically estimate body fat percentage to be 4-8 percent lower than measures obtained via a DEXA scan.

Tests of Movement

From a performance plan perspective, the purpose of movement tests is to determine whether an athlete has limitations or excesses in range of motion that would be relevant to altering their performance program. Additionally, the standing tests (discussed in a later section) investigate whether an athlete can coordinate their joints optimally. Movement testing is a safety check to protect against poor exercise selection. For example, if an athlete lacks ankle mobility, it is likely that other joints—the midfoot, the knee, the hips, and the lumbar spine—will take on load because the body must compensate to move. Therefore, the goal of movement testing is twofold: 1) to derive a plan to optimize movement and 2) to protect the athlete against unnecessary joint stress by improving exercise selection for high-force or high-velocity exercise. We cover four global movement tests in the following sections (see figure 2.6).

| Global movement tests | • Toe touch
• Squat
• Split squat
• Single-leg stance |

Figure 2.6   Tests of global movement.

Toe Touch

Importance to Basketball

The toe touch informs a coach of an athlete's ability to bend their hips and spine, as well as shift their weight posteriorly to properly load those structures. If an athlete cannot touch their toes, there are structures that are not allowing for proper hip loading and posterior weight shift. Hip hinge exercises, like a deadlift, may need to be modified (i.e., use blocks to raise the start position of the lift) to improve safety and protect the lumbar spine.

Test Protocol

The athlete stands with the feet at hip-width. Keeping the knees straight throughout the movement, the athlete bends at the hips and attempts to touch the toes (see figure 2.7).

Figure 2.7   Toe touch test.

Squat

Importance to Basketball

The squat tests an athlete's ability to bend their lower extremity joints (ankles, knees, and hips) in a balanced, coordinated fashion. The ability to squat and load the ankles, knees, hips, and spine is a precursor to two-leg jumping. If the squat movement test shows movement deficiencies or asymmetry, it is highly likely those deficiencies will be evident in the athlete's countermovement jump and rebound jump tests (discussed later in the chapter).

Test Protocol

The athlete stands with their feet at hip-width. Keeping their feet flat, the athlete bends their knees and hips, squatting as low as they can (see figure 2.8). The depth to which an athlete can squat should inform the coach about how low an athlete should squat in the weight room under load, or whether squatting is even appropriate for an athlete in their current body structure. Athletes with long femurs, restricted ankles, and weak quadriceps will struggle with squatting. Additionally, asymmetry between the right and left halves of the body should be considered as well. Greater asymmetry should prompt coaches to make changes in the performance plan by using unilateral exercises (i.e., split squats, lunges, single-leg squats) to protect against asymmetrical loading while still gaining lower-extremity strength. Limb length will certainly be a factor, and its implications will be captured within the test.

Figure 2.8   Squat test.

Split Squat

Importance to Basketball

A split squat shows the athlete's ability to coordinate the lower body with one hip flexed and one hip extended, a position achieved during sprinting. On the flexed-hip side of the body (the forward leg), the limb is in a loading or deceleration position, while on the extended-hip side of the body (the backward leg), the limb is in a propulsive or acceleration position. Therefore, the demands are different on each side, and limitations in range of motion and coordination affect movement performance.

Test Protocol

The athlete stands with one foot in front of the body and one foot behind the body, at hip width. The athlete lowers their body as far as possible while keeping the front foot fully on the ground and their trunk as upright as possible (see figure 2.9). From the front, coaches should pay attention to the athlete's ability to maintain the foot, ankle, and hip in a straight line and their ability to keep their weight distributed evenly. From the side, coaches should pay attention to the athlete's ability to maintain an even distribution of weight and their ability to maintain an upright trunk. Lack of split squat depth may speak to range-of-motion deficits or lack of strength.

Figure 2.9   Split squat test.

Single-Leg Stance

Importance to Basketball

Single-leg stance is a movement test of balance and hip range of motion. Standing on one leg may be a challenge for athletes with a history of ankle sprains and therefore should be noted in a performance plan. Balance training can be added to a plan to improve ankle stability. Additionally, this test asks the athlete to create active hip flexion while the stance leg is supporting the body in hip extension. The reciprocal hip flexion and extension are like in the split squat test, but the lower extremity biomechanics of the stance leg better represent the midstance of maximal speed sprinting (where the leg is directly underneath the body). Therefore, the split squat and single-leg stance tests complement each other.

Test Protocol

The athlete starts standing with feet together. Keeping one leg straight (foot flat, knee straight, hip straight), the athlete flexes the hip and knee of the opposite leg, lifting the leg as high as possible (see figure 2.10). The athlete should lift the knee only if they can keep the stance leg straight.

Figure 2.10   Single-leg stance test.

Tests of Athleticism

Assessments of athleticism determine the force and velocity outputs an athlete can achieve in movements that are required in basketball. Jumping, sprinting, and agility (or changing direction) are three elements of athletic movement performed on a basketball court. The tests that follow attempt to capture the specific physiological qualities expressed through jumping, sprinting, and agility. The capacity to perform those movements repeatedly, via fitness, is the fourth element (see figure 2.11).

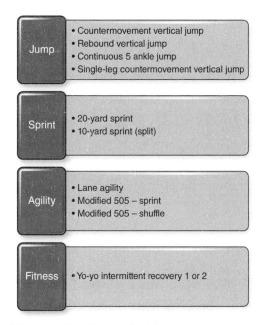

Figure 2.11 Tests of athleticism.

Jump Tests

In jump testing, several distinct types of strategies and physical qualities can be assessed. The standard countermovement jump provides a baseline of lower-body power. Another basketball-specific quality, "second-jump ability," is often touted by players, coaches, and scouts as being different than the simple countermovement. Second-jump ability can be divided into two types: full, maximum-effort second-jump ability; and quick, bouncy second-jump ability. Physiologically, second-jump ability measures the player's ability to quickly coordinate braking forces, absorb energy through the musculoskeletal system, and instantly reapply that energy into a second jump. Inefficiencies in absorbing and reapplying energy will result in lower jump output. Lastly, a player's ability to express single-leg power can be measured with a single-leg countermovement jump.

Countermovement Vertical Jump

Importance to Basketball

For a basketball player, maximizing vertical power is a significant advantage to improve shooting distance, rebounding ability, and shot blocking. The countermovement vertical jump is a test of two-leg vertical power. It is simple but extremely effective.

Test Protocol

This test is dependent on the equipment being used. Discussed here are procedures for Vertec devices and force plates. However, other technology, like smartphone applications, can be used to derive jump height from video recording. This can be an effective and economical way to track vertical jump performance.

If using a Vertec device: The athlete stands next to the Vertec with their jumping arm directly below the Vertec flags. The reaching arm needs to be the same used in the standing reach test described earlier in the chapter. The athlete must keep their feet on the ground during the descent of the counter-movement, although their heels are allowed to come off the floor if the balls of their feet remain on the ground. The player should attempt to jump as high as possible, reaching for the highest flag they can touch. Multiple attempts are encouraged. The NBA combine allows for three attempts, but more may be allowed depending on the setting and time availability. For the safety of the athlete, to ensure their best performance, and to protect equipment, athletes are asked not to swing their arm and hand at the Vertec flags. Rather, they are encouraged to simply reach and touch to displace them.

If using a force plate: The coach has the option to use an arm swing or not. The advantage of an arm swing is that it is more basketball-specific and natural for the athlete and increases the impulse and realistic force output of the athlete. However, with an arm swing, the variability between jumps is likely to increase, which decreases the reliability of the test. The advantage of not using an arm swing is the coach gets a more specific measure of lower-body output because the upper extremity cannot contribute to increasing forces. Additionally, the reliability and overall variability is improved. However, the more restrictive and unnatural movement of jumping without using their arms takes time for athletes to learn. Coaches must be strict with execution because athletes will try to use their arms.

See table 2.5 for average range data for the countermovement vertical jump for high school and college players.

Table 2.5 Countermovement Vertical Jump Average Range: High School and College

	Average range
Males	
High school: 9th-10th grade	15 to 19.5 inches
High school: 11th-12th grade	19.5 to 24 inches
College	24.25 to 32 inches
Females	
High school: 9th-10th grade	12 to 16 inches
High school: 11th-12th grade	16.5 to 20.5 inches
College	20 to 26 inches

Data from BAMTESTING "Test Like the Best"

Rebound Vertical Jump

Importance to Basketball

Second-jump ability is often touted by coaches as an important skill for basketball players. Multiple jumps are often required in putback shots after rebounds and for contesting shots around the rim. Physically, an athlete's second-jump ability is their capacity to quickly coordinate two phases of a jump in sequence: 1) deceleration with braking forces in landing from the first jump and 2) and immediate reacceleration with propulsive forces to jump a second time. The ability to express this skill demonstrates superior coordination, energy absorption and release through the musculoskeletal system, and rapid force production. Athletes who lack this skill will jump lower on their second jump compared to the countermovement jump. This test is very similar to the demands of a drop jump (i.e., a coordinated effort of landing and jumping immediately), but more sport specific.

Test Protocol

This test is highly dependent on the equipment being used.

If using a Vertec device: The athlete stands in the same starting position as the countermovement jump (see previous section). The athlete is instructed to jump twice, the first jump being a maximum-effort vertical jump without reaching for the Vertec flags, followed immediately by a second maximum-effort vertical jump where the athlete reaches for the Vertec flags. Athletes should be encouraged to bend their ankles, knees, and hips for the rebound jump (as opposed to maintaining a straighter body in the continuous ankle jump test, discussed later). The height of the second jump is recorded.

If using a force plate: The athlete stands on the force platform so it can accurately measure force at the starting position. The coach then commands the athlete to jump, and the athlete performs two maximum-effort countermovement jumps in immediate succession, as explosively as possible. The athlete needs to land on the force plate after both jumps. Upon landing after the second jump, the athlete should hold their position through the landing phase to ensure landing metrics are recorded.

Continuous 5 Ankle Jump

Importance to Basketball

In basketball, being "bouncy" is often touted as a positive attribute. Physically, the ability to "bounce" off the ground, or exhibit short ground contact times, demonstrates the elastic qualities of the musculotendon unit and the musculoskeletal system. The continuous 5 ankle jump test, otherwise known as the 5 pogo jump test, measures the ability of an athlete to maximize air time while minimizing ground contact time. Jump height (or flight time) and ground contact time are the critical measures. A useful metric is the reactive strength index (RSI), which is calculated as a ratio of vertical jump height divided by ground contact time, or a ratio between flight time and ground contact time. (These are two different ratios, so a coach must pick one or the other depending on what technology is available.) A higher RSI represents more bounciness.

Test Protocol

A coach will need technology to perform this test, as a Vertec device will not work. Technology could be a smartphone with video (using flight and contact time), a contact mat or optical sensors that capture flight and contact time, or a force plate. The athlete performs five jumps in a row, with the first jump being a maximum-effort vertical jump. The athlete should be instructed to execute the following four jumps as high and fast as possible, with minimal bending of the ankles, knees, and hips (i.e., like a pogo stick).

Single-Leg Countermovement Jump

Importance to Basketball

Basketball is not always played with two feet on the ground. The single-leg countermovement jump is a test of single-leg power production and allows for an assessment of asymmetry. Exploding off one leg for a dunk or performing Euro-step skills in the lane to finish a layup requires significant single-leg power. This test tries to capture the athlete's ability to do that.

Test Protocol

This test is dependent on the equipment being used. Discussed in the next section are procedures for Vertec devices and force plates. However, other technology, like smartphone applications, can be used to derive jump height from video recording. This can be an effective and economical way to track vertical jump performance.

If using a Vertec device: The athlete stands next to the Vertec with their jumping arm directly below the Vertec flags. The reaching arm needs to be the same used in the standing reach test (described previously). The athlete must keep their foot on the ground during the descent of the countermovement, although the heel is allowed to come off the floor if the ball of the foot remains on the ground. The player should attempt to jump as high as possible, reaching for the highest flag they can touch. Multiple attempts are encouraged. The test is performed on each leg. The NBA combine allows for three attempts, but more may be allowed depending on the coaches' setting and time availability. For the safety of the athlete, to ensure their best performance, and to protect equipment, athletes are asked not to swing their arm and hand at the Vertec flags. Rather, they are encouraged to simply reach and touch to displace them.

If using a force plate: The coach has the option to use an arm swing or not. The advantage of an arm swing is that it is more basketball-specific and natural for the athlete and increases the impulse and realistic force output of the athlete. However, with an arm swing, the variability between jumps is likely to increase, which decreases the reliability of the test. The advantage of not using an arm swing is the coach gets a more specific measure of lower-body output because the upper extremity cannot contribute to increasing forces. Additionally, the reliability and overall variability is improved. However, the more restrictive and unnatural movement of jumping without using their arms takes time for athletes to learn. Coaches must be strict with execution because athletes will try to use their arms.

The athlete stands on the force platform so it can accurately measure force at the starting position. (The amount of time standing still may depend on the force plate system being used, but it is usually 2 to 5 seconds.) The coach then commands the athlete to jump, and the athlete performs the countermovement as explosively as possible. The athlete should land on the force plates and hold their position through the landing phase to ensure landing metrics are recorded.

Sprint Test

Whereas jumping is used to measure the vertical expression of power, sprinting can be used to assess horizontal power. In basketball, the court is not long enough to reach maximum speeds, so sprint tests become a measure of acceleration ability. The ability to accelerate quickly ultimately leads to better performance.

Sprint Test

Importance to Basketball

Due to the constraint of the court being 94 feet (29 m) long, achieving maximal speed in basketball is rare at higher levels, although it could be achieved at the youth level due to lack of physical maturity. Regardless, the ability to accelerate quickly is paramount in all levels. Speed in fast-break opportunities is a major advantage for teams looking to push the pace of a game and create scoring opportunities. The NBA combine uses a 25-yard (23 m) test (called the 3/4 court sprint); however, a 20-yard (18 m) test with an optional 10-yard (9 m) split is more consistently performed in performance testing research to capture acceleration ability. The 20-yard (18 m) sprint test with a 10-yard (9 m) split is proposed here. This test can be performed with a stopwatch or timing gates. If using timing gates, there are methodological considerations, like starting position, beam height, and beam technology (single versus dual) that should be considered.

Test Protocol

The athlete starts in a two-point stance and must come to a complete stop before starting the sprint. The athlete initiates the test. If using a stopwatch, coaches start the time on the athlete's first movement. The time is stopped once the athlete's center of mass crosses the finish line (or optional 10-yard [9 m] split). If multiple coaches are available to time trials with a stopwatch, the NBA combine protocol recommends averaging the times.

See table 2.6 for average range data for the 3/4 court sprint for high school and college players.

Table 2.6   3/4 Court Sprint Average Range: High School and College

	Average range
Males	
High school: 9th-10th grade	3.70 to 3.99 seconds
High school: 11th-12th grade	3.45 to 3.69 seconds
College	3.20 to 3.45 seconds
Females	
High school: 9th-10th grade	3.84 to 4.17 seconds
High school: 11th-12th grade	3.61 to 3.84 seconds
College	3.44 to 3.60 seconds

Data from BAMTESTING "Test Like the Best"

Agility Tests

The agility tests offer different methods to measure change of direction ability without any reactive interference. The lane agility test is a longer test that provides the athletes with multiple direction changes and two modes of locomotion (sprinting and shuffling) within the test. The shorter modified 505 focuses on a single change of direction and a single mode of locomotion (either sprint or shuffle) to help differentiate the different skills an athlete has.

Lane Agility Test

Importance to Basketball

The lane agility, or pro lane drill, is a classic NBA combine test. This test captures the ability to linearly accelerate forward and backward and perform 90-degree and 180-degree changes of direction in multiple planes, while incorporating a sport-specific movement in lateral shuffling.

Test Protocol

A stopwatch or timing gates can be used for this test. Four 18-inch (46 cm) cones are placed at the four corners of the NBA key (19 × 16 feet [5 × 4 m]) (see figure 2.12). If the athlete is facing the baseline, they would start on the left elbow of the key, behind the free throw line extended. The athlete starts in a two-point stance and must come to a complete stop before starting the test. The athlete initiates the test. If using a stopwatch, coaches start the time on the athlete's first movement. In this drill the athlete will complete the following steps.

1. Sprint to the baseline.
2. Transition around the cone 90 degrees and lateral shuffle right to the opposite side of the lane.
3. Transition around the cone 90 degrees and backpedal to the level of the free throw line.
4. Transition around the cone 90 degrees and lateral shuffle left to the opposite side of the lane.
5. Touch the line that is extended from the lane line (midway point of the drill) and change direction 180 degrees, continuing to lateral shuffle right to the opposite side of the lane.

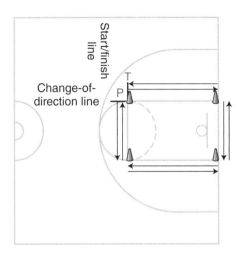

Figure 2.12 Lane agility test.

6. Transition around the cone 90 degrees and sprint to the baseline.
7. Transition around the cone 90 degrees and lateral shuffle left to the opposite side of the lane.
8. Transition around the cone 90 degrees and backpedal through the free throw line extended to finish the drill.

The time is stopped once the athlete's center of mass crosses the finish line. It is important for coaches to ensure that proper technique is used during the test. Potential disqualifications are crossing the feet during a defensive lateral shuffle, touching a cone, or missing the line at the midway point. If multiple coaches are available to time trials with a stopwatch, the NBA combine protocol recommends averaging the times.

See table 2.7 for average range data for the lane agility test for high school and college players.

Table 2.7 Lane Agility Average Range: High School and College

	Average range
Males	
High school: 9th-10th grade	12.26 to 13.38 seconds
High school: 11th-12th grade	11.41 to 12.24 seconds
College	10.80 to 11.50 seconds
Females	
High school: 9th-10th grade	13.01 to 14.08 seconds
High school: 11th-12th grade	12.21 to 12.99 seconds
College	11.64 to 12.30 seconds

Data from BAMTESTING "Test Like the Best"

Modified 505: Sprint and Shuffle Agility Test

Importance to Basketball

An advantage of the modified 505 versus the lane agility test is that it is shorter, which limits fatigue and allows the athlete to focus on a single 180-degree change of direction. With this test, the coach can test a linear acceleration (sprint) or a lateral shuffle leading to the direction change, providing insights into different movement patterns.

Test Protocol

This test can use a stopwatch or timing gates. A turning-point line is set 5 yards (4 m) away from the start/finish line (see figure 2.13). If testing linear acceleration, the athlete starts in a two-point stance and must come to a complete stop before starting the test. If testing lateral shuffle ability, the athlete would start in a defensive stance, perpendicular to and fully behind the start/finish line. The athlete initiates the test. If using a stopwatch, coaches start the time on the athlete's first movement. The athlete sprints or lateral shuffles to the turning point line, changes direction 180 degrees, and sprints or lateral shuffles back through the finish line. If multiple coaches are available to time trials with a stopwatch, the NBA combine protocol recommends averaging the times.

See table 2.8 for average range data for the modified 505 test for high school and college players.

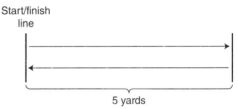

Figure 2.13   Modified 505 setup.

Table 2.8   Modified 505 Average Range: High School and College

	Average range
Males	
High school: 9th-10th grade	3.5 to 3.80 seconds
High school: 11th-12th grade	3.21 to 3.50 seconds
College	2.97 to 3.20 seconds
Females	
High school: 9th-10th grade	3.98 to 4.42 seconds
High school: 11th-12th grade	3.58 to 3.97 seconds
College	3.29 to 3.57 seconds

Data from BAMTESTING "Test Like the Best"

Fitness and Health Tests

Being able to repeat high-intensity movement, like sprinting, is the best way to assess fitness. The yo-yo intermittent recovery test provides objective data on how well an athlete can recover between bouts of high-intensity exercise. It is also a psychologically challenging test. Health and wellness tests provide a way to objectively monitor an athlete's physiological state. Rating of perceived exertion (RPE) can be used to assess how hard a practice or conditioning session feels to an athlete. Wellness questionnaires provide an opportunity for athletes to share how nutrition, sleep, and outside stress are affecting their lives, which allows coaches an opportunity to find strategies to help them.

Yo-Yo Intermittent Recovery Test (Level 1 or Level 2)

Importance to Basketball

Fitness is critical to the physical success of basketball players. Athletes need a robust cardiorespiratory system to help them recover during and after games. They also need excellent muscle buffering capacity to shuttle the waste products that build with fatigue from high-intensity activities like jumping, sprinting, and changing direction. Strong anaerobic and aerobic systems help athletes produce power and recover. The yo-yo intermittent recovery (YYIR) test is a running test with one change of direction that increases speed over the course of the test. It provides a significant challenge to the anaerobic and aerobic systems.

Test Protocol

An audio file of the YYIR Level 1 or Level 2 is required. The Level 2 test simply starts at a faster speed and is meant for a more elite population. A 20-meter (22-yard) distance is required between two points, with a 5-meter (16.4-foot) recovery area (a total of 25 meters [82 feet] of space is required) (see figure 2.14). On the start beep, the athlete runs 20 meters down to a marked line, where another beep is heard. The athlete then changes direction and runs 20 meters back to cross the starting line before a subsequent beep. The athlete then walks or jogs the recovery distance of 5 meters, changes direction, and jogs or walks back to the starting line in preparation for the next beep. Athletes must come to a complete stop before the next beep. Athletes continue until they miss two beeps at either end of the 20 meters. Athletes are required to wait for the audible signal before starting their run and touch each line before the beep. The test can be recorded as the level an athlete achieves or the total distance covered in the last successfully completed shuttle.

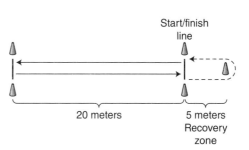

Figure 2.14   Setup for the yo-yo intermittent recovery test.

Rating of Perceived Exertion

The term *load monitoring* has become a part of the NBA vernacular in recent years, and teams go to great lengths to monitor their athletes with expensive wearable devices. However, rating of perceived exertion (RPE) is an effective and free method to gather load. RPE is a simple questionnaire that can be handed to an athlete following a game or practice to measure the difficulty of the training session (see table 2.9). The RPE that the athlete records is often multiplied by the duration of time spent in training. If the athlete records the RPE as a 7 and the practice session lasted 90 minutes, we would record the load as 630. Tracking load over time can help determine practice design, nutrition protocols, recovery sessions, or the need for extra conditioning. RPE can also be integrated with other forms of monitoring to give a more complete picture of the athlete's response to stress. Player load is discussed in greater detail in chapter 10.

Table 2.9 Sample RPE Questionnaire

RPE Scale	Rating of perceived exertion
0	**Max effort activity** Feels almost impossible to keep going. Completely out of breath, unable to talk. Cannot maintain for more than a very short time.
9	**Very hard activity** Very difficult to maintain exercise intensity. Can barely breathe and speak only a few words.
7-8	**Vigorous activity** Borderline uncomfortable. Short of breath, can speak a sentence.
4-6	**Moderate activity** Breathing heavily, can hold a short conversation. Still somewhat comfortable, but becoming noticeably more challenging.
2-3	**Light activity** Seems easy to maintain for hours. Can comfortably breathe and carry on a conversation.
1	**Very light activity** Hardly any exertion, but more than sleeping, watching TV, etc.

Wellness Questionnaires

Importance to Basketball

As mentioned in chapter 1, the physical and psychological domains often overlap. For example, physical fatigue can disrupt decision making. Additionally, psychological stress can manifest itself in physical stress for an athlete, leading to decreases in performance. Therefore, measuring psychological wellness can be helpful in determining athletes' physical readiness. Wellness questionnaires can help a coach gauge how athletes are handling stress or assess their routines (i.e., nutrition, sleep, recovery). While there are standard questionnaires, coaches can choose questions they feel are important to their program and are most practical.

Test Protocol

The athlete is provided with the questionnaire. This can be done online or with pen and paper. A rating scale of 1 through 5 is common, correlated to these five responses: Poor = 1, Below average = 2, Average = 3, Above average = 4, Great = 5. Common questions include: How well did you sleep last night? What is your current level of muscle soreness? How is your mood? How is your appetite? What is your current energy level? What is your current level of focus? Total and evaluate responses individually, keeping the answers confidential. Closely inspect each athlete's questionnaire to identify any areas of concern that need to be addressed in a private meeting, and with the athlete's approval, take the necessary steps to do so.

CONCLUSION

Body structure, movement, and athleticism form the physical profile of a basketball player. With the proper performance plan, physical profiles can be developed and improved.

Physical profiles are best used in two different scenarios: 1) talent identification and 2) tracking athletes over time to monitor development. With talent identification, such as the NBA combine, coaches usually collect data from tests of body structure, movement, and athleticism on one day. Then they compare the athlete's physical profile against a historical database to determine how a player of interest stacks up against other players. Typically, athletes would be divided by position or position group (i.e., guard, wing, big) to help make better comparisons. The more a coach can collect data over time, the better the historical database and more accurate the analysis of an athlete's physical profile for talent identification.

For coaches tracking their own athletes over time, a historical database can be useful to provide context to the athlete. However, it is far more useful and important for coaches to compare an athlete's physical profile to their own data over time to see changes and trends. Reassessment is critical. New physical profiles can be created every 4 to 6 weeks. Testing doesn't necessarily have to occur on one day, and many tests of athleticism can be performed over the course of a training cycle. Updated physical profiles help to create effective goals and provide proper focus on an athlete's strengths and weaknesses, particularly during distinct parts of a basketball season (i.e., off-season versus in-season).

As a reminder, physical assessments are only one aspect of a basketball performance plan. Technical, tactical, and psychological assessments should be performed to create a complete picture of a basketball player. After the assessment, goals can be created and performance plans can be developed to help athletes achieve their best performance.

Chapter 3

Movement Preparation

Michael Gonzales/Getty Images

In basketball, as in all team sports, athletes aim to optimize performance for competition. The game requires athletes to perform dynamic, multiplanar movements, meaning their joints must be able to move fluidly and proficiently through more than one plane of motion. Success on the court is linked to time spent rehearsing proper dynamic stretching and movement patterns prior to play.

General warm-ups have long been regarded as a routine that helps prime the cardiorespiratory and musculoskeletal systems for more intense activity. Athletes benefit from a general warm-up because it elevates core temperature, reduces muscle tension, and increases joint range of motion. As we've evolved in our understanding of human movement, and more specifically the movements that occur in basketball, there has been a shift in what an optimal preparatory training routine should look like. Current thinking holds that implementing a purposeful three-dimensional movement routine develops specific muscles and neural recruitment pathways that are necessary for skill transference on the court. The movement preparation can be performed pregame, during halftime, and prepractice. It's important to note that the movement prep routine doesn't replace the general warm-up but should be combined with exercises that elevate the heart rate.

Basketball players' bodies must be prepared to meet challenging mechanical and physiological demands. Thus, it's crucial to establish movement competency in all three planes of motion to bolster robustness and performance. A dedicated movement preparation routine readies the athlete for acceleration, deceleration, jumping, and changes of direction.

MOVEMENT PREP WARM-UP

An appropriate movement preparation warm-up starts with a gradual progression of dynamic stretching and flows into more intense movements. The aim is to expose the athlete to the mobility and stability movements necessary for sound locomotive technique, while preparing the muscles, tendons, joints, ligaments, and stretch-reflex cycle to respond appropriately to faster in-play intensities.

In this chapter, we provide a three-dimensional movement framework that targets specific muscle groups and motor skills in the sagittal, frontal, and transverse planes. First, we focus on sagittal plane flexion and extension joint motions, which are key factors in linear forward and backward running. Next, we progress into frontal plane–focused exercises that prepare the athlete to move side to side and rotationally.

The goal of dynamic stretching is to increase the range of motion and then start to move with a higher intensity, increasing the tissues' ability to generate power. For the purpose of elevating the core body temperature and keeping the athlete in a good rhythm, we include running, cutting, backpedaling, and shuffling along with the specific dynamic exercises outlined in this chapter.

LINEAR ACCELERATION EXERCISES

The following exercises are examples of movements that involve bending and lengthening the body to enhance forward and back motions. Linear acceleration is a key skill in basketball, which requires athletes to exhibit good running technique with short ground contact times. In fact, patterning triple extension of the ankles, knees, and hips prior to play promotes more efficient running and jumping. The first four movement prep exercises focus on progressively increasing range of motion of the hips, quadriceps, hamstrings, and calves. They are followed by dynamic stability exercises that emphasize short ground contact times. Six of the eight movements are performed to half-court, about 15 yards (14 m) followed by a light jog, stride, or sprint to the opposite baseline, about 15 yards (14 m).

Knee to Chest

Purpose

To improve unilateral hip flexion range of motion while integrating stability from the opposite foot and hip

Execution

1. Start standing tall with your legs a little less than hip-width apart and arms down at your sides.

2. Begin the movement by flexing your torso to grasp your shin with both hands.

3. Slowly pull the knee upward into flexion toward your chest, keeping the toes pointed up, and extend the hip of the support leg. Push tall through your midfoot (figure 3.1).

4. Be sure to keep your chest upright and back straight.

5. Repeat the movement to half-court, alternating legs each rep. Jog forward to the opposite baseline.

Figure 3.1   Knee to chest.

Reverse Lunge With Reach to Quad Stretch

Purpose

To increase tissue extensibility of the hip flexors and quads

Execution

1. Begin by taking a big step backward, flexing through your hips and bending your knee until the front shin is over the ankle joint.
2. With the trailing leg straight, slowly reach the same side arm up to the sky (i.e., left arm with left leg and right arm with right leg) until you feel a slight stretch on the front side of the hip (figure 3.2a).
3. Next, flex the back leg, bringing your heel toward the gluteus, and grasp the top of your foot with the reaching hand. Push upward with the front leg and hold the quad stretch for two seconds (figure 3.2b).
4. Take a step forward and repeat the stretch with the opposite leg.
5. Repeat the movement to half-court, alternating legs each rep. Jog forward to the opposite baseline.

Figure 3.2   Reverse lunge with reach to quad stretch.

Forward/Backward Hip Rotation to Drop Squat

Purpose

To improve hip rotational ability and deceleration while incorporating a timing and rhythm aspect to the bilateral squat

Execution

1. Start by externally rotating the right leg and driving the knee up and over an imaginary hurdle (figure 3.3a). Follow with the left leg moving forward, again placing the foot straight down on the floor.
2. Take a mini hop forward and drop into a quarter squat with the feet slightly farther than shoulder-width apart and the arms extended out at chest level for counterbalance (figure 3.3b).
3. With an upright chest, push up to a standing position. Alternate legs on each repetition to half-court.
4. At half-court run backward to the starting line.
5. Repeat the same movement sequence going backward followed by one stride forward to the start position.

Figure 3.3 Forward hip rotation to drop squat.

Walking Single-Leg Romanian Deadlift to Reach

Purpose

To improve single-leg hip flexion while integrating stability from the opposite foot, hip, and core

Execution

1. Stand with the feet shoulder-width apart, knees slightly flexed and one leg off the ground.
2. Start the motion by hinging at the hips, reaching one arm forward and parallel with the ground as the back leg lifts up. Keep your torso and pelvis squared and parallel to the floor (figure 3.4a).
3. Maintaining stability on the down leg, briefly pause at the bottom.
4. Push through the ground to extend the hips and torso back to the standing position. Bring the trailing leg up to a flexed position in front of the body (figure 3.4b).
5. Alternate legs to half-court and stride to the opposite baseline.

Figure 3.4   Walking single-leg Romanian deadlift to reach.

Backward Low Walk to Backward Run

Purpose

To increase calf flexibility and improve backside (rear leg and pelvis) mechanics

Execution

1. Start in a flexed position with back facing opposite lane line. The hips, knees, and ankles are bent, and the shoulders are over the hips.
2. Walk backward, toe to heel, to get a calf stretch. The goal is to increase calf range of motion on each step (figure 3.5a).
3. At half-court, transition into an upright position and backpedal as quickly as possible to the baseline. Stay on the balls of the feet (figure 3.5b).

Figure 3.5 Backward low walk to backward run.

Ankle Flips

Purpose

To improve foot and ankle stiffness while priming the elastic structures in the lower legs

Execution

1. Start in upright posture with hands at your sides.
2. Moving forward, keep the legs straight and lift one foot off the ground with the toe dorsiflexed (figure 3.6a). Next, bounce quickly off the ground, landing on the ball of the opposite foot (figure 3.6b).
3. As you move forward, stay as tall as possible and let the arms follow a natural reciprocal motion with the legs.
4. Start with short-range flips to half-court. As you pass half-court, increase the distance of each skip to cover the full length of the court.

Figure 3.6 Ankle flips.

Hands Overhead A-Skip

Purpose

To improve linear single-leg stability while improving sprint mechanics

Execution

1. Stand upright with your feet shoulder-width apart and both hands over your head.
2. Begin the movement by skipping forward, driving your knee up, drawing the toes up toward your shin, and maintaining an upright posture (figure 3.7). After a small skip, land on the same foot and then switch legs.
3. Execute the movement by extending the ankles, knees, and hips on each skip. The arms overhead will challenge stability, so do your best to stay straight, avoiding rotation.
4. Complete the movement to half-court, then sprint to the opposite baseline.

Figure 3.7   Hands overhead A-skip.

45-Degree Hop

Purpose

To establish proper joint position for vertical and horizontal propulsion

Execution

1. Stand erect on the right foot with an imaginary ball held at the right ear. Keep the left leg up.
2. Begin the movement by tilting the body forward at a 45-degree angle, landing on the ball of the left foot (figure 3.8).
3. Simultaneously, swing the arms across the body to the left ear.
4. Repeat with the right leg.
5. On each hop, hold the position, ensuring that the knee is properly aligned with the foot and hip. On each landing, ensure the hip is flexed.
6. Complete four reps to the free throw line followed by a three-quarter-court sprint to the opposite baseline.

Figure 3.8 45-degree hop.

LATERAL CHANGE OF DIRECTION EXERCISES

Fundamentally, basketball players need to shuffle side to side and rotate their hips to cut and change direction. These lateral rotational movements involve more activity from the hip abductors than forward acceleration. Hence, in this section we work on dynamic stability in the frontal and transverse planes. A key requisite for changing direction in basketball is an athlete's ability to create the proper angle of force opposite the direction of the anticipated movement. The first three exercises focus on range of motion in the feet, trunk, adductors, and abductors. The next four are dynamic stability exercises for footwork and hip dissociation. These movements increase foot reaction time and the hips' ability to rotate, providing more degrees of multidirectional freedom to move on the basketball court.

Single-Leg Lateral Reach With Hands Overhead

Purpose

To improve frontal plane single-leg stability while integrating the entire kinetic chain

Execution

1. Start in a standing position on the left leg, with a slight knee bend and arms reaching out at chest level.
2. The left leg should be rooted in the ground for stability, while the right foot is in a plantar flexed (toes pointing down) position.
3. Reach sideways away from the body, flexing the hip of the planted leg, and drive both hands overhead toward the opposite side of the body (figure 3.9a).
4. Next, push the hips vertical, reaching the right foot across the body, while swinging the arms in the opposite direction (figure 3.9b).
5. Perform 10 total reaches in place on each leg.

Figure 3.9   Single-leg lateral reach with hands overhead.

Lateral Lunge With Rotation

Purpose

To increase range of motion in the adductor complex while activating hip internal rotation muscles

Execution

1. Stand upright and perpendicular to the lane line with the feet parallel and shoulder-width apart.
2. Take an exaggerated long step to the right away from your midline. Slightly flex the hip and knee, shifting weight to the flexed leg. The right knee should be over the ankle while the left leg is straight (figure 3.10a).
3. Next, rotate the upper body to the right while reaching the left arm across the body (figure 3.10b).
4. Straighten the flexed leg, pause, take two shuffles, and repeat the motion in the same direction.
5. Repeat this sequence to half-court and return back to the baseline, lunging and shuffling in the opposite direction.

Figure 3.10   Lateral lunge with rotation.

Lateral Explosive Step

Purpose

To improve foot position during a lateral change of direction

Execution

1. Start perpendicular to the lane line in a defensive position with your feet more than hip-width apart. The hips and knees should be flexed, and the gluteus should be down and back.
2. Keeping the shoulders forward over the hips, raise the foot of the inside leg off the ground a few inches. Maintain an upright torso position, bringing both arms out roughly parallel to the ground, while keeping the foot raised.
3. Begin the movement by planting the foot of the up leg into the ground (figure 3.11a).
4. Push off the inside of the foot and open the hip of the outside leg (figure 3.11b).
5. Perform two shuffles. Pause. Assume a defensive position and repeat to half-court. Face the same direction to get to the other side when coming back to the baseline.

Figure 3.11   Lateral explosive step.

Lateral Push-Off Skip

Purpose

To increase frontal plane foot and ankle stiffness while grooving lateral agility technique

Execution

1. Stand upright and perpendicular to the baseline with arms bent 90 degrees at your waist.
2. Begin by moving laterally, driving the knee of the outside leg up to the waist, pulling the foot up into dorsiflexion (figure 3.12).
3. Keep the trailing leg as straight as possible, placing the foot of the outside leg under the hip on each repetition. Pump your arms in a running motion.
4. Continue moving laterally, staying as tall as possible, and push from the balls of the feet.
5. Repeat to half-court and return to the baseline facing the same direction to work the other leg.

Figure 3.12   Lateral push-off skip.

Quick Feet Carioca to High Knee Carioca

Purpose

To improve lateral movement, agility, and footwork

Execution

1. Stand upright and perpendicular to the lane line.
2. Start by moving laterally, rapidly crossing the feet over one another. Limit ground contact time by quickly swiveling your hips and swinging your arms. Stay as tall as possible, keeping the hips squared (figure 3.13a).
3. Transition into a high knee carioca by extending the front hip and driving the trailing leg, hip, and knee to the sky and across the body (figure 3.13b).
4. Let the arms swing in synchrony with the lower body.
5. Perform quick feet carioca to half-court and high knee carioca to the opposite baseline.
6. Repeat this sequence facing the same direction with the opposite leg leading in front.

Figure 3.13 Quick feet carioca to high knee carioca.

Hip Poppers

Purpose

To improve hip disassociation and improve hip rotational power

Execution

Figure 3.14 Hip poppers.

1. Stand with your feet slightly more than shoulder-width apart.
2. Flex the ankles, knees, and hips and bend the torso forward.
3. Staying on the balls of the feet, powerfully rotate the right leg to the midline of your body, while the left leg moves backward. Keep your upper body facing forward (figure 3.14).
4. Quickly swivel the feet back to the starting position.
5. Perform 10 repetitions in place with both legs.

Lateral Crossover Step to Base

Purpose

To improve the hips' ability to rotate during a change of direction

Execution

Figure 3.15 Lateral crossover step to base.

1. Start perpendicular to the lane line in a defensive position with your feet more than hip-width apart. The hips and knees should be flexed, and the gluteus should be down and back.
2. Execute a crossover step by taking the leg across your midline in the direction of the opposite lane line.
3. Next, push off the inside leg to propel the knee vertically and across the body. Simultaneously, extend the hip of the outside leg to help propel the leg laterally (figure 3.15).
4. Transition the crossover step back into a defensive position. Keep your shoulders level and squared with the hips.
5. Repeat to half-court. Face the same direction and repeat coming back to the baseline.

MOVEMENT PREPARATION ROUTINES

Basketball players should undertake a movement prep warm-up to promote blood flow to the active muscles, mitigate injury risk, and improve movement patterns. The exercises discussed in this chapter provide a template of movements that can be applied prepractice, pregame, and at halftime. Prior to intense activity, athletes should allocate 8-12 minutes for movement preparation. A proper warm-up means athletes are not using practice or the game as the day's first high-intensity movements. Thus, the movement sequences are progressive, so the body can progress from slower dynamic stretching movements to higher-tempo drills. To appropriately ramp up the body for play, the movement prep routines should be combined with running, skipping, and shuffling.

In addition to specific mobility and stability exercises discussed in chapter 4, the following movement prep drills allow the athlete to rehearse progressive movement sequences and increase kinesthetic sense. Our goal is to wake up the nervous system, prepare the mind, and prime the body for play.

Prepractice Movement Routine

The sequence of exercises presented in table 3.1 is an example of a movement preparation routine that can be performed before training and/or shootaround. Using dynamic stretching as a form of active mobilization pretraining provides an excellent opportunity to increase range of motion. During this sequence we blend stationary and movement exercises to increase tissue extensibility, core activation, and proprioceptive awareness.

Table 3.1 Prepractice Movement Routine

Exercise
1. Knee to chest (p. 37)
2. Reverse lunge with reach to quad stretch (p. 38)
3. Walking single-leg Romanian deadlift to reach (p. 40)
4. Single-leg lateral reach with hands overhead (p. 45)
5. Lateral lunge with rotation (p. 46)
6. Forward/backward hip rotation to drop squat (p. 39)
7. Hip poppers (p. 50)
8. Quick feet carioca to high knee carioca (p. 49)

Pregame Movement Routine

The sequence of exercises presented in table 3.2 is an example of a pregame movement routine. A neural drive warm-up, it should be performed after doing the mobility and stability exercises explained in chapter 4. These eight exercises are useful when there is a limited amount of time for a warm-up because they comprise quick, intense movements that improve proprioception before playing.

With the greater amount of time usually allotted for a general practice, the prepractice and pregame movement routines can be combined.

Table 3.2   Pregame Movement Routine

Exercise
1. Forward/backward hip rotation to drop squat (p. 39)
2. Backward low walk to backward run (p. 41)
3. Ankle flips (p. 42)
4. Hands overhead A-skip (p. 43)
5. 45-degree hop (p. 44)
6. Lateral explosive step (p. 47)
7. Lateral push-off skip (p. 48)
8. Lateral crossover step to base (p. 50)

Halftime Movement Routine

After an extended period of rest during halftime, muscles get cold and the body stiffens up. Performing a dynamic warm-up during halftime rewarms the body for competition, and doing movement exercises maximizes the athlete's ability to perform when the game starts back up. Table 3.3 provides an example of a halftime movement routine to increase the athlete's core temperature while stimulating muscle activation and organizing the body to perform efficiently.

Table 3.3   Halftime Movement Routine

Exercise
1. Knee to chest (p. 37)
2. Lateral lunge with rotation (p. 46)
3. Forward/backward hip rotation to drop squat (p. 39)
4. Backward low walk to backward run (p. 41)
5. 45-degree hop (p. 44)
6. Single-leg lateral reach with hands overhead (p. 45)
7. Lateral explosive step (p. 47)
8. Quick feet carioca to high knee carioca (p. 49)

CONCLUSION

To wrap up this chapter, remember that the margin between winning and losing in basketball is very small. Daily improvements in movement literacy add up, creating positive adaptations over time. Similarly, a preventative approach can reduce athletes' injury risk and improve their performance.

Chapter 4

Mobility and Flexibility Training

Tim Nwachukwu/Getty Images

Mobility and flexibility are very important to a basketball player's health and performance. Mobility and flexibility enhance each other in a way that improvement in one area benefits the other: Increased flexibility improves mobility and vice versa.

In this chapter we demonstrate areas of flexibility and how they relate to mobility—for example, using a band to increase ankle flexibility and pairing it with a mobility exercise such as a slant board dorsiflexion step-over. We will move up the chair from the ankle, knees, hips, back, and shoulders, pairing two of the targeted body movements with each other.

A simple definition of flexibility is the ability to bend without breaking. The exercise-specific definition of flexibility is the ability for a joint or a series of joints to move through an unrestricted and pain-free range of motion.

WAYS TO IMPROVE MOBILITY AND FLEXIBILITY

One way to increase flexibility is to warm up properly before beginning your workout. Proper warm-up before exercise is important because it allows the body to increase in temperature, heart rate, blood flow, and respiratory rate, drawing more oxygen to the muscles. All this helps in lubricating the joints and making tendons and ligaments more pliable and ready for exercise. (See chapter 3 for three movement preparation routines.)

The second way to improve flexibility is to do stretches for the targeted muscle group. This can be done by doing a "static stretch," in which a person holds a stretch for a certain amount of time—for example, a hamstring stretch in a supine position where the athlete raises the right leg upward, toward the sky, while keeping the left leg on the ground. The athlete grabs the right leg to help hold and maintain the stretch in the muscle. A static stretch can be held for 10 to 60 seconds or athlete preference. Another type of stretch is a dynamic stretch. This is where you are actively moving a joint and muscles to create tension and stretch over a muscle. An example of a dynamic stretch for the hamstring would be a standing toe touch in which you kick your leg upward to touch your outstretched hand, then repeat the process with the other leg.

The third way to improve flexibility is through mobility. Mobility is defined as the ability of a joint to move through a range of motion. With mobility we have a combination of movement and flexibility, each element enhancing the other.

Lack of mobility in one area of the body can often lead to stiffness in surrounding areas. For example, the lack of mobility in the ankle joint can cause an athlete to compensate in a negative way in the squat pattern. Often the athlete will compensate in the knees and hips if there is a lack of dorsiflexion in the ankle. The knees may go past the toes, or the feet will tend to turn outward in the squat.

MOBILITY AND FLEXIBILITY EXERCISES

The following exercises, when performed correctly and consistently, will improve flexibility and mobility of specific areas of the body. We start with the ankle and move up the body to the shoulder.

Ankle and Calf Flexibility: Box Stretch

Execution

1. Start with one foot raised on a box.
2. Make sure to keep the foot flat and do not let the heel come off the box (figure 4.1a)
3. Line the lower leg directly over the ankle and then slowly start to move the lower leg forward, allowing the knee to pass over the toes (figure 4.1b).
4. You will feel a stretch in the Achilles tendon and calf, with possible restriction on top of the ankle.
5. Move the lower leg in three directions: middle, left, and right. Perform for 5 reps or 10 to 20 seconds in each direction.
6. Repeat with the other foot on the box.

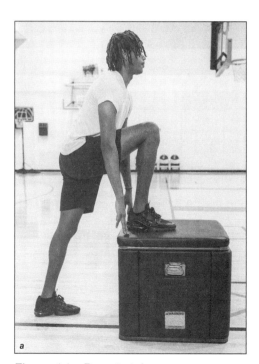 

Figure 4.1   Box stretch.

Ankle Mobility: Three-Way Slant Board Step-Over

Execution

1. Start with the heel in contact with the ground and half of the foot on the slant board.

2. First position is a straight line over the slant board. Take the opposite foot and step over the slant board in the same direction the foot on the slant board is facing.

3. As you step over, you will feel some restriction on top of the ankle as dorsiflexion increases. Allow the heel to lift up as you step over.

4. Turn the foot on the board slightly to the left and repeat the above steps, making sure to follow the direction of the foot. Now you will have different pinch points on the foot that is on the slant board.

5. The foot on the slant board is placed in three different positions: middle (figure 4.2a and 4.2b), left (figure 4.2c and 4.2d), and right (figure 4.2e and 4.2f). Step over 3 to 10 times, more if there are restrictions in a particular direction.

6. Repeat with the other foot on the slant board.

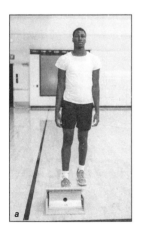  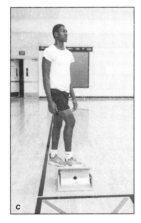 

Figure 4.2 Three-way slant board step-over: (a-b) foot facing forward, (c-d) foot facing to the left, and (e-f) foot facing to the right.

Quadriceps Flexibility: Half-Kneeling Stretch

Execution

1. Start in a half-kneeling position with a pad to support the knee that is on the ground (figure 4.3a).
2. Slowly move the hips forward without bending at the waist (figure 4.3b). With your back foot on the ground, you will feel the stretch over the quadriceps. Hold for 20 to 30 seconds.
3. Repeat on the opposite side.

Figure 4.3   Half-kneeling stretch.

(continued)

Variations

- To increase the stretch, raise the back foot slightly with a roller or yoga block (figure 4.4*a*). Slowly increase the stretch by bringing the back foot closer to the butt.
- This could be modified using a stretch cord around the foot or by grabbing the foot with one hand and pulling upward to bring the back foot closer to the butt (figure 4.4*b*).

Figure 4.4 Half-kneeling stretch variations: *(a)* rear foot elevated with foam roller; *(b)* grabbing the foot to increase the stretch.

Quadriceps Mobility: Slant Board Step-Up

Execution

1. Step onto a slant board with the right foot pointed downward. The left foot is positioned behind the slant board, slightly to the side and in a quarter-lunge position (figure 4.5a).
2. Lift the left foot and stand with the right foot on the slant board with the left leg in a 90-degree running position (figure 4.5b). Repeat the movement 5 to 10 times.
3. Switch to the left foot on the slant board and repeat.

Figure 4.5   Slant board step-up.

Hamstring Flexibility: Lying Hamstring Stretch

Execution

1. Wrap a stretch cord or resistance band around the middle of the right foot and lie on your back with both legs flat on the ground (figure 4.6a).

2. For the first stretch position, pull the band with your hands toward the head, keeping the right leg as straight as possible. Keep the left leg flat on the ground (figure 4.6b).

3. Move the right leg up and down three times and hold the stretch on the third raise for 5 to 10 seconds. Repeat with the left leg.

4. For the second stretch position, place the leg at a 45-degree angle and pull the band upward toward the head while keeping the leg straight. Repeat three times, holding for 5 to 10 seconds on the third raise (see figure 4.6c).

5. For the third stretch position, move the band leg across the body and lift three times, holding the third raise for 5 to 10 seconds (see figure 4.6d).

6. Repeat with the other leg.

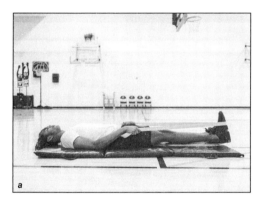

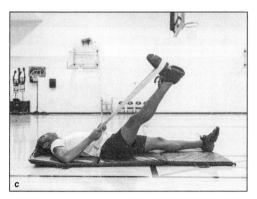
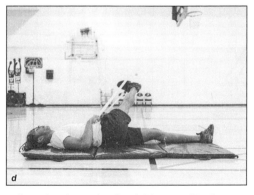

Figure 4.6 Lying hamstring stretch: *(a-b)* leg directly above body; *(c)* leg at 45-degree angle; *(d)* leg across body.

Hamstring Mobility: Lying Hip Thrust

Execution

1. Start by lying on your back with both knees bent and feet flat on the ground, close to the buttocks (see figure 4.7a).
2. Lift your hips, keeping the hips and shoulders square and feet flat on the ground. Make sure to engage the abs by contracting your core as if you were about to take a punch (see figure 4.7b).
3. Lift the hips up and down five times slowly and in control. You will feel the lower back, glutes, and hamstrings engaged.
4. Now move the feet away from the buttocks about six inches. Lift the toes so the weight is on the heels (figure 4.7c). Now lift the hips again for five reps at a slow pace with the abs engaged.
5. Now move the feet as far out as possible but still have the knees bent slightly. Stay on the heels and lift for five reps again (figure 4.7d). As the feet move away from the buttocks, hamstring engagement will vary.

Figure 4.7 Lying hip thrust: (a-b) initial position with feet close to buttocks; (c) feet 6 inches further away from buttocks; (d) feet as far out as possible while keeping the knees slightly bent.

Glute Flexibility: Figure 4 Stretch

Execution

1. Lie on your back with the knees bent. Cross your right leg over your left so that it resembles the number 4 (figure 4.8a).
2. Place your hands under your left thigh and lift the left foot off the ground (figure 4.8b). You will feel a stretch in your right glutes.
3. Hold for 5 to 10 seconds, keeping the back flat to the floor.
4. Repeat on the opposite side.

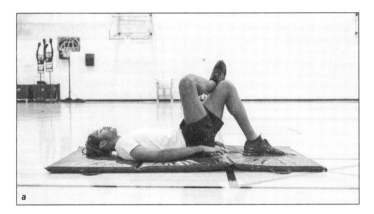

Figure 4.8   Figure 4 stretch.

Glute Mobility: Hip Drops

Execution

1. Start by placing one forearm on a mat and propping your body in a side plank position. The bottom leg is slightly bent and the weight is on the outside of the knee (figure 4.9a). When propped up, the top shoulder, hip, knee, and foot are in a straight line.

2. Lower the hip toward the floor from the side plank position and dip down slightly before moving up to the original position (figure 4.9b).

3. Do 5 to 10 reps up and down slowly, not allowing the bottom hip to touch the floor.

4. Repeat on the opposite side.

Figure 4.9   Hip drops.

Shoulder Flexibility: Three-Way Shoulder Stretch

Execution

1. Start on hands and knees, then rest one forearm on top of a physio ball.
2. The first position is straight overhead and pressing down to stretch the shoulder, lats, and triceps (figure 4.10a).
3. The second position is slightly angled to the left about 45 degrees across the body, also pressing down to increase the stretch (figure 4.10b).
4. The third position is across your body at about 90 degrees (see figure 4.10c).
5. Hold each position for 20 to 30 seconds.
6. Repeat with the opposite arm.

Figure 4.10 Three-way shoulder stretch: *(a)* straight overhead, *(b)* 45 degrees across the body, and *(c)* 90 degrees across the body.

Shoulder Mobility: Three-Way Shoulder Activation

Execution

1. Stand tall with a band or cord attached to a pulley system. Bend the knees slightly. Grab the cord or handles with your thumbs facing upward (figure 4.11*a*).
2. First pull is to move the cord apart overhead, opening your arms in a Y pattern (4.11*b*).
3. Second pull is across the chest, moving the cord in a T pattern (4.11*c*).
4. Third pull is moving the cord directly overhead with arms straight up in an I pattern (4.11*d*).
5. Do 5 to 10 reps for each movement.

Figure 4.11   Three-way shoulder activation: *(a)* start position, *(b)* Y position, *(c)* T position, and *(d)* I position.

CONCLUSION

None of the exercises mentioned in this chapter take a lot of time. The more you do them the easier they get, and this keeps the athlete prepped before the actual workout. These movements can be imagined as daily doses of vitamins. Instead of swallowing the vitamins, you are preparing your body for activity. Just like taking vitamins, to be effective these exercises should be done daily and consistently.

Strength Training

The best basketball players in the world are amazing athletes. Underlying their impressive athleticism is a tremendous amount of strength. This chapter shows you how to increase strength and explosiveness for more stability when boxing out, how to jump higher, be more agile, and shoot with more ease and from greater range, all of which will boost confidence and result in better performance on the court.

Strength training not only helps players perform better on the court but also helps reduce the risk and severity of injuries. To reduce injury risk, it is important to understand the nature of the sport. Basketball is a high-intensity sport that requires many multidirectional efforts performed at various speeds and angles for varying lengths of time. The primary goal of a good basketball strength training program is to improve overall athletic abilities and ensure that the new abilities transfer to the basketball movements on the court.

A by-product of a properly structured basketball-specific program is the reduced risk of injury resulting from the development of bigger and stronger muscles and tendons. Stronger muscles and tendons are more capable of handling the large forces that they are exposed to while playing, which helps reduce the risk of injury. Another important goal of strength training is to improve the body's ability to tolerate progressively increasing practice and game workloads over time. Stronger and better-prepared tissue is able to recover faster between games and practices, and thus the risk of overuse injuries is lower. These benefits are not restricted solely to muscles and tendons but are also seen in developing stronger bones.

Muscle imbalances are a component that must be well understood and addressed in a complete training program. It is typical for athletes to perform an incredibly high number of repetitions and movements daily to improve their game. The sheer volume of repetitions and drills can create muscle imbalances where one side of the body naturally becomes "dominant" and stronger compared to the other side. In order to combat the overuse of one side of the body it is important that basketball players perform unilateral (single arm or leg) training in their program. Unilateral training will help to identify a lack of symmetry between the right and left sides of the body. Once identified, the weaker side can be strengthened to provide better symmetry and protection against injuries.

Before presenting the exercises that most effectively help players develop functional basketball strength and prevent injuries, it's important to review some key information you should know and consider in developing and maintaining this key physical component of basketball performance.

TYPES OF STRENGTH

Strength can be defined as the capability to overcome a certain resistance or muscular tension acting against a certain resistance. There are three main types of strength capacity:

- Maximum strength
- Explosive strength
- Strength endurance (Schmolinsky 1993)

The maximal effort method is defined as lifting a maximal load, the dynamic effort method is defined as lifting or throwing medium and light loads with maximum speed, the repeated effort method is defined as lifting medium loads to failure, and the submaximal effort is defined as lifting medium loads an intermediate number of times (not to failure) (Zatsiorsky 1995).

Maximum Strength

Maximum strength is defined as the maximum force produced in a single voluntary contraction. In the weight room, it would be the maximum weight that an athlete can squat for one repetition, for example. Training for maximum strength requires large loads lifted for few repetitions, which in turn requires a tremendous amount of coordination between muscles. Maximum strength can be viewed in one of two ways:

- **Absolute strength:** maximum force generated
- **Relative strength:** maximum force generated relative to the player's body weight

A practical example of the need for maximum strength in basketball would be when two opponents are fighting for position around the basket. If both players are of similar size and use similar technique, then the player with the greater maximal strength will win the position.

Explosive Strength

Strength development also must be considered in relation to the time and the speed (rate) at which strength is utilized in a game. Being maximally strong without the ability to generate strength rapidly is not very helpful, since basketball is a sport characterized primarily by explosive actions.

Explosive strength is the ability to generate maximum strength in minimal time. Since that time factor is so important we refer to explosive strength as rate of force development (RFD). In the weight room, it would be how fast an athlete can squat a particular weight for one repetition, and on the court, how fast an athlete can create force to drive out of the bottom position of a jump.

Now imagine how this RFD factor transfers to the basketball court. Say two explosive athletes weigh the same, both squat 400 pounds (181 kg), and both jump 40 inches (1 m). Player A drops deeper in the squat portion of his jump and takes significantly longer to complete his jump compared to player B. Both players jump 40 inches, but practically speaking, if both players initiate their jumps for a rebound at the same exact time, Player B will get to the ball before Player A. So, although both players have the same maximum strength, Player B has greater explosive strength and therefore has the advantage in rebounding over Player A.

Strength Endurance

Strength endurance is the combination of the very different attributes of strength and endurance. Strength endurance can be thought of as the ability to sustain the various types of strength efforts. In the weight room it could be the ability to sustain great speed and explosiveness throughout a set of explosive squat jumps, for example. On the court, strength endurance is evidenced when players defend in the proper stance, box out and jump repetitively to rebound, drive to the basket through contact, or shoot from range through the course of a game.

THREE PHASES OF MUSCLE CONTRACTIONS

The three phases of muscular contraction are eccentric, isometric, and concentric. Each of these phases can be trained with maximal effort strength training methods, explosive or dynamic strength training methods, or submaximal strength training methods.

All three phases of muscle contraction are involved in every movement a player makes on the court. To fully understand and plan the training that enhances performance, each phase's characteristics must be fully understood.

Eccentric Muscle Actions
- An increase of muscle tension by the lengthening of the muscle
- The muscle lengthens and force is produced in order to yield against the load.
- For example, in the barbell squat the eccentric phase would be from the beginning of the squat, when the lifter lowers the weight by squatting down to a determined depth.

Isometric Muscle Actions
- An increase in muscle tension without a change in the length of the muscle
- Fibers contract and maintain the muscle length to keep the load motionless or to push against an immovable load.
- For example, in the barbell squat this would be at the bottom of the squat exercise where there is a brief moment when the squat is held stationary prior to lifting the weight back up to the standing position.

Concentric Muscle Actions
- An increase in muscle tension by the shortening of the muscle
- The muscle shortens and force is produced in order to overcome the load.
- For example, in the barbell squat this would be the lifting of the weight from the bottom of the squat up to the standing position.

BASKETBALL-SPECIFIC STRENGTH TRAINING

Basketball has its own specific multidirectional movement patterns that need to be performed skillfully to have success in playing the game. Jump shots, layups, and defensive slides are some of the many movements that are frequently repeated in a training session or game. These movements involve not only coordination but also strength and endurance of the muscles involved. Basketball-specific training helps athletes meet higher physiological and mechanical demands as their game improves and they reach higher levels of competition.

Put simply, specificity means that within reason, the closer training is to the game of basketball, the better the results will be. Therefore, in theory, the more specific the exercises used in the resistance training program are to the movements and speeds found in a sport (i.e., the actual speed of movement, type of muscle action, joint angles, and so on), the better the adaptations transfer to the sport. However, playing and practicing basketball alone is insufficient because it takes specific resistance training to develop the qualities needed to improve health and performance.

Programs that are specific to basketball focus on the demands of the game, such as duration, type of action, speed of action, and rest between action during the game as well as the cardiorespiratory, neurological, and muscular systems. All should be considered when designing the optimal training program.

Basketball is a three-dimensional game because it includes forward, backward, vertical, lateral, and rotational actions on the court. To support the three-dimensional aspects of the game, it is important to include strength exercises that utilize the various planes of motion.

- **Sagittal plane:** forward and backward, such as a forward lunge or backward lunge
- **Frontal plane:** side to side, such as a lateral side lunge
- **Transverse plane:** rotational, for example, a rotational lunge

STRENGTH TRAINING BASICS

Muscle growth or hypertrophy is the goal of strength training. Muscle fibers are enlarged through heavy resistance training (French and Ronda 2021). There are two types of muscle fibers, type I and type II. Type I are the "slow twitch" fibers, which are more fatigue resistant and have high endurance capability. Type II are the "fast twitch" fibers, which have a great capacity for explosive actions or anaerobic power but are not optimal for endurance. Training of both fiber types is necessary to be able to play basketball at a high level.

Muscle hypertrophy is achieved through progressive overload. Progressive overload entails placing greater than normal demands (training volume) on the exercising musculature over time. Studies show that the training volume known for optimal results in the hypertrophy phase is about 3 to 6 sets per muscle group. The load should be moderate, 67 to 85 percent of the 1 repetition maximum (RM), and the goal repetitions 6 to 12 for a period up to 6 weeks (French and Ronda 2021).

Strength training properly and safely is essential for optimal results and avoiding injury. Here are some key measures to ensure the best results.

- **Maintaining proper and safe spacing.** Examine the workout area and make sure there is enough space to work out safely and efficiently. Look for unracked dumbbells or weight plates, loose collars, medicine balls, stability balls, or anything else on the floor that could cause an injury. Also check the flooring to make sure it is clean, dry, and not slippery. Make sure the ceiling is high enough to safely perform overhead exercises. Check for low-hanging overhead lighting or anything hanging from the ceiling. Make sure there is enough room to perform the exercise without bumping into a wall, equipment, or other athletes. This is just common sense, but common sense goes a long way in preventing injuries.

- **Determining the correct weight.** Different methods can be used to determine the correct weight for an exercise. A popular method involves calculating certain percentages based on the maximum weight the athlete can lift for one repetition. We prefer using the trial-and-error method: Start by warming up with a very light weight to prevent injury and to prepare the muscles. Move up to a light, comfortable weight for the first set. Then move the weight up each additional set until the weight is very hard to lift on the last two or three repetitions without compromising good technique for the prescribed sets and repetitions.

- **Bracing the core.** When lifting weights it is important to tighten the core in order to provide stability in your trunk and spine. Bracing your core means engaging your entire trunk—abdominals, pelvic floor, diaphragm, and spinal erectors—to create the stability required to lift effectively and safely. A braced core provides not only safety but also an effective force transfer through your body to move the weight.

- **Breathing.** Proper breathing technique is very important when strength training. The simple rule is to take a deep breath and hold it during the beginning of the exercise, or the eccentric phase (lengthening of the muscle). Exhale during the finishing part of the movement, or the concentric phase (shortening of the muscle). For example, when doing the bench press, as your arms are extended straight up, take a deep breath and hold it while lowering the bar to your chest, and exhale during the finish part of the pressing movement. Repeat this process throughout each repetition. This method of breathing will allow for a large blood return to your heart, which reduces heart stress. For the explosive, Olympic-type movements, there are exceptions to the breathing rules. The lifter holds their breath during the exertion phases of an Olympic-type movement and inhales between the exertion phases.

- **Performing barbell safety checks.** Before lifting with a barbell, always check the following:

  – The same weight is loaded on each end of the bar.
  – Each end of the bar has a collar.
  – The collars are secure.

- **Spotting.** Proper spotting is extremely important in any strength training program. Spotting involves observing or helping a person through an exercise. "Helping" means helping to raise the weight or helping to balance it when the lifter performs an exercise. When spotting, be sure to keep your eyes on the bar and the lifter at all times. Look for a breakdown in technique, a loss of balance, or a sticking point during the exercise—all indicate that assistance is needed.

  Some exercises (such as the bench press, incline bench press, and seated dumbbell shoulder press) may require a lift-off to start the movement. For a balanced lift-off, the spotter's hands should be evenly spaced on the bar with one hand over the bar and one hand under the bar. Here is a good procedure to follow:

  1. The lifter or spotter counts to 3.
  2. On the count of 3, the spotter and the lifter lift the bar to the starting position together.
  3. Once the lifter has the bar under control, the spotter removes their hands from the bar and the lifter starts the exercise.
  4. The spotter should also help the lifter rerack the weight at the completion of the exercise.

  When spotting a lifter who is using dumbbells, watch to see if the dumbbells stray from the proper exercise groove. If they do, grab the lifter's wrists and help guide the dumbbells into the proper groove.

- **Training through the proper range of motion.** To keep flexibility and mobility in the muscles and joints, train through the proper range of motion. Failure to train through the proper range of motion creates a chance that the muscles will shorten, causing a lack of flexibility and increasing your chance of injury. For example, during the biceps curl, the arms should hang straight down at the start and be fully flexed at the elbow joint at the top of the movement. Imagine the effect of shooting a basketball if the biceps had lost some flexibility and incurred a limited range of motion during the follow-through. If you continually shorten the movement in this exercise, the biceps may begin to lose its range of motion, which could affect proper shooting technique. This may also lead to an injury.

- **Controlling the speed of movement.** The speed at which an exercise is performed is very important. Once you have mastered the technique of the exercise, more explosive speed can be utilized on exercises as determined by the program. However, a large proportion of strength training involves controlling both the lowering and the raising phases of the lift. Each repetition should be a smooth, controlled movement. An exception is the explosive Olympic movements used to target explosive strength. Perform those movements as fast as possible with proper technique as dictated in the program.

• **Resting between sets.** Rest periods between sets vary according to strength training goals. For example, low-intensity, high-volume workouts, such as circuit training with lighter weights, require less recovery time. The rest period between these sets can be 30 to 60 seconds. The goal is to increase muscular endurance and conditioning. High-intensity low-volume training that uses sets and repetitions with heavy weight requires more rest and recovery time. The rest period between those sets can be 3 to 5 minutes. The goal is to increase strength and power. A good general guideline for recovery between sets is 30 seconds to 2 minutes for lower-intensity, lighter-weight workouts and 3 to 5 minutes for higher-intensity, heavier-weight workouts.

• **Planning exercise order.** When planning a workout, outline a plan of attack for each training session. A general rule of thumb is to do explosive exercises early in the workout, then target the major muscle groups before the smaller muscle groups. When doing a lower-body workout, first perform hang cleans, squats, leg presses, lunges, and step-ups. When doing a total-body program in the same day, follow the exercise order for both upper-body and lower-body exercises. The exercises in the strength training programs in chapter 12 are in the proper exercise order.

STRENGTH TRAINING EXERCISES

This section contains the strength training exercises that we have found most beneficial for basketball players. Each includes explanations and photos presenting the correct technique to get the best results. The exercises are organized into the following three categories: total-body/power, lower-body strength, and upper-body strength.

Some words of caution: No two people are exactly alike. You need to be aware of individual differences as they relate to proper technique in strength training exercises. First you should adjust the equipment and weight to fit your body and individual needs for each exercise. Very few people are capable of perfect technique on all lifts. Technique may vary depending on individual differences. You might have to make adjustments in range of motion, grips, stances, and grooves. To be on the safe side, have a qualified coach or instructor evaluate your lifting technique.

TOTAL-BODY/POWER EXERCISES

Trap Bar Clean Pull

Execution

1. Begin by standing inside the curve of the bar with your feet hip-width apart.
2. Grip the bar with both hands. Keep your back tight and flat and your shoulders over your feet as you bend your knees and lower your hips to prepare for the first pull (figure 5.1*a*).
3. First pull: Slowly lift the bar from the floor using your legs, keeping your shoulders over your feet and your back flat (figure 5.1*b*). Don't jerk the bar from the floor. Keep your butt down until the bar clears your knees. Lift your butt a little to prepare for the second pulling phase of the lift.
4. Second pull: Initiate the second pull by explosively extending your legs, hips and back, keeping your arms straight. Thrust your shoulders back and up. Thrust your hips forward and up.
5. Straighten your legs and extend up onto your toes while shrugging the shoulders upward (figure 5.1*c*).
6. As you complete the explosive portion of the lift, slightly bend your knees to prevent back strain at the end of the rep.
7. Slowly lower the bar back to the floor using your legs, keeping your shoulders over your feet and your back flat. Keep your butt down until the bar reaches the floor.
8. Repeat for the desired number of repetitions.

Figure 5.1 Trap bar clean pull.

Dumbbell Power Drop Pause Jump

Execution

This exercise can be done with dumbbells or kettlebells. The focus of this exercise is to achieve the greatest possible speed on the drop portion of the lift, pausing and exploding up into the air taking great care to maintain the best possible technique and body position.

1. Begin by standing tall and holding a dumbbell in each hand (figure 5.2*a*).
2. For the explosive portion of the lift, rapidly drop down to the bottom of the half-squat position (i.e., slightly above thighs parallel to the ground) or quarter-squat position (figure 5.2*b*) and hold there for a count of 2.
3. After the two count, initiate the pull by explosively extending your legs, hips, and back, keeping your arms straight. Thrust your shoulders back and up. Thrust your hips forward and up.
4. Straighten your legs and jump up into the air (figure 5.2*c*).
5. As you complete the jump it is important to land in a good position, with knees bent, hips back, chest up, and the back flat.
6. Standing tall, return to the starting position for the next repetition.
7. When you have performed all repetitions, slowly lower the weight to the floor or place the dumbbells safely on a box or bench.

Figure 5.2 Dumbbell power drop pause jump.

Rear Foot Elevated Drop Catch

Execution

This exercise can be done with dumbbells, kettlebells, or body weight. This exercise is performed in the rear foot elevated position with the foot up on a bench behind you.

1. If using dumbbells or kettlebells, hold them at your sides.
2. Stand a few feet in front of a bench and reach your right foot back to place it on top of the bench while keeping your left leg directly under your hips and your head, shoulders, and torso perpendicular to the ground (figure 5.3a). Keep your shoulders and hips square as you maintain your balance.
3. Quickly drop into the bottom of a split squat by bending the knee of the standing leg and allowing a free fall.
4. Catch yourself by decelerating quickly, just before the knee of the rear support leg touches the ground (figure 5.3b).
5. Extend the knee of the stance leg to return to a tall standing position, making sure to keep your back straight and the weights by your sides.
6. Complete all repetitions on the right leg before moving on to the left leg.

Figure 5.3   Rear foot elevated drop catch.

Push Press

Execution

1. Begin by standing tall with dumbbells set on the front of each shoulder or the barbell in the hang-clean racked position. Perform a one-eighth to one-quarter squat while maintaining a tight, flat back as the bar rests on the front part of your shoulders (figure 5.4a).

2. Explosively extend your legs as your hips come forward, up, and through. Push the bar with your arms straight up overhead (figure 5.4b). Reach complete lockout in one explosive motion with slightly bent knees as a safety cushion.

3. Return the bar with control to the original starting position on the front of your shoulders using your legs as a cushion.

4. When you have performed all desired repetitions, slowly lower the weight to the floor.

Figure 5.4   Push press.

Kettlebell Snatch

Execution

1. Stand with the feet shoulder-width or slightly wider apart with the kettlebell on the floor in front of and in between the feet.
2. Bending slightly at the knees but hinging mainly at the hips, grasp the kettlebell with your right hand and pull it back between your legs to create momentum (figure 5.5*a*).
3. Drive your hips forward and straighten your back to begin moving the kettlebell upward.
4. Once the bell passes chest height, gently pull it back and slide your fist around and under the bell, then punch it upward so it nestles softly on the back of your wrist with your arm straight above your head (figure 5.5*b*).
5. You should punch the bell upward at the end of the move just as it nestles onto the back of your wrist. If it slaps the back of your wrist with a thud, that means the timing of the movement is off and should be adjusted.
6. Perform for the desired number of repetitions, then repeat with the left arm.

Figure 5.5 Kettlebell snatch.

Dumbbell Single-Leg Snatch to Box

Execution

1. Stand in front of a box or bench with your feet shoulder-width apart and hold a dumbbell in each hand.

2. Perform a single-leg Romanian deadlift by hinging back and reaching the dumbbells down toward the foot of the supporting leg (figure 5.6a).

3. Quickly explode out of the bottom position by swinging the dumbbells to an overhead position while also bringing the lifted leg forward and high to the top of the bench.

4. Keep the dumbbells close to your body as you pull it up in a straight line. As the dumbbells reach chest level, flip your wrists so that your palms face forward and catch the weight (figure 5.6b).

5. Lower the weight back down to the starting position. Repeat for the desired number of repetitions and then switch legs.

Figure 5.6 Dumbbell single-leg snatch to box.

Hang Pull

Execution

1. Stand with your feet hip-width apart, bar near your shins. Hold the bar in a closed pronated grip, palms turned toward the body.

2. Slowly stand up with the bar close to your body. Maintain an upright head and shoulders. Use your legs to lift the weight. Maintain a tight, flat back and straight arms.

3. Bend over by sliding the bar down your thighs to the power pulling position, just above your knees (figure 5.7a).

4. Initiate the pull by explosively extending your legs, hips, and back, keeping your arms straight. Thrust your shoulders back and up. Thrust your hips forward and up.

5. Straighten your legs and extend up onto your toes before pulling with your arms. Keep the bar close to your body.

6. As the bar reaches your upper chest, slightly bend your knees (figure 5.7b).

7. Slowly lower the bar, keeping it close to your body. To prevent lower-back strain, as the bar descends it should brush your thighs and your knees should be slightly bent. Stand straight up and then lower the bar to thigh level just above your knees and perform the next repetition.

8. After performing all repetitions, slowly lower the weight to the floor, reversing the technique in step 2.

Figure 5.7 Hang pull.

Hang Clean

Execution

1. Stand with your feet hip-width apart, bar near your shins. Grip the bar in a closed pronated wide grip, palms turned toward the body.

2. Slowly stand up with the bar, keeping it close to your body. Keep your head and shoulders up. Use your legs to lift the weight. Maintain a tight, flat back and straight arms.

3. Bend over by sliding the bar down your thighs to the power pulling position, just above your knees (figure 5.8a).

4. Initiate the pull by explosively extending your legs, hips, and back, keeping your arms straight. Thrust your shoulders back and up. Thrust your hips forward and up.

5. Straighten your legs and extend up onto your toes before pulling with your arms (figure 5.8b). Keep the bar close to your body.

6. As the bar reaches your upper chest, lower your body to one-eighth to one-quarter squat position before the bar starts to descend in preparation for catching or racking the bar on your shoulders. Rotate your wrists back around and under the bar, lifting your elbows high out in front of the bar. Carry the bar on your shoulders with your knees slightly bent to cushion the impact (figure 5.8c). Stand up straight with the bar racked.

7. Slowly lower the bar, keeping it close to your body. To prevent lower-back strain, as the bar descends it should brush your thighs and your knees should be slightly bent. Stand straight up and then lower the bar to thigh level just above your knees and perform the next repetition.

8. When you have performed all repetitions, slowly lower the weight to the floor, reversing the technique in step 2.

Figure 5.8   Hang clean.

Power Clean From the Ground

Execution

1. Stand with your feet hip-width apart, bar near your shins. Grip the bar with a closed pronated grip, palms turned toward your body, hands shoulder-width apart.

2. Keep your back tight and flat and your shoulders over the bar, then bend your knees and lower your hips to prepare for the first pull (figure 5.9a).

3. First pull: Slowly lift the bar from the floor using your legs, keeping your shoulders over the bar and your back flat. Don't jerk the bar from the floor. Keep the bar close to your body and your butt down until the bar clears your knees. Lift your butt a little to prepare for the scoop (the second pulling phase of the lift).

4. Second pull: Initiate the second pull by explosively extending your legs, hips and back, keeping your arms straight. Thrust your shoulders back and up. Thrust your hips forward and up (figure 5.9b).

5. Straighten your legs and extend up onto your toes before pulling with your arms. Keep the bar close to your body.

6. A proper finish to this lift is critical. As the bar reaches your upper chest, lower your body to a one-eighth to one-quarter squat position before the bar starts to descend in preparation for the catching or racking the bar on your shoulders. Rotate your wrists back around and under the bar, lifting your elbows high out in front of the bar. Carry the bar on your shoulders with your knees slightly bent to cushion the impact (figure 5.9c). Stand up straight with the bar racked.

7. Slowly lower the bar, keeping it close to your body. To prevent lower-back strain, as the bar descends it should brush your thighs and your knees should be slightly bent. Lower the bar to the floor, using your legs, keeping your shoulders over the bar and your back flat. Keep the bar close to your body and your butt down until the bar reaches the floor.

Figure 5.9 Power clean from the ground.

LOWER-BODY STRENGTH EXERCISES

Stability Ball Leg Curl

Execution

1. Begin by lying face up on the floor with your lower legs on top of a stability ball, your ankles dorsiflexed (toes and feet pulled up toward your shins), and your arms out to the sides for stability.
2. Straighten the lower back, knees, and hips by raising the back and hips off the floor (figure 5.10a).
3. Keeping your hips and low back straight, bend your knees and pull them toward your butt. Allow the feet to roll up onto the ball (figure 5.10b).
4. Return to the starting position by straightening the knees until the body is back to the supine position described in step 2 of this exercise.
5. Repeat for the desired number of repetitions.

Variation

This exercise can be done single leg with the same technique.

Figure 5.10   Stability ball leg curl.

Standing Calf Raise

Execution

1. This exercise can be done on a standing calf machine or as a single-leg version, holding a dumbbell while standing on the edge of a small box or platform.

2. For the single-leg version, hold a dumbbell in the hand on the same side as the leg you are working. Stand with the toes of the working leg on the edge of the platform with the heel down and the calf stretched.

3. Raise up on the toes of the working leg and hold for a count of 2 (figure 5.11).

4. Return to the starting position slowly by lowering for a count of 3 seconds. The only joint movement is in the ankle.

5. Repeat for the desired number of repetitions. Be sure to complete each set with both legs if doing the single-leg version.

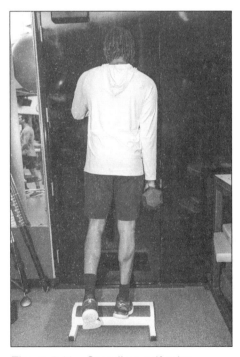

Figure 5.11 Standing calf raise.

Seated Calf Raise

Execution

1. This exercise is ideally done on a seated calf machine, or the single-leg version can be done seated on a bench with a heavy dumbbell placed on the knee.

2. Begin seated with your feet on the seated calf machine and the knees underneath the pads, heels down, calves stretched.

3. Raise up on your toes as high as possible and hold for a count of 2 (figure 5.12).

4. Return to the starting position slowly by lowering for a count of 3 seconds. The only joint movement is in the ankles.

5. Repeat for the desired number of repetitions. Be sure to complete each set with both legs if doing the single-leg version.

Figure 5.12   Seated calf raise.

Back Extension

Execution

1. On a back extension bench, place your heels under the heel pads and your thighs on the thigh pad with enough room to bend over.
2. Start at the bottom position with your torso perpendicular to the ground and your arms crossed on your chest (figure 5.13a).
3. Raise your torso, keeping your back straight, until it is parallel to the ground or slightly above the thigh pad (figure 5.13b).
4. Slowly return to the starting position, keeping your back straight.
5. Repeat for the desired number of repetitions.

Note: Control both the raising and lowering phases. Do not hyperextend your lower back at the top of the movement.

Variation

This exercise can also be done with one leg by slipping the off leg outside the heel pads so that it is hanging freely in the air. Perform the single-leg version exactly the same as the double-leg version, completing the required number of repetitions for each leg.

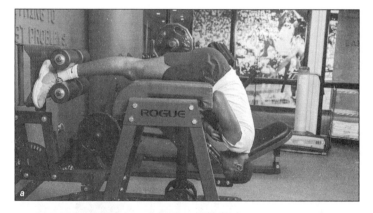

Figure 5.13   Back extension.

Supported Single-Leg Romanian Deadlift

1. Stand tall with a dumbbell in the left hand and the right hand lightly holding onto a rack for stability (figure 5.14a).
2. With the right knee slightly bent, lift the left leg off of the ground and slowly bend over, keeping your back straight, and lower the dumbbell along your leg toward the top of your foot (figure 5.14b). Do not round your back. Do not bang the weight on the floor or bounce at the bottom of the movement.
3. Slowly return to a full standing position, keeping your back straight.
4. If possible, complete each repetition without the foot touching the ground in between.
5. After completing all of the desired repetitions on one leg, switch to the other leg.

Figure 5.14   Supported single-leg Romanian deadlift.

Single-Leg Romanian Deadlift to Hip Lock Iso

Execution

1. Stand tall with a dumbbell in each hand down by your sides. Lift one leg off the floor and slowly bend forward at the hips, keeping your back straight and lowering the dumbbells along your leg toward the top of your foot (figure 5.15a). Do not round your back. Do not bang the weight on the floor or bounce at the bottom of the movement.

2. Quickly extend through your hips, driving up to a standing position. Keep your back straight and drive the opposing leg upward into a hip-flexed position. While driving your knee upward, also actively pull the dumbbells upward, relying heavily on momentum and making sure to keep the weight close to your body.

3. As you approach a single-leg standing position, allow both arms to extend overhead while maintaining control of the dumbbells (figure 5.15b).

4. Carefully lock out the standing leg and both arms while in the single-leg standing position.

5. After completing the desired number of repetitions on one leg, switch to the other leg.

Figure 5.15   Single-leg Romanian deadlift to hip lock iso.

Single-Arm Dumbbell Lateral Lunge

Execution

1. Stand tall with a dumbbell in your right hand resting on the front of your thigh (figure 5.16a).
2. Step laterally to the left with the left foot.
3. As your foot contacts the floor, bend at the knee and hips and allow your chest to drop slightly toward the floor. Reach with the dumbbell in the direction of motion, making sure to keep the weight on the inside of the leg (figure 5.16b).
4. Drive the outside foot into the ground and extend at the knee and hips to return to a standing position.
5. Repeat for the desired number of repetitions and then switch legs, making sure to also switch the hand holding the dumbbell.

Figure 5.16   Single-arm dumbbell lateral lunge.

Lunge Matrix

Execution

This exercise can be done with dumbbells, kettlebells, a medicine ball, or body weight. It has three parts: forward lunge, lateral lunge, and 45-degree backward lunge.

1. Start in a standing position. If using dumbbells or kettlebells, hold them at your sides (figure 5.17a). If using a medicine ball, hold it against your chest.

2. Lunge forward until your thigh is parallel to the ground and your shin is relatively vertical (figure 5.17b). Do not allow the knee on the trailing leg to touch the floor.

3. Push off with your right leg and step back to the starting position.

4. For the lateral lunge, step to the side with your right leg, keeping your head, shoulders and torso upright and square until your thigh is almost parallel to the floor (figure 5.17c). The trailing leg should be straight (knee locked out).

5. Push off with your right leg and step back to the starting position.

6. To execute the 45-degree backward lunge, step and turn the body until you are facing 45 degrees to the side (one-quarter turn) while maintaining a straight (near locked out) front leg. Drop down into the lunge while maintaining an upright chest (figure 5.17d).

7. Push back to the forward-facing start position. Complete the desired number of repetitions before switching to the other leg. For example, 9 reps would be alternating between the three positions until 3 reps have been completed on each.

Figure 5.17 Lunge matrix: (a) starting position, (b) forward lunge, (c) lateral lunge, and (d) 45-degree backward lunge.

Resisted Lateral Drive

Execution

1. Stand in an athletic position with your feet shoulder-width apart and knees bent with an anchored resistance band around your waist pulling from a lateral direction (figure 5.18a).
2. Slightly lift the outside foot and drive from the inside foot in a lateral jumping motion against the resistance of the band (figure 5.18b).
3. Land carefully on both feet, stabilizing your landing position.
4. Step back toward the starting position and repeat for the desired number of repetitions. After completing all the repetitions on one leg, turn to switch sides and repeat on the other leg.

Figure 5.18 Resisted lateral drive.

Dumbbell Iso Lunge With Floating Heel

Execution

1. Stand tall in a split stance with a dumbbell in each hand down by your sides. Make sure your feet are hip-width apart and the heel of your front foot is up and actively avoiding contact with the ground. You can place the ball of your foot on a small riser or bumper plate lying flat on the floor to help keep the heel up if desired.

2. Flex both knees and descend into the bottom of a split squat position, making sure to maintain about 90 degrees of hip and knee flexion on the front leg and 90 degrees of knee flexion on the back leg (figure 5.19).

3. Hold this position for the desired amount of time and then switch legs.

Figure 5.19   Dumbbell iso lunge with floating heel.

Back Squat

Execution

1. Place the bar on the rack just below your shoulders so it is necessary to squat slightly to place the bar on the back of your shoulders.

2. Grip the barbell, hands in a medium to wide overhand grip. Raise your elbows to create a muscular shelf for the bar across the posterior deltoids and upper trapezius. Do not put the bar on your neck; it should be below your neck.

3. Stand with both feet and hips under the bar, then straighten your legs to lift the bar off the rack.

4. Step back from the rack and get in a set position. Stand with feet slightly wider than the hips and toes pointed out slightly (figure 5.20a).

5. Keep your eyes, head, shoulders, and chest up, and maintain a tight back throughout the lift.

6. Squat down under control, leading with your hips, until your thighs are parallel to the ground (figure 5.20b). Do not bounce at the bottom of the movement. Keep your knees in line with your toes; don't allow your knees to move inside or outside the normal tracking of the knee joint or move out in front of your toes. Keep your weight evenly distributed over your feet; do not shift your weight forward to your toes.

7. Raise the bar by straightening your hips and knees while maintaining correct body position. Keep your hips underneath your torso; do not round your back or lean forward on your feet.

8. Repeat for the desired number of repetitions. When you have finished the set, slowly walk back into the rack with both feet and hips underneath the bar. Squat down and lower the bar back into the rack.

Spotting: Spot from behind, helping the lifter out of the rack. Squat each repetition with the lifter, hands underneath the bar or underneath the lifter's arm near the lifter's chest. Assist only if necessary by grabbing the bar or chest from underneath; then the spotter and lifter together squat the weight up to a safe position. Walk forward and help the lifter safely into the rack. Adjust the safety bars inside the rack to just below parallel to catch the bar if need be.

Figure 5.20   Back squat.

Goblet Squat

Execution

1. Start by holding a kettlebell or dumbbell with both hands in front of the chest. Stand with your feet slightly wider than the hips and the toes pointed out slightly (figure 5.21*a*).

2. Keep your eyes, head, shoulders, and chest up and maintain a tight back throughout the lift.

3. Squat down under control, leading with your hips, until your thighs are parallel to the ground (figure 5.21*b*). Do not bounce at the bottom of the movement. Keep your knees in line with your toes; don't allow your knees to move inside or outside the normal tracking of the knee joint or move out in front of your toes. Keep your weight evenly distributed over your feet; do not shift your weight forward to your toes.

4. Stand up by straightening your hips and knees while maintaining correct body position. Keep your hips underneath you; do not round your back or lean forward on your feet.

5. When you have finished the desired number of repetitions, slowly squat down and lower the weight onto the floor.

Figure 5.21 Goblet squat.

Front Squat

Execution

1. Stand with the bar racked on the front your shoulders in either a clean rack grip or cross-shoulder position (figure 5.22a).

2. Keep your eyes, head, shoulders, and chest up and maintain a tight back throughout the lift.

3. Squat down under control, leading with your hips, until your thighs are parallel to the ground (figure 5.22b). Do not bounce at the bottom of the movement. Keep your knees in line with your toes; don't allow your knees to move inside or outside the normal tracking of the knee joint or move out in front of your toes. Keep your weight evenly distributed over your feet; do not shift your weight forward to your toes.

4. Raise the bar by straightening your hips and knees while maintaining correct body position. Keep your hips underneath you; do not round your back or lean forward on your feet.

5. When you have finished the desired number of repetitions, slowly walk the barbell back into the rack and set it down safely.

Figure 5.22　Front squat.

Trap Bar Deadlift

Execution

1. Begin by standing inside the curve of the bar with your feet hip-width apart. Grip the bar with both hands.

2. Keep your back tight and flat and your shoulders over your feet, then bend your knees and lower your hips to prepare to lift the weight (figure 5.23a).

3. Slowly lift the bar from the floor using your legs, keeping your shoulders over your feet and your back flat. Don't jerk the bar from the floor. Keep your butt down throughout the lift.

4. Straighten your legs and stand tall to complete the lift (figure 5.23b).

5. Slowly lower the bar back to the floor using your legs, keeping your shoulders over your feet and your back flat. Keep your butt down until the bar reaches the floor.

6. Repeat for the desired number of repetitions.

Figure 5.23   Trap bar deadlift.

Rear Foot Elevated Split Squat

Execution

This exercise can be done with a barbell, dumbbells, kettlebells, or body weight.

1. Start in a standing position. If using dumbbells or kettlebells, hold them at your sides. If using a barbell, begin with the barbell on the back of your shoulders.

2. Begin with your right foot behind you, supported on a low bench. Step forward with your left leg, keeping your head, shoulders, and torso vertical to the ground. Keep your shoulders and hips square to maintain balance.

3. Slowly squat down until your left thigh is parallel to the ground and the shin is close to vertical (figure 5.24). Your back (supported) leg will lower until the knee is near, but not touching, the floor.

Figure 5.24   Rear foot elevated split squat.

4. Push hard with your left leg to rise straight up and return to the starting position. Note that this is an up-and-down movement and not a forward-and-backward movement.

5. Complete all repetitions on the left leg prior to moving on to the right leg.

Single-Leg Wall Sit

Execution

1. Lean against a wall with your back flat and hands by your sides.

2. Lift one leg off the floor and slowly bend the other knee, lowering your body toward the floor until your support leg is bent at about 90 degrees (figure 5.25).

3. Stabilize your weight at this position and hold for the prescribed amount of time before switching to the other leg.

Variation

You can hold a dumbbell or kettlebell to increase the difficulty.

Figure 5.25   Single-leg wall sit.

Pistol Squat

Execution

The exercise can be done with body weight (arms straight out in front of you) or a dumbbell or kettlebell held with both hands in front of the body, touching the chest (goblet). A bench or box should be approximately 6 inches (15 cm) behind your foot and of sufficient height that when you squat down you will be in a half-squat position, with the thigh parallel to the ground and knee slightly forward yet not pushing out in front of the toes.

1. Stand tall on your left leg with your right foot raised slightly off the floor and your arms out in front at chest height (figure 5.26a).
2. Keeping your back flat, core engaged, and right leg held out in front of you, slowly push your hips back and bend your left knee to squat down until your butt touches the bench (figure 5.26b).
3. Reverse the movement to push back up to the starting position.
4. Repeat for the desired number of repetitions, then switch legs.

Figure 5.26 Pistol squat.

Step-Up

Execution

The bench, platform, or step required for this exercise should be high enough for the thigh to be parallel to the floor when your foot is resting on the bench. This exercise can be done with a barbell, dumbbells, kettlebells, or body weight.

1. Start in a standing position, facing the bench or platform. If using dumbbells, hold the dumbbells at your sides. If using a barbell, begin with the barbell on the back of your shoulders.
2. With your right leg, step up onto the bench or platform (figure 5.27a). Then lift your left (trailing) leg and stand on the bench or platform on your right leg with your left leg flexed in front of you so your thigh is parallel with the ground (figure 5.27b).
3. Step down under control, left leg first and right leg following.
4. Repeat this sequence, beginning with your left leg. Alternate right-leg, left-leg step-ups until the set is complete.

Variations

- This exercise can also be done with one arm holding a weight overhead in the single-arm overhead step-up.
- For another variation, this exercise can be completed as a power step-up with an explosive emphasis by lifting the foot 2 inches (5 cm) above the step, then powerfully stepping onto the box and exploding upward to the top position.

Figure 5.27 Step-up.

Hip Thrust

Execution

This exercise is done with a barbell and a bench or a hip thrust machine.

1. Sit on the floor with your back to the long side of a bench and your legs straight out in front of you with a barbell at your feet. Roll the barbell over your legs until it is centered over your hips. You can use some cushioning for the bar such as a towel or pad.

2. Next, place your shoulders on the edge of the bench. Place your feet on the floor about shoulder-width apart, knees bent and hands on the barbell more than shoulder-width apart for stability (figure 5.28a).

3. Raise the hips until they are fully extended (figure 5.28b) and then slowly lower the bar back to the start position.

4. Repeat for the desired number of repetitions.

Note: The isometric version is holding each rep for the desired amount of time.

Variation

This exercise can also be done with one leg (figure 5.28c). The technique is the same, but the single-leg version is more challenging and requires a lighter weight.

Figure 5.28 *(a-b)* Hip thrust and *(c)* single-leg hip thrust.

Bench Glute Lift Iso

Execution

1. Lie on your back with your arms out to your sides, palms down. Place your heels on a stable elevated surface like a bench with a knee bend angle of about 60 degrees.
2. Drive your hips up by contracting through the hamstrings and glutes while actively pulling your heels into the bench throughout the duration of the set (figure 5.29).
3. Hold this position for the desired amount of time.

Figure 5.29   Bench glute lift iso.

Single-Leg Long Leg Bridge Iso

Execution

1. Start lying face up on the ground with your hands by your sides and knees bent about 30 degrees.
2. Actively drive your hips upward toward the ceiling, keeping the shoulders, hips, and knees aligned.
3. Lift one leg off the floor and hold it in the air for the prescribed amount of time (figure 5.30).

Figure 5.30   Single-leg long leg bridge iso.

4. Once the time has been reached, return the leg to the floor and repeat with the opposite leg.

Bench Hip Extension With Alternating Leg Raise

Execution

1. Lie with your back flat on the floor, arms at your sides, heels of your feet elevated on a bench, and knees slightly bent.
2. Extend your hips upward toward the ceiling.
3. While maintaining an extended hip position, lift one leg off the bench by driving your knee upward toward your head, stabilizing your weight at the hip and engaging your glute and hamstring muscles (figure 5.31).
4. Place your foot back down on the bench and lift the other foot, stabilizing the transfer of body weight from one leg to the other.
5. Repeat for the desired number of repetitions for each leg.

Figure 5.31   Bench hip extension with alternating leg raise.

Nordic Curl

Execution

1. Kneel on a pad and secure your heels under something stable, like the heel pads of a machine (or a partner can hold your heels if necessary).
2. Start at the top position with your torso vertical to the ground and your arms at your sides.
3. Lower your torso with a straight back (figure 5.32) until your knees are straight and you are chest down on the ground.
4. Bend your knees to slowly return to the starting position with your torso back to vertical.
5. Control both the raising and lowering phases. Don't hyperextend your lower back too much on the way up. Be sure that both your feet are secure.

Variation

To make the exercise easier with band assistance, wrap a band around your chest and have a partner hold it or secure it to a rack behind you.

Figure 5.32   Nordic curl.

Front Foot Elevated Dumbbell Ankle Pops

Execution

1. Stand tall with a dumbbell in each hand down by your sides, with one foot elevated on a box or bench in front of you and your weight shifted toward the standing leg.
2. Quickly hop up and down on the tall standing leg, being sure to bend slightly at the ankle and knee.
3. Stabilize the weights in each hand and maintain a tall posture throughout the repetitions, making sure to stay on the ball of the foot during the jumping actions (figure 5.33).
4. After completing all the repetitions on one leg, switch to the other leg.

Figure 5.33   Front foot elevated dumbbell ankle pops.

Leg Press Achilles Iso

Execution

1. Sit in the leg press machine with your back flat and your butt touching the pad. Begin with a weight that is approximately 1.5 to 2 times your body weight, including the weight of the sled itself. For safety do not rotate the safety catches outward, as you will not need to move them for this exercise.

2. Press up with both legs until your knees are fully extended, then remove one leg so that you are holding the weight on the forefoot of one leg with the heel slightly in the air (figure 5.34).

3. Hold for 5 seconds and then switch to the other leg without letting the platform move up or down during the switch.

4. Continue to alternate back and forth until each leg has done 5 repetitions of 5-second isometric holds. That is considered one set.

5. Slowly set the weight down after the set is completed.

Note: Due to the nature of the Achilles tendon, it can be helpful to perform one set with the toes straight, one set with the toes slightly pointed inward, and one set with the toes slightly pointed outward.

Figure 5.34 Leg press Achilles iso.

UPPER-BODY STRENGTH EXERCISES

Push-Up Rotation

Execution

1. Lie face down on the floor supported by your hands in the standard push-up position.
2. Perform a push-up by extending the arms powerfully (figure 5.35a).
3. At the top of the push-up, lift the right arm from the floor and raise it toward the ceiling while twisting your torso along with the raised arm (figure 5.35b). Allow your heels to shift to the left with the arm pointing toward the ceiling and keep your body straight, similar to a side plank position.
4. Slowly rotate the torso, returning to the push-up position, and then slowly lower yourself to the ground.
5. Repeat with the opposite side and alternate sides until the set is complete.

Figure 5.35   Push-up rotation.

Half-Kneeling Single-Arm Overhead Press

Execution

1. Begin in the half-kneeling position by kneeling on your right leg (back leg) and bending your left leg (front leg) in front of you with your foot flat on the floor.
2. Hold a dumbbell in your right hand so that the dumbbell touches your right shoulder and your palm faces the shoulder. This is the bottom phase of the press (figure 5.36a).
3. Now press the dumbbell overhead (figure 5.36b).
4. Slowly lower the dumbbell back to the starting position and complete all the repetitions on that arm.
5. Switch your leg positions, move the dumbbell to the left hand, and repeat the sequence for the desired number of repetitions.

Figure 5.36   Half-kneeling single-arm overhead press.

Single-Arm Cable Chest Press

Execution

1. This exercise can be done with a cable chest press machine or cable crossover machine. Set the handle of the cable at chest height.

2. Grab a handle with one hand and stand facing away from the machine with your feet shoulder-width apart and one foot staggered about a foot in front of the other. If the right arm is working, the right leg should be the back leg in the stagger (figure 5.37a).

3. Before pressing, make sure your head is up, your core is engaged, and the rest of your body is stable and stationary without leaning forward.

4. Press the handle forward by extending the arm until it is straight out in front of you (figure 5.37b).

5. Slowly lower the handle back to the start position and continue for the desired number of repetitions, then repeat with the other arm.

Figure 5.37   Single-arm cable chest press.

Split Stance Cable Single-Arm High Row

Execution

1. Stand facing a cable machine with the handle set at the highest position.
2. Grab the handle with your right hand and take a step back with your right leg. When the right arm is working you will be in a high lunge position with your right leg as the rear leg.
3. Allow the shoulder of the right arm to be pulled forward while slightly twisting the torso (figure 5.38*a*).
4. Begin the row by pulling the right arm to the side of your body while slightly rotating your torso to the right. Pull the right shoulder back as the left shoulder rotates forward (figure 5.38*b*).
5. Slowly return the arm back to the start position until the arm is fully extended and the right shoulder is pulled forward.
6. Repeat for the desired number of repetitions. After the right-arm set is complete, repeat the sequence with your left arm.

Figure 5.38   Split stance cable single-arm high row.

Split Stance Cable Single-Arm Low Row

Execution

1. Stand facing a cable machine with the handle set at the lowest position.
2. Grab the handle with your right hand and take a step back with your right leg. When the right arm is working you will be in a high lunge position with your right leg as the rear leg.
3. Allow the shoulder of the right arm to be pulled forward while slightly twisting the torso (figure 5.39*a*).
4. Begin the row by pulling the right arm to the side of your body while slightly rotating your torso to the right. Pull the right shoulder back as the left shoulder rotates forward (figure 5.39*b*).
5. Slowly return the arm back to the start position until the arm is fully extended and the right shoulder is pulled forward.
6. Repeat for the desired number of repetitions. After the right-arm set is complete, repeat the sequence with your left arm.

Figure 5.39 Split stance cable single-arm low row.

Half-Kneeling Single-Arm Pulldown

Execution

1. Stand facing a cable machine with the handle set at the highest position.
2. Grab the handle with your left hand and take a step back and kneel down on your left knee. When the left arm is working you will be in a half-kneeling position with your left leg as the rear leg.
3. Maintain your torso in a slightly forward 45-degree position so that the exercise remains a pulldown instead of a row.
4. Allow the shoulder of the left arm to be pulled forward while maintaining a rigid torso (figure 5.40a).
5. Begin the row by pulling the left arm to the side of your body (figure 5.40b).
6. Slowly return the arm back to the start position until the arm is fully extended and the left shoulder is pulled forward.
7. Repeat for the desired number of repetitions. After the left-arm set is complete, repeat the sequence with your right arm.

Figure 5.40   Half-kneeling single-arm pulldown.

Inverted Row

Execution

1. Lie underneath a barbell that is in a fixed, stable position on a squat rack, approximately 3 to 4 feet (1 m) from the floor. It is important that the bar is safely hooked in place so that it does not fall during the exercise.

2. Reach up and grasp the bar with a wide overhand grip and straighten the body with the arms locked out and heels on the floor (figure 5.41a).

3. Keeping your body straight, use your arms to pull your chest up to the bar (figure 5.41b).

4. Return to the start position by lowering your body until your arms are straight. Be sure to keep the body straight.

5. Repeat for the desired number of repetitions.

Variations

- The exercise can be made easier with a higher bar height (higher body angle) or made more difficult with your feet placed on a bench instead of on the floor.

- A suspension trainer is also a great device to use for this exercise (figure 5.41c).

Figure 5.41 (a-b) Inverted row and (c) variation using a suspension trainer with the feet on a bench.

Lat Pulldown

Execution

1. Sit on the bench of the lat pulldown machine with your legs underneath the thigh pads. Keep your torso perpendicular to the floor.
2. Hold the bar in a pronated grip, arms straight, palms facing away, hands wider than shoulder-width apart (figure 5.42a).
3. Pull the bar straight down, without moving your torso, to just below your chin (figure 5.42b).
4. Return the bar under control to the starting position.
5. Repeat for the desired number of repetitions.

Variation

For the single-arm version you will need to change the bar attachment to a single handle. The technique is mostly the same except that the grip is pronated (facing away from the body) at the top and rotates during the pulldown to finish facing you at the bottom.

Figure 5.42   Lat pulldown.

Barbell Bench Press

Execution

1. Lie flat on the bench with your head, shoulders, and butt touching the bench. Feet are flat and planted firmly on the floor. Maintain this position throughout the lift.

2. Your eyes should be directly underneath the bar; this will prevent the bar from hitting the rack during the exercise. You may need help in getting the bar out of and back into the rack.

3. Your grip on the barbell can vary; in general, it should be a little more than shoulder-width (figure 5.43a).

4. Slowly lower the bar to your nipple area (4 to 6 inches [10-15 cm] range on your chest) (figure 5.43b). Although the grooves vary, this range should fit everyone. Gently touch the bar to your chest without bouncing it, and then push it back up to full extension.

5. Repeat for the desired number of repetitions.

Spotting: The spotter holds the bar in an alternating grip. On the count of 3, the spotter helps you lift the barbell from the rack as you begin the exercise. When the bar is in the starting position, the spotter releases it. During the exercise, the spotter follows the bar with their hands, not touching the bar unless needed. When you are finished with your repetitions, the spotter helps you rerack the bar.

Figure 5.43 Barbell bench press.

Dumbbell Bench Press

Execution

1. After removing the dumbbells from the rack, sit on the weight bench, placing the dumbbells on your thighs. Use your thighs to help lift the dumbbells to the starting position.

2. Lie flat on the bench with your head, shoulders, and butt touching the bench. Feet are flat and planted firmly on the floor. Maintain this position throughout the lift.

3. Arms and elbows are down with the dumbbells touching your anterior deltoids, similar to the barbell position (figure 5.44a).

4. Press both dumbbells to a fully extended position over your chest and gently touch them together (figure 5.44b). Try to press each arm at the same speed and exercise groove. Slowly lower the dumbbells in the same exercise groove back to the starting position. Controlling the dumbbells is very important.

5. Repeat for the desired number of repetitions. After the last repetition, finish with the dumbbells over your chest. Lower them to your thighs and lift the torso off the bench. Don't drop the dumbbells; this could cause injury or damage the equipment.

Figure 5.44 (a-b) Dumbbell bench press and (c) single-arm variation.

Spotting: Dumbbells may deviate inside, outside, below, or above the correct exercise groove. The spotter should spot the dumbbells from behind by grabbing the lifter's wrists and guiding, if necessary.

Variation

The single-arm dumbbell bench press technique is the same, but you may prefer the feet to be a little bit wider for stability. The off arm can either be pointing straight up toward the ceiling or placed alongside the body or on the hip (figure 5.44c).

Dumbbell Alternating Incline Bench Press

Execution

1. Adjust the weight bench so that it has an incline of about 35 to 45 degrees.

2. After removing the dumbbells from the rack, sit on the weight bench, placing the dumbbells on your thighs. Lift one knee and one dumbbell at a time up to your chest to the starting position. Dumbbells should be touching your anterior deltoids, and the arms and elbows are down.

3. Lie on the incline bench with your head, shoulders, and butt in contact with the bench, feet firmly planted on the floor. Maintain this position throughout the lift.

4. Press both dumbbells to a fully extended position over your chest and gently touch them together (figure 5.45a). Slowly lower one dumbbell from the extended position to just outside the shoulder (figure 5.45b) and then press to return to the starting position. Controlling the dumbbells is very important.

5. Repeat with the other arm and continue to alternate for the desired number of repetitions. After the last repetition, finish with the dumbbells over your chest. Lower them to your thighs and then get up off the bench. Don't drop the dumbbells; this could cause injury or damage the equipment.

Spotting: Dumbbells may deviate inside, outside, below, or above the correct exercise groove. The spotter should spot the dumbbells from behind by grabbing the lifter's wrists and guiding, if necessary.

Figure 5.45 Dumbbell alternating incline bench press.

Dumbbell Floor Press

Execution

1. Begin by sitting on the floor in an upright position with your legs straight and the dumbbells on the floor.
2. Pick up each dumbbell and set it in your hip crease while maintaining a tight grip.
3. While keeping the dumbbells close to your chest, slowly lie back until your elbows rest on the floor with your forearms perpendicular to the ground (figure 5.46a).
4. Press the weights overhead by extending the arms until they are straight (figure 5.46b).
5. Slowly lower the dumbbells until the elbows lightly touch the floor, then press both dumbbells back to the starting position. To complete the exercise slowly, lower the weights to the floor in a "controlled drop." It should be a smooth motion, but not one that requires excessive effort or one that puts the shoulder under unnecessary risk.
6. Repeat for the desired number of repetitions.

Figure 5.46 Dumbbell floor press.

Barbell Bent-Over Row

Difficulty

Intermediate

Execution

1. Set up facing a barbell on the floor or in a rack.
2. Facing the rack, take the bar out and walk it a step away from the rack. While keeping your back flat, bend over (similar to the Romanian deadlift) until the chest is slightly above parallel to the floor.
3. Bend over with your knees slightly bent and back flat.
4. Grasp the bar with an underhand grip (palms facing forward) and the hands approximately shoulder-width apart.
5. Initiate the row by pulling with your arms and back muscles until the barbell touches your stomach near your belly button (figure 5.47).
6. Slowly lower the weight until the arms are fully extended. Do not bend from the back or try to touch the ground with the bar.
7. Repeat for the desired number of repetitions.

Note: Ensure that the lower back does not round during this exercise. If it is impossible to keep your back flat, then either bend your knees a little more or don't go as low with your chest.

Figure 5.47   Barbell bent-over row.

Single-Arm Dumbbell Row

Execution

1. Place your right knee and right hand on a flat bench with your torso parallel to the floor. Your left leg is next to the bench with a slightly bent knee.
2. Hold a dumbbell in your left hand, arm hanging straight down.
3. Pull the dumbbell up toward the outside of your shoulder with a high elbow at the top of the pull. Touch the dumbbell to your shoulder or side of your body (figure 5.48a). Don't jerk the weight; use a steady pull.
4. Slowly lower the weight to the starting position.
5. Repeat for the desired number of repetitions. After completing a set with your left arm, repeat the sequence with your right arm.

Variation

To make the exercise more intense, perform a bird dog row. Start in the quadruped position on top of a flat bench with a dumbbell in your right hand, arm hanging straight down. Extend your left leg back until it is parallel with the ground and perform rows with your right arm for the desired number of repetitions (figure 5.48b), then lift your right leg and row with your left arm.

Figure 5.48   (a) Single-arm dumbbell row and (b) bird dog row variation.

Pull-Up

Execution

1. Hang from a pull-up bar with hands slightly more than shoulder-width apart. Hold onto the bar with a pronated grip, palms facing away. Body and arms are straight.
2. Pull up until your chin clears the bar (figure 5.49). Keep your legs fairly straight and don't jerk your body while pulling up but instead pull smoothly.
3. Slowly return to the starting (hanging) position with straight arms.
4. Repeat for the desired number of repetitions.

Variation

An easier variation of this exercise is the chin-up, which is performed the same way but with an underhand grip in which the palms are rotated toward your face so that the biceps are more involved.

Figure 5.49 Pull-up.

Push-Up

Execution

1. Start lying face down on the ground with your hands under your shoulders and your elbows extended. Keep the back and legs straight with your toes touching the ground (figure 5.50a).
2. Lower your body until the upper arms are parallel to the ground (figure 5.50b).
3. Reverse the movement and raise your body until the arms are extended back to the start position. Keep your body as flat as a board with your head in a neutral position, neither hanging downward or extended upward.
4. Repeat for the desired number of repetitions.

Variation

Perform a weighted version for increased difficulty. Have a partner place a weight plate on your back that you are capable of using for the desired repetitions while maintaining a flat torso.

Figure 5.50   Push-up.

Push-Up Push-Away

Execution

1. The start position is the bottom of a push-up position, lying face down on the ground with your hands under the shoulders and your elbows bent until the upper arms are parallel to the ground and the torso is completely flat.

2. Begin the exercise by pushing backward with the arms, allowing the hips to rise up into the air until you are in a downward dog yoga or pike position (figure 5.51).

3. Lower back to the start position and repeat for the desired number of repetitions.

Figure 5.51   Push-up push-away.

Plyo Push-Up

Execution

1. The start position is the top of the push-up position, with your hands under your shoulders and your elbows extended. Keep the back and legs straight with your toes touching the ground.
2. Rapidly lower your body until the upper arms are parallel to the ground.
3. Quickly reverse the movement and raise your body until your arms are extended and your hands completely leave the ground briefly (figure 5.52).
4. Immediately perform the next rep as soon as your hands return to the floor.
5. Keep your body as flat as a board with your head in a neutral position, neither hanging downward or extended upward. The hands should be quiet and soft when making contact with the floor.

Variation

This exercise can be made easier or more explosive by performing it with the hands on a flat bench instead of the floor.

Figure 5.52   Plyo push-up.

Dumbbell Split Stance Curl and Press

Execution

1. With a dumbbell in each hand step out into a high lunge position with your torso upright.

2. While holding the lunge position, flex your elbows and curl the dumbbells up toward your shoulders (figure 5.53a).

3. Pivot your arms up and out to press the dumbbells overhead.

4. At the top, stack your wrists over your elbows and shoulders, with your forearms facing forward (figure 5.53b).

5. Reverse the motion to lower the dumbbells back down.

6. Repeat for the desired number of repetitions, alternating which leg is in front each set.

Figure 5.53   Dumbbell split stance curl and press.

Stork Press

Execution

1. Begin with your right leg as your stance leg and your left knee held isometrically at hip height with a dumbbell in your right hand, resting on the front of the right shoulder.

2. Hold a stable position while you press the dumbbell directly overhead (figure 5.54), then return it to the front of the right shoulder.

3. Repeat for the desired number of repetitions, then repeat on the other side.

Figure 5.54   Stork press.

Cable Face Pull

Execution

1. Set a cable machine to chest height and add a rope attachment. Grip the rope so that the palms are facing the floor.

2. Stand facing the machine and take a step backward into a shoulder-width or staggered stance with your arms extended at shoulder level.

3. Pull the rope toward your face, pulling the handles apart as you do so (figure 5.55).

4. Return to the start position and repeat for the desired number of repetitions.

Figure 5.55   Cable face pull.

Landmine Split Stance Shoulder Shift

Execution

1. Stand tall in a split stance with your left leg in front and the right behind you while keeping a slight bend in both knees to achieve an athletic position. Hold the end of the barbell landmine in front of your right shoulder with both hands interlocked (figure 5.56a).

2. Raise the barbell and slowly shift it from the right side to the left side of your body while maintaining a strong and stable split stance position (figure 5.56b).

3. After completing all the repetitions on one side, switch legs and repeat, shifting from the left to the right side with the right leg forward.

Figure 5.56　Landmine split stance shoulder shift.

Cable Scarecrow

Execution

1. Set two cables with handle attachments to the lowest height with a relatively light weight.

2. Stand facing the cables with your feet shoulder-width apart and knees slightly bent and a cable handle in each hand. Hold the right cable handle in the left hand and vice versa so the cables cross over one another (figure 5.57*a*).

3. Pull upward with the shoulders. As your hands approach head level, begin rotating backward at the shoulders so the backs of your hands face behind you (figure 5.57*b*).

4. Briefly pause with your shoulders abducted and elbows flexed around 90 degrees before returning to a tall standing position with the weight lowered.

5. Repeat for the desired number of repetitions.

Figure 5.57   Cable scarecrow.

Blackburn Isometric Series

Execution

1. Begin by lying face down on an incline bench holding a light (3 to 10 pound [1.4-4.5 kg]) weight in each hand.

2. The exercise consists of 10-second isometric holds in six positions performed consecutively without rest.

3. Position 1: Face down with the arms straight and almost touching the sides of the hips. Raise the arms straight up with palms rotated toward the ceiling (figure 5.58a).

4. Position 2: Face down with the arms straight out to the side (shoulder level) with the shoulders rotated so that the thumbs are pointing toward the floor (figure 5.58b).

5. Position 3: Face down with the arms straight out to the side (shoulder level) with the shoulders rotated so that the thumbs are pointing toward the ceiling (figure 5.58c).

6. Position 4: Face down with the arms held straight at a 45-degree angle (Y position) above shoulder height and the thumbs pointing toward the ceiling (figure 5.58d).

7. Position 5: Face down with the arms held straight at a 45-degree angle (Y position) above shoulder height and the thumbs pointing toward the floor (figure 5.58e).

8. Position 6: Face down with the elbows held at 90 degrees (field goal position) with the palms facing toward the floor (figure 5.58f).

Figure 5.58   Blackburn isometric series.

Prone Ys, Ts, Is

Execution

1. Begin by lying face down on an incline bench holding a light (3 to 8 pound [1.4-3.6 kg]) weight in each hand.

2. Y: With your thumbs up, squeeze your shoulder blades down and back and lift your arms up and forward at an angle into the Y position (figure 5.59a). Hold for 1 second, then lower your arms back down.

3. T: With your thumbs up, put your arms straight out to your sides to form the letter T (figure 5.59b). Hold for 1 second, then lower your arms back down.

4. I: Keep your arms straight and lift them up in front of you with your thumbs up, forming the letter I (figure 5.59c). Hold for 1 second, then lower your arms back down.

5. Repeat the series for the desired number of repetitions.

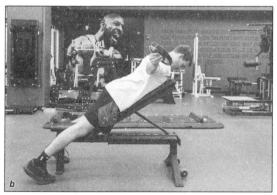

Figure 5.59 Prone (a) Ys, (b) Ts, (c) Is.

D2 Shoulder Pattern

Execution

1. Set a cable machine to the lowest height. Stand sideways to the machine in a single-leg balance stance on the near leg and reach across your body to grasp the cable handle with your far hand.

2. The start position is with the far arm reaching across the body with the shoulder rotated so that the thumb is facing downward toward the floor (figure 5.60*a*).

3. Initiate the movement by raising the arm up and diagonally across the body while rotating the palm to face forward in the top position (figure 5.60*b*).

4. Repeat for the desired number of repetitions, then switch sides.

Figure 5.60   D2 shoulder pattern.

Wall Plate Push

Execution

1. Lean your butt against a wall with your knees slightly bent and your torso at a 45-degree angle forward. Grip a 5-, 10-, or 25-pound (2.3, 4.5, or 11.3 kg) weight plate, depending on your strength level, with both hands with your arms hanging down in front of you.

2. Lift the plate with both arms to an overhead position with your biceps near your ears (figure 5.61).

3. While in this position attempt to protract/reach your arms an extra inch overhead.

4. Reverse the steps to return to the start position and complete for the desired number of repetitions.

Figure 5.61 Wall plate push.

PHASES OF A STRENGTH TRAINING PROGRAM

All strength training programs for basketball players should have very clear and specific goals. The off-season program derived from these goals consists of a short active rest period (2 or 3 weeks) followed by four phases beginning with low intensity and progressing to higher intensity (see table 5.1). It is important to follow the guidelines for each of the phases for the number of sets and repetitions and the intensity and volume of lifts at each phase.

Table 5.1   Four Progressive Phases of an Off-Season Strength Training Program

	Phase			
	Muscular endurance/ general physical preparation	Hypertrophy	Base strength	Power and speed
Sets	2-3	3-4	3-5	3-5
Repetitions	12-15	7-10	3-6	2-4
Intensity	Low	Moderate	High	High
Volume	High	High	Moderate	Low

After a long season, the active recovery phase is the time for the athlete to recover from accumulated stress and strain on the mind and body. This phase is typically 2 or 3 weeks in duration and consists of a balance of rest and light activity or cross training 2 or 3 times per week. Cross training can take many forms, such as playing other sports or participating in activities such as hiking or biking. Taking time away from basketball allows the athlete to lay the foundation of physical and mental rejuvenation needed to adapt optimally to the upcoming phases. While it is necessary to take time away from training during the active rest phase, it is important to maintain activity to avoid becoming completely deconditioned. Deconditioning can happen in as little as 2 weeks, which is why it is imperative to maintain some level of activity.

The first training phase of the off-season program is the general preparation phase (GPP). When organized properly, this phase will allow the athlete to build a muscular endurance base and prepare the body for the higher-intensity strength training phases that follow. In the 2-week GPP phase, the training intensity is low and the volume is high. The recommendation for this phase is to train 3 or 4 times per week with the exercises in each session contained to 2 or 3 sets of 12 to 15 repetitions. The exercises in this phase are to be performed slowly to challenge the body to improve tissue quality of tendons and muscles, and the exercises selected will explore various movement patterns to address the deficiencies and muscle imbalances accrued during the season.

The next phase of the training program is the hypertrophy phase. The purpose of this phase is to lay a foundation of muscle and connective tissue development as well as muscular endurance to support the upcoming off-season phases. Another objective of this phase is to slowly increase the overall workload in preparation for a seamless transition to the subsequent strength phase. The exercises selected for this phase emphasize neuromuscular adaptations, movement patterns, and optimization of base core stability. In this phase, we recommend training 3 or 4 times per week with the majority of the exercise prescription being 2 to 4 sets of 7 to 10 repetitions. In this phase the athlete should approach near maximal effort on each set by selecting a weight where at the completion of each set the athlete could only have performed another 1 to 3 additional repetitions.

For the strength exercises the athlete's focus is to develop technical efficiency throughout the high volume of slow repetitions. The focus of the core exercises in this phase is to develop muscular endurance and stability with the goal of preparing the athlete to maintain proper position and posture during the more stressful training of the next phase. The final week of this phase is what is called a deload week in which there is a reduction of volume and intensity of exercises, which allows for the body to recover and be optimally ready to benefit from the stressful workload in the following strength phase. This is called *supercompensation*. Failure to allow the body to recover prior to the initiation of the next phase can result in stagnation of results and adaptations or in some cases can result in overtraining and injuries.

Following the hypertrophy phase is the strength phase, where the major focus is improving maximal force production or strength. The training load and intensity increase each week to achieve the desired training effect of increased force production. The total volume is reduced during this phase as the intensity increases. To increase maximal strength, exercises are selected and implemented with the goal of progressively increasing the weight used without compromising technique. In this phase the exercises are performed in a controlled manner, not as slow as in the hypertrophy phase nor as fast as in the upcoming power and speed phase. There will also be an increase in the more specific supportive exercises necessary to target the patella and Achilles tendon, which at present are two of the most commonly injured areas for young basketball athletes. During this phase we recommended training 3 or 4 times per week with 3 to 5 sets of 3 to 6 reps. As in the hypertrophy phase prior, the final week will see a reduction of volume and intensity to deload the body for the final phase.

The final off-season phase focuses on power and speed development. While an emphasis of this phase is explosive strength, a portion of the training will seek to maintain the force-generating and physiological qualities developed in previous blocks. As such, the primary exercises will target high movement speed with lower repetitions, while supportive exercises will range from targeting higher-intensity and lower-repetition maximal force maintenance to higher-repetition and lower-intensity exercises to maintain hypertrophy. The emphasis, however, is shifted to strength exercises requiring a great power requirement such as Olympic lifts and derivatives while concurrently addressing the unilateral and mulitdirectional nature of basketball. These exercises have been shown to be effective in increasing the rate of force development (power). Due to the increased speed of movement, the technical mastery of these exercises is crucial to develop power in a safe manner. Weight or speed should never be increased at the expense of technique. During this phase we recommended training 3 or 4 days per week with 3 to 5 sets and 2 to 4 reps on primary exercises. As the power phase is the final phase prior to the start of preseason, the deload week workload reduction is essential in order to arrive at camp or the first day of practice in the most optimal condition physically and mentally.

The preseason phase bridges the gap between general training in the weight room and the basketball actions required for high performance on the court. Due to the increased percentage of training time dedicated to on-court practices and games during the preseason, there must be a subsequent reduction in workload in the weight room to account for this. During this phase we recommended training with 2 or 3 total-body sessions per week.

After the completion of the progressive off-season program and an optimal preseason program, the in-season maintenance phase is characterized by continuing to develop the qualities needed for basketball actions while maintaining the strength qualities developed over the course of the off-season.

STRENGTH TRAINING PROGRAMS

When planning a strength training program, it is important to consider the individual athlete's needs, including strengths, weaknesses, priorities, sport and position specificity, and injury history. It is also important to consider all of the general training principles when designing the annual training plan. In this book, the age group we have targeted is high school and older for the programs. Because we cannot prescribe an individual program for everyone who reads this book, the programs provided are developed as a general guide for any basketball player but can be tailored by an experienced coach to address the individual athlete's needs. The 16-week programs in tables 12.1 and 12.2 will address the full off-season calendar, and tables 12.3 and 12.4 provide examples of preseason and in-season programming.

Regardless of the time of year (off-season or in-season), it is important to provide adequate time for the body to recover between workouts. Muscle and connective tissues require 48 to 96 hours to fully recover and repair from a training session to be ready for the next session. This does not mean, however, that players should take multiple days off without working out. Each program includes 1 to 3 days between workout type, such as 2 full days between lower-body training sessions in the 4-day split program.

Off-Season Strength Training Programs

We have included two off-season training programs for basketball players:

- 3-day total-body program
- 4-day split program

3-Day Total-Body Program

This program may be used by any level of athlete. It is designed for athletes who have only 3 days per week to strength train. You may use this program Monday, Wednesday, and Friday; or Tuesday, Thursday, and Saturday; or even Monday, Wednesday, and Saturday. See table 5.2 on page 140 for a sample 3-day total-body off-season lifting schedule. Allow 1 day between workouts. The Wednesday workout (or second workout of the week) works the same muscle groups as the Monday and Friday workouts (or first and third workouts of the week); however, each day may emphasize either the lower or upper body, and the suggested exercises are different for each day. You will notice that we opted to superset exercises (blocks) in each phase of the 3-day, 16-week program.

4-Day Split Program

This program may also be used by any level of athlete. This design allows a 2- or 3-day recovery time between workouts for the same muscle groups and allows you to focus on one body segment, upper or lower body, per workout (see table 5.3 on page 147). The workouts may be shorter depending on whether you superset (perform a set of two different exercises back-to-back with little rest in between sets) and how many exercises you perform.

The workout days are Monday, Tuesday, Thursday, and Friday. You may choose what days (Monday and Thursday or Tuesday and Friday) to work either the upper body or the lower body. This program is also forgiving. If you miss a day, you should still have enough open days to get all your workouts in. The exercises work opposing muscle groups or are exercises that will not interfere with each other. You will notice that we opted to superset exercises (blocks) in each phase of this program. Some advantages of supersetting include the following:

- Faster workouts
- Proper muscle balance
- Increased conditioning levels
- Cleaner neuromuscular signal, recruitment, and function
- Increased blood flow to body segments being exercised

The 16-week off-season cycle starts 16 weeks before the first practice; for best results, please follow the complete program the way it was designed.

Preseason and In-Season Strength Training Programs

In general, in-season programs should have fewer exercises and reduced frequency and level of intensity compared to the off-season program. High-risk lifts or lifts that require a high level of technique proficiency should be adjusted or eliminated during the in-season depending on a multitude of factors that the coach can determine to be optimal for each athlete. These adjustments are made to avoid overtraining between practices, games, and workouts; overtraining may lead to decreased performance or injury.

We have opted for a total-body training program for our preseason (see table 12.3) and in-season (see table 12.4) programs because there is often less time to devote to training in the weight room during these phases, and total-body strength training sessions ensure that the entire body is trained with optimal frequency with the fewest sessions per week. Consider the following when developing a preseason or in-season strength training program:

- In-season programs cut back on the number of exercises, sets, reps, or intensity.
- Try to do two or three strength training workouts per body part each week during the preseason and in-season. If you have 2 days or more before your next game, you may lift heavier. If you have only 1 day off between games, you may lift lighter or cut out some of the sets, reps, or exercises.
- On lighter lifting days or when working around injuries, you may substitute exercises—for example, step-up instead of squat, single-leg Romanian deadlift instead of hang clean, or dumbbell bench press instead of barbell bench press.
- Depending on game, practice, and travel schedules, some weeks may leave time for only one workout.

Table 5.2 Sample 16-Week Basketball Off-Season Lifting Calendar: 3 Total-Body Workouts per Week

Exercise	Page #	Week 1	Week 2
Weeks 1-2 (Mondays): General physical preparation, total body with lower-body focus			
Block #1 (circuit style)			
Goblet squat	96	2 × 15	3 × 12
Inverted row	114	2 × 15	3 × 12
Bench hip extension with alternating leg raise	104	2 × 15	3 × 12
Block #2 (circuit style)			
Rear foot elevated split squat	99	1 × 15 each leg 2 × 12 each leg	3 × 12 each leg
Single-arm cable chest press	110	1 × 15 each arm 2 × 12 each arm	3 × 12 each arm
Front plank with alternating shoulder taps	172	2 × 30 sec	3 × 30 sec
Block #3 (circuit style)			
Stability ball leg curl	84	2 × 10	2 × 12
Half-kneeling cable chop	170	2 × 10 each side	2 × 10 each side
Side plank	177	2 × 30 sec each side	2 × 30 sec each side
Weeks 1-2 (Wednesdays): General physical preparation, total body with upper-body focus			
Block #1 (circuit style)			
Push-up	123	2 × 15	2 × 12 1 × 10
Step-up	101	2 × 15	2 × 12 1 × 10
Paloff press	175	2 × 10 each side	3 × 10 each side
Block #2 (circuit style)			
Lat pulldown	115	2 × 15	2 × 12 1 × 10
Dumbbell split stance curl and press	126	2 × 15	2 × 12 1 × 10
Cable dead bug	161	2 × 10	3 × 10
Block #3 (circuit style)			
Single-leg hip thrust	102	2 × 10 each leg	2 × 10 each leg
Seated mini-band clamshell	163	2 × 10	2 × 10
Prone Ys, Ts, Is	132	2 × 10	2 × 10

Exercise	Page #	Week 1	Week 2
Weeks 1-2 (Fridays): General physical preparation, total body			
Block #1 (circuit style)			
Trap bar deadlift	98	1 × 15 2 × 12	1 × 12 2 × 10
Half-kneeling single-arm overhead press	109	1 × 15 each arm 2 × 12 each arm	1 × 12 each arm 2 × 10 each arm
Curl-up	160	3 × 5 (5 sec)	3 × 5 (5 sec)
Block #2 (circuit style)			
Single-arm dumbbell lateral lunge	90	1 × 15 each side 2 × 12 each side	1 × 12 each side 2 × 10 each side
Single-arm dumbbell row	121	1 × 15 each arm 2 × 12 each arm	1 × 12 each arm 2 × 10 each arm
Bird dog	162	3 × 20	3 × 20
Block #3 (circuit style)			
Back extension	87	1 × 15 1 × 12	1 × 12 1 × 10
Push-up rotation	108	1 × 15 1 × 12	1 × 12 1 × 10
Seated calf raise	86	1 × 15 1 × 12	1 × 12 1 × 10

Exercise	Page #	Week 3	Week 4	Week 5	Week 6	Week 7 (deload)
Weeks 3-7 (Mondays): Hypertrophy, total body with lower-body focus						
Block #1						
Front squat	97	3 × 10	3 × 8	4 × 8	1 × 8 3 × 7	2 × 6
Single-arm dumbbell row	121	3 × 10 each arm	3 × 8 each arm	4 × 8 each arm	1 × 8 each arm 3 × 7 each arm	2 × 6 each arm
Hip thrust	102	3 × 10	3 × 8	4 × 8	1 × 8 3 × 7	2 × 6
Block #2						
Half-kneeling single-arm overhead press	109	3 × 10 each arm	3 × 8 each arm	3 × 8 each arm	3 × 7 each arm	2 × 8 each arm
Step-up	101	3 × 10	3 × 8	3 × 8	3 × 7	2 × 8
Front plank	171	3 × 45 sec	3 × 45 sec	3 × 45 sec	3 × 45 sec	2 × 45 sec

(continued)

Table 5.2 *(continued)*

Exercise	Page #	Week 3	Week 4	Week 5	Week 6	Week 7 (deload)
Block #3						
Stability ball leg curl	84	2 × 10	2 × 8	2 × 8	2 × 7	2 × 7
Single-leg wall sit	99	2 × 20 sec each leg	3 × 20 sec each leg	3 × 25 sec each leg	3 × 25 sec each leg	2 × 25 sec each leg
Copenhagen side plank	178	2 × 20 sec each side	3 × 20 sec each side	3 × 30 sec each side	3 × 30 sec each side	2 × 30 sec each side
Weeks 3-7 (Wednesdays): Hypertrophy, total body with upper-body focus						
Block #1						
Bench press	116-117	2 × 10 1 × 8	2 × 8 1 × 7	3 × 8 1 × 7	4 × 7	2 × 12
Rear foot elevated split squat	99	2 × 10 each leg 1 × 8 each leg	2 × 8 each leg 1 × 7 each leg	3 × 8 each leg 1 × 7 each leg	4 × 7 each leg	2 × 12 each leg
Paloff press	175	3 × 10 each side	3 × 10 each side	3 × 10 each side	3 × 10 each side	2 × 10 each side
Block #2						
Lat pulldown or pull-up	115 or 122	2 × 10 1 × 8	2 × 8 1 × 7	3 × 8	3 × 7	2 × 12
Dumbbell split stance curl and press	126	2 × 10 1 × 8	2 × 8 1 × 7	3 × 8	3 × 7	2 × 12
Leg press Achilles iso	107	3 × 5 (5 sec)	3 × 5 (5 sec)	3 × 5 (5 sec)	3 × 5 (5 sec)	3 × 5 (5 sec)
Block #3						
Single-leg RDL to hip lock iso	89	3 × 10 each leg	3 × 8 each leg	3 × 8 each leg	3 × 7 each leg	2 × 6 each leg
Vertical Paloff press	176	2 × 10	2 × 10	2 × 10	2 × 8	2 × 8
Cable face pull	127	3 × 12	3 × 12	3 × 10	3 × 10	2 × 8
Weeks 3-7 (Fridays): Hypertrophy, total body						
Block #1						
Trap bar dead-lift	98	1 × 10 2 × 8	3 × 7	2 × 8 2 × 7	2 × 8 2 × 7	2 × 8
Dumbbell alternating incline bench press	118	1 × 10 2 × 8	3 × 7	2 × 8 2 × 7	2 × 8 2 × 7	2 × 8
Ab wheel rollout	173	3 × 10	3 × 10	3 × 8	3 × 8	2 × 8

Exercise	Page #	Week 3	Week 4	Week 5	Week 6	Week 7 (deload)
Block #2						
Single-arm dumbbell lateral lunge	90	2 × 10 each side	3 × 8 each side	1 × 8 each side 2 × 7 each side	3 × 7 each side	2 × 7 each side
Bird dog row	121	2 × 10 each arm	3 × 8 each arm	1 × 8 each arm 2 × 7 each arm	3 × 7 each arm	2 × 7 each arm
Medicine ball rips	180	3 × 10	3 × 10	3 × 10	3 × 10	2 × 10
Block #3						
Nordic curl	105	2 × 10 1 × 8	2 × 8 1 × 7	1 × 8 2 × 7	3 × 7	2 × 5
Weighted push-up	123	3 × 10	3 × 8	3 × 8	3 × 7	2 × 12
Seated calf raise	86	3 × 15	3 × 15	3 × 12	3 × 12	2 × 10

Exercise	Page #	Week 8	Week 9	Week 10	Week 11	Week 12 (deload)
Weeks 8-12 (Mondays): Base strength, total body with lower-body focus						
Block #1						
Hang clean	82	2 × 5 1 × 4	1 × 5 2 × 4	2 × 4 2 × 3	5 × 3	2 × 6
Back squat	94	2 × 7 1 × 6	3 × 5	4 × 4	5 × 3	1 × 10 1 × 8
Bird dog iso	162	3 × 5 (5 sec)	3 × 5 (5 sec)	3 × 5 (5 sec)	3 × 5 (5 sec)	2 × 5 (5 sec)
Block #2						
Hip thrust iso	102	1 × 7 (4 sec) 2 × 6 (4 sec)	3 × 5 (4 sec)	3 × 4 (4 sec)	3 × 4 (4 sec)	2 × 4 (4 sec)
Single-arm dumbbell row	121	2 × 7 each arm 1 × 6 each arm	3 × 6 each arm	3 × 5 each arm	3 × 5 each arm	2 × 6 each arm
Ab wheel rollout	173	3 × 10	3 × 10	3 × 10	3 × 10	2 × 10
Block #3						
Weighted push-up	123	2 × 7 1 × 6	3 × 6	3 × 5	3 × 5	2 × 6
Single-leg wall sit	99	3 × 30 sec each leg	3 × 30 sec each leg	3 × 30 sec each leg	3 × 30 sec each leg	2 × 30 sec each leg
Copenhagen side plank	178	3 × 30 sec each side	3 × 30 sec each side	3 × 30 sec each side	3 × 30 sec each side	2 × 30 sec each side

(continued)

Table 5.2 *(continued)*

Exercise	Page #	Week 8	Week 9	Week 10	Week 11	Week 12 (deload)
Weeks 8-12 (Wednesdays): Base strength, total body with upper-body focus						
Block #1						
Bench press	116-117	2 × 5 1 × 4	1 × 5 2 × 4	2 × 4 2 × 3	5 × 3	2 × 6
Rear foot elevated split squat	99	2 × 5 each leg 1 × 4 each leg	1 × 5 each leg 2 × 4 each leg	2 × 4 each leg 2 × 3 each leg	5 × 3 each leg	2 × 6 each leg
Medicine ball rotational throw	182	3 × 10	3 × 10	3 × 8	3 × 8	2 × 8
Block #2						
Lat pulldown or pull-up	115 or 122	2 × 7 1 × 6	3 × 6	3 × 5	3 × 5	2 × 6
Supported single-leg RDL	88	2 × 7 each leg 1 × 6 each leg	3 × 6 each leg	3 × 5 each leg	3 × 5 each leg	2 × 6 each leg
Landmine straight-arm rotation	167	3 × 10	3 × 10	3 × 8	3 × 8	2 × 8
Block #3						
Landmine split stance shoulder shift	128	3 × 10	3 × 8	3 × 8	3 × 7	2 × 6
Leg press Achilles iso	107	3 × 5 (5 sec)	3 × 5 (5 sec)	3 × 5 (5 sec)	3 × 5 (5 sec)	3 × 5 (5 sec)
Cable scarecrow	129	3 × 10	3 × 8	3 × 8	3 × 7	2 × 8
Weeks 8-12 (Fridays): Base strength, total body						
Block #1						
Push press	78	3 × 6	1 × 5 2 × 4	2 × 4 2 × 3	1 × 4 4 × 3	2 × 5
Trap bar deadlift	98	3 × 6	3 × 5	4 × 4	5 × 3	1 × 8 1 × 7
Weighted front plank	171	3 × 45 sec	3 × 45 sec	3 × 45 sec	3 × 45 sec	2 × 45 sec

Exercise	Page #	Week 8	Week 9	Week 10	Week 11	Week 12 (deload)
Block #2						
Single-arm dumbbell lateral lunge	90	2 × 5 each side 1 × 4 each side	2 × 5 each side 1 × 4 each side	1 × 5 each side 2 × 4 each side	3 × 4 each side	2 × 6 each side
Bird dog row	121	2 × 7 (each arm) 1 × 6 (each arm)	3 × 6 (each arm)	3 × 5 (each arm)	3 × 5 (each arm)	2 × 6 (each arm)
Weighted Copenhagen side plank	178	3 × 30 sec each side	3 × 30 sec each side	3 × 30 sec each side	3 × 30 sec each side	2 × 30 sec each side
Block #3						
Single-leg long leg bridge iso	103	3 × 6 (3 sec) each leg	3 × 6 (3 sec) each leg	3 × 6 (3 sec) each leg	3 × 6 (3 sec) each leg	2 × 6 (3 sec) each leg
Push-up rotation	108	2 × 10 1 × 8	2 × 8 1 × 7	1 × 8 2 × 7	3 × 7	2 × 6
Single-leg wall sit	99	3 × 30 sec each leg	3 × 30 sec each leg	3 × 30 sec each leg	3 × 30 sec each leg	2 × 30 sec each leg

Exercise	Page #	Week 13	Week 14	Week 15	Week 16 (deload)
Weeks 13-16 (Mondays): Power and speed, total body with lower-body focus					
Block #1					
Power clean	83	1 × 4 1 × 3 3 × 2	2 × 3 3 × 2	1 × 3 4 × 2	3 × 5
Barbell pause front squat	97	5 × 3 (2 sec)	5 × 3 (2 sec)	5 × 2 (2 sec)	3 × 5 (2 sec)
Dumbbell power drop pause jump (25-40 lb dumbbells)	76	3 × 5 (2 sec)	3 × 5 (2 sec)	3 × 5 (2 sec)	2 × 5 (2 sec)
Block #2					
Bench hip extension with alternating leg raise	104	3 × 8	3 × 7	3 × 7	2 × 6
Split stance cable single-arm high row	111	3 × 8 each arm	3 × 6 each arm	3 × 6 each arm	2 × 6 each arm
Box out iso	179	3 × 10 sec each side	3 × 10 sec each side	3 × 10 sec each side	2 × 10 sec each side
Block #3					
Single-arm cable chest press	110	3 × 8 each arm	3 × 6 each arm	3 × 6 each arm	2 × 6 each arm
Dumbbell iso lunge with floating heel	93	3 × 30 sec each leg	3 × 30 sec each leg	3 × 30 sec each leg	2 × 30 sec each leg
Cable hip flexion to hip lock	164	3 × 10 each leg	3 × 10 each leg	3 × 8 each leg	2 × 8 each leg

(continued)

Table 5.2 *(continued)*

Exercise	Page #	Week 13	Week 14	Week 15	Week 16 (deload)
Weeks 13-16 (Wednesdays): Power and speed, total body with upper-body focus					
Block #1					
Plyo push-up	125	4 × 5	4 × 4	5 × 3	3 × 5
Bench press	116-117	4 × 5	4 × 4	5 × 3	3 × 5
Weighted crunch with leg lift	159	3 × 10	3 × 10	3 × 8	2 × 8
Block #2					
Pistol squat	100	3 × 6 each leg	3 × 5 each leg	3 × 4 each leg	2 × 5 each leg
Lat pulldown or pull-up	115 or 122	2 × max reps	2 × max reps	2 × max reps	2 × 5
Front foot elevated dumbbell ankle pops	106	3 × 15 sec each leg	3 × 15 sec each leg	3 × 15 sec each leg	2 × 15 sec each leg
Block #3					
Stork press	127	3 × 8 each side	3 × 6 each side	3 × 6 each side	2 × 5 each side
Nordic curl	105	3 × 8	3 × 6	3 × 6	2 × 5
Blackburn isometric series	130	2 × 6 (10 sec)	2 × 6 (10 sec)	2 × 6 (10 sec)	2 × 6 (10 sec)
Weeks 13-16 (Fridays): Power and speed, total body					
Block #1					
Push press	78	3 × 6	3 × 5	4 × 4	2 × 5 1 × 3
Trap bar clean pull	75	3 × 4	3 × 3	4 × 3	2 × 5
Medicine ball rotational chest pass	181	3 × 6 each side	3 × 5 each side	3 × 4 each side	2 × 4 each side
Block #2					
Rear foot elevated split squat	99	2 × 5 each leg 1 × 4 each leg	1 × 5 each leg 2 × 4 each leg	3 × 4 each leg	2 × 6 each leg
Barbell bent-over row	120	3 × 6	3 × 5	3 × 4	2 × 5 1 × 3
Weighted Copenhagen side plank	178	3 × 20 sec each side	3 × 20 sec each side	3 × 30 sec each side	2 × 30 sec each side
Block #3					
Supported single-leg RDL	88	3 × 6 each leg	3 × 5 each leg	3 × 5 each leg	2 × 5 each leg
Weighted push-up	123	3 × 6	3 × 5	3 × 5	2 × 5
Weighted single-leg wall sit	99	3 × 20 sec each side	3 × 20 sec each side	3 × 30 sec each side	2 × 30 sec each side

Table 5.3 Sample 16-Week Basketball Off-Season Lifting Calendar: 4 Workouts per Week, Upper-Body/Lower-Body Split Routine

Exercise	Page #	Week 1	Week 2
Weeks 1-2 (Mondays): General physical preparation, lower body			
Block #1 (circuit style)			
Goblet squat	96	2 × 15	3 × 12
Single-leg hip thrust	102	2 × 15 each leg	3 × 12 each leg
Bird dog	162	2 × 20	3 × 12
Block #2 (circuit style)			
Supported single-leg RDL	88	2 × 15 each leg	3 × 12 each leg
Step-up	101	2 × 15	3 × 12
Front plank with alternating shoulder taps	172	2 × 30 sec	3 × 30 sec
Block #3 (circuit style)			
Stability ball leg curl	84	2 × 15	2 × 12
Bench glute lift iso	103	2 × 30 sec	2 × 30 sec
Half-kneeling cable chop	170	2 × 10 each side	2 × 10 each side
Weeks 1-2 (Tuesdays): General physical preparation, upper body			
Block #1 (circuit style)			
Bench press	116-117	2 × 15	3 × 12
Single-arm dumbbell row	121	2 × 15 each arm	3 × 12 each arm
Paloff press	175	2 × 10 each side	3 × 10 each side
Block #2 (circuit style)			
Lat pulldown	115	2 × 15	3 × 12
Push-up	123	2 × 15	3 × 12
Cable dead bug	161	2 × 10	3 × 10
Block #3 (circuit style)			
Dumbbell split stance curl and press	126	2 × 12	2 × 12
Seated mini-band clamshell	163	2 × 12	2 × 12
Prone Ys, Ts, Is	132	2 × 12	2 × 12
Weeks 1-2 (Thursdays): General physical preparation, lower body			
Block #1 (circuit style)			
Trap bar deadlift	98	1 × 15 2 × 12	3 × 12 1 × 10
Bench hip extension with alternating leg raise	104	1 × 15 2 × 12	3 × 12
Side plank	177	3 × 30 sec each side	3 × 30 sec each side

(continued)

Table 5.3 *(continued)*

Exercise	Page #	Week 1	Week 2
Block #2 (circuit style)			
Rear foot elevated split squat	99	1 × 15 2 × 12	1 × 12 2 × 10
Nordic curl	105	1 × 15 2 × 12	1 × 12 2 × 10
Curl-up	160	3 × 5 (5 sec)	3 × 5 (5 sec)
Block #3 (circuit style)			
Single-arm dumbbell lateral lunge	90	2 × 10 each arm/leg	2 × 10 each arm/leg
Back extension	87	2 × 10	2 × 10
Seated calf raise	86	2 × 15	2 × 15
Weeks 1-2 (Fridays): General physical preparation, upper body			
Block #1 (circuit style)			
Half-kneeling single-arm overhead press	109	1 × 15 each arm 2 × 12 each arm	3 × 12 each arm 1 × 10 each arm
Inverted row or barbell bent-over row	114 or 120	1 × 15 2 × 12	3 × 12 1 × 10
Vertical Paloff press	176	3 × 10	3 × 10
Block #2 (circuit style)			
Single-arm cable chest press	110	1 × 15 each arm 2 × 12 each arm	1 × 12 each arm 2 × 10 each arm
Split stance cable single-arm high row	111	1 × 15 each arm 2 × 12 each arm	1 × 12 each arm 2 × 10 each arm
Medicine ball rips	180	3 × 10	3 × 10
Block #3 (circuit style)			
Push-up rotation	108	2 × 12	2 × 12
Cable face pull	127	2 × 12	2 × 12
D2 shoulder pattern	133	2 × 12 each side	2 × 12 each side

Exercise	Page #	Week 3	Week 4	Week 5	Week 6	Week 7 (deload)
Weeks 3-7 (Mondays): Hypertrophy, lower body						
Block #1						
Front squat	97	3 × 10	3 × 8	4 × 8	1 × 8 3 × 7	2 × 12
Hip thrust	102	3 × 10	3 × 8	4 × 8	1 × 8 3 × 7	2 × 12
Bird dog	162	3 × 20	3 × 20	3 × 20	3 × 20	2 × 20
Block #2						
Single-leg RDL to hip lock iso	89	3 × 10 each leg	3 × 8 each leg	3 × 8 each leg	3 × 7 each leg	2 × 12 each leg
Step-up	101	3 × 10	3 × 8	3 × 8	3 × 7	2 × 12

Exercise	Page #	Week 3	Week 4	Week 5	Week 6	Week 7 (deload)
Front plank	171	3 × 45 sec	3 × 45 sec	3 × 45 sec	3 × 45 sec	2 × 45 sec
Block #3						
Stability ball leg curl	84	2 × 10	2 × 10	2 × 10	2 × 10	2 × 10
Single-leg wall sit	99	3 × 20 sec each leg	3 × 20 sec each leg	3 × 25 sec each leg	3 × 25 sec each leg	3 × 25 sec each leg
Leg press Achilles iso	107	3 × 5 (5 sec)	3 × 5 (5 sec)	3 × 5 (5 sec)	3 × 5 (5 sec)	3 × 5 (5 sec)
Weeks 3-7 (Tuesdays): Hypertrophy, upper body						
Block #1						
Bench press	116-117	3 × 10	3 × 8	4 × 8	1 × 8 3 × 7	2 × 12
Single-arm dumbbell row	121	3 × 10 each arm	3 × 8 each arm	4 × 8 each arm	1 × 8 each arm 3 × 7 each arm	2 × 12 each arm
Paloff press	175	3 × 10 each side	3 × 10 each side	3 × 10 each side	3 × 10 each side	2 × 10 each side
Block #2						
Lat pulldown	115	3 × 10	3 × 8	3 × 8	3 × 7	2 × 12
Weighted push-up	123	3 × 10	3 × 8	3 × 8	3 × 7	2 × 12
Cable dead bug	161	3 × 10	3 × 10	3 × 10	3 × 10	2 × 10
Block #3						
Rotational plate lift	165	2 × 10 each side	2 × 10 each side	2 × 10 each side	2 × 10 each side	2 × 10 each side
Seated mini-band clamshell	163	3 × 10	3 × 10	3 × 10	3 × 10	3 × 10
Prone Ys, Ts, Is	132	3 × 10	3 × 10	3 × 10	3 × 10	3 × 10
Weeks 3-7 (Thursdays): Hypertrophy, lower body						
Block #1						
Trap bar dead-lift	98	2 × 10 1 × 8	2 × 8 1 × 7	2 × 8 2 × 7	4 × 7	2 × 12
Bench hip extension with alternating leg raise	104	3 × 10	3 × 10	3 × 10	3 × 10	2 × 12
Copenhagen side plank	178	3 × 20 sec each side	3 × 20 sec each side	3 × 30 sec each side	3 × 30 sec each side	2 × 30 sec each side

(continued)

Table 5.3   *(continued)*

Exercise	Page #	Week 3	Week 4	Week 5	Week 6	Week 7 (deload)
Block #2						
Rear foot elevated split squat	99	2 × 10 each leg 1 × 8 each leg	2 × 8 each leg 1 × 7 each leg	1 × 8 each leg 2 × 7 each leg	3 × 7 each leg	2 × 12 each leg
Nordic curl	105	2 × 10 1 × 8	2 × 8 1 × 7	1 × 8 2 × 7	3 × 7	2 × 5
Ab wheel roll-out	173	3 × 10	3 × 10	3 × 8	3 × 8	2 × 8
Block #3						
Single-arm dumbbell lateral lunge	90	2 × 10 each arm/leg	3 × 8 each arm/leg	1 × 8 each arm/leg 2 × 7 each arm/leg	3 × 7 each arm/leg	2 × 7 each arm/leg
Medicine ball rotational throw	182	2 × 10 each side	3 × 10 each side	3 × 8 each side	3 × 8 each side	2 × 8 each side
Seated calf raise	86	3 × 15	3 × 15	3 × 12	3 × 12	2 × 10
Weeks 3-7 (Fridays): Hypertrophy, upper body						
Block #1						
Half-kneeling single-arm overhead press	109	2 × 10 each arm 1 × 8 each arm	2 × 8 each arm 1 × 7 each arm	2 × 8 each arm 2 × 7 each arm	4 × 7 each arm	2 × 12 each arm
Bird dog row	121	2 × 10 each arm 1 × 8 each arm	2 × 8 each arm 1 × 7 each arm	2 × 8 each arm 2 × 7 each arm	4 × 7 each arm	2 × 12 each arm
Vertical Paloff press	176	3 × 10	3 × 10	3 × 8	3 × 8	2 × 8
Block #2						
Dumbbell alternating incline bench press	118	2 × 10 1 × 8	2 × 8 1 × 7	1 × 8 2 × 7	3 × 7	2 × 12
Split stance cable single-arm high row	111	2 × 10 each arm 1 × 8 each arm	2 × 8 each arm 1 × 7 each arm	1 × 8 each arm 2 × 7 each arm	3 × 7 each arm	2 × 12 each arm
Medicine ball rips	180	3 × 10	3 × 10	3 × 8	3 × 8	2 × 8

Exercise	Page #	Week 3	Week 4	Week 5	Week 6	Week 7 (deload)
Block #3						
Push-up rotation	108	2 × 10	3 × 10	3 × 8	3 × 8	2 × 8
Cable face pull	127	2 × 10	3 × 10	3 × 8	3 × 7	2 × 7
D2 shoulder pattern	133	2 × 10 each side	3 × 10 each side	3 × 8 each side	3 × 8 each side	2 × 8 each side

Exercise	Page #	Week 8	Week 9	Week 10	Week 11	Week 12 (deload)
Weeks 8-12 (Mondays): Base strength, lower body						
Block #1						
Hang clean	82	2 × 5 1 × 4	1 × 5 2 × 4	2 × 4 2 × 3	5 × 3	2 × 6
Back squat	94	1 × 7 2 × 6	3 × 5	4 × 4	5 × 3	1 × 10 1 × 8
Bird dog iso	162	3 × 5 (5 sec)	3 × 5 (5 sec)	3 × 5 (5 sec)	3 × 5 (5 sec)	2 × 5 (5 sec)
Block #2						
Hip thrust iso	102	1 × 7 (4 sec) 2 × 6 (4 sec)	3 × 5 (4 sec)	3 × 4 (4 sec)	3 × 4 (4 sec)	2 × 4 (4 sec)
Rear foot elevated split squat	99	1 × 7 each leg 2 × 6 each leg	3 × 5 each leg	3 × 4 each leg	3 × 3 each leg	1 × 10 each leg 1 × 8 each leg
Front plank with alternating shoulder taps	172	3 × 20	3 × 20	3 × 20	3 × 20	2 × 20
Block #3						
Nordic curl	105	2 × 7	3 × 6	3 × 5	3 × 5	2 × 5
Single-leg long leg bridge iso	103	2 × 6 (3 sec) each leg	3 × 6 (3 sec) each leg	3 × 6 (3 sec) each leg	3 × 6 (3 sec) each leg	2 × 6 (3 sec) each leg
Leg press Achilles iso	107	3 × 5 (5 sec)	3 × 5 (5 sec)	3 × 5 (5 sec)	3 × 5 (5 sec)	2 × 5 (5 sec)
Weeks 8-12 (Tuesdays): Base strength, upper body						
Block #1						
Bench press (slow)	116-117	1 × 7 (3 sec) 2 × 6 (3 sec)	3 × 5 (3 sec)	4 × 4 (3 sec)	5 × 3 (3 sec)	1 × 10 2 × 8
Lat pulldown or pull-up	115 or 122	1 × 7 2 × 6	3 × 5	4 × 4	5 × 3	1 × 10 1 × 8
Paloff press (split stance)	175	3 × 10 each side	3 × 10 each side	3 × 8 each side	3 × 8 each side	2 × 8 each side

(continued)

Table 5.3 *(continued)*

Exercise	Page #	Week 8	Week 9	Week 10	Week 11	Week 12 (deload)
Block #2						
Push press	78	3 × 6	3 × 5	3 × 4	3 × 4	1 × 10 1 × 8
Split stance cable single-arm low row	112	1 × 7 each arm 2 × 6 each arm	3 × 5 each arm	3 × 4 each arm	3 × 4 each arm	1 × 10 each arm 1 × 8 each arm
Kettlebell half dead bug press	160	3 × 10 each side	3 × 10 each side	3 × 8 each side	3 × 8 each side	2 × 8 each side
Block #3						
Weighted push-up	123	1 × 7 2 × 6	1 × 7 2 × 6	1 × 6 2 × 5	3 × 5	1 × 10 1 × 8
Weighted front plank	171	2 × 30 sec	2 × 30 sec	2 × 45 sec	2 × 45 sec	2 × 45 sec
Blackburn isometric series	130	2 × 6 (10 sec)	2 × 6 (10 sec)	2 × 6 (10 sec)	2 × 6 (10 sec)	2 × 6 (10 sec)
Weeks 8-12 (Thursdays): Base strength, lower body						
Block #1						
Kettlebell snatch	79	2 × 5 each arm 1 × 4 each arm	1 × 5 each arm 2 × 4 each arm	2 × 4 each arm 2 × 3 each arm	1 × 4 each arm 2 × 3 each arm 2 × 2 each arm	2 × 5 each arm
Trap bar deadlift	98	3 × 6	3 × 5	4 × 4	5 × 3	1 × 8 1 × 7
Weighted Copenhagen side plank	178	3 × 20 sec each side	3 × 20 sec each side	3 × 30 sec each side	3 × 30 sec each side	2 × 30 sec each side
Block #2						
Pistol squat	100	3 × 6 each leg	3 × 5 each leg	3 × 4 each leg	3 × 3 each leg	1 × 8 each leg 1 × 7 each leg
Supported single-leg RDL	88	3 × 6 each leg	3 × 5 each leg	3 × 4 each leg	3 × 4 each leg	1 × 8 each leg 1 × 7 each leg
Ab wheel rollout	173	3 × 10	3 × 10	3 × 8	3 × 8	2 × 8

Exercise	Page #	Week 8	Week 9	Week 10	Week 11	Week 12 (deload)
Block #3						
Single-arm dumbbell lateral lunge	90	2 × 6 each arm/leg	3 × 5 each arm/leg	3 × 4 each arm/leg	3 × 4 each arm/leg	1 × 8 each arm/leg 1 × 7 each arm/leg
Single-leg wall sit	99	2 × 30 sec each leg	3 × 30 sec each leg	3 × 30 sec each leg	3 × 30 sec each leg	2 × 20 sec each leg
Standing calf raise	85	2 × 10	3 × 10	3 × 8	3 × 8	1 × 8 1 × 7
Weeks 8-12 (Fridays): Base strength, upper body						
Block #1						
Landmine split stance shoulder shift	128	3 × 6	3 × 5	4 × 4	5 × 4	1 × 10 1 × 8
Barbell bent-over row	120	3 × 6	3 × 5	4 × 4	5 × 3	1 × 10 1 × 8
Vertical core	174	3 × 10 each side	3 × 10 each side	3 × 8 each side	3 × 8 each side	2 × 8 each side
Block #2						
Dumbbell floor press	119	3 × 6	3 × 5	3 × 4	3 × 3	1 × 10 1 × 8
Half-kneeling single-arm pull-down	113	3 × 6 each arm	3 × 6 each arm	3 × 5 each arm	3 × 5 each arm	1 × 10 each arm 1 × 8 each arm
Medicine ball rotational throw	182	3 × 10 each side	3 × 10 each side	3 × 8 each side	3 × 8 each side	2 × 8 each side
Block #3						
Push-up push-away	124	2 × 10	3 × 10	3 × 8	3 × 8	1 × 10 1 × 8
Cable scarecrow	129	2 × 10	2 × 10 1 × 8	3 × 8	3 × 8	2 × 8
Landmine straight-arm rotation	167	2 × 10	3 × 10	3 × 8	3 × 8	2 × 8

(continued)

Table 5.3 *(continued)*

Exercise	Page #	Week 13	Week 14	Week 15	Week 16 (deload)
Weeks 13-16 (Mondays): Power and speed, lower body					
Block #1					
Power clean	83	1 × 4 1 × 3 3 × 2	2 × 3 3 × 2	1 × 3 4 × 2	3 × 5
Barbell pause front squat (explosive eccentric)	97	5 × 3 (2 sec)	5 × 3 (2 sec)	5 × 2 (2 sec)	3 × 5 (2 sec)
Dumbbell power drop pause jump (25-40 lb dumbbells)	76	3 × 5 (2 sec)	3 × 5 (2 sec)	3 × 5 (2 sec)	2 × 5 (2 sec)
Block #2					
Hip thrust	102	3 × 6	3 × 6	3 × 6	2 × 5
Dumbbell iso lunge with floating heel	93	3 × 30 sec each leg	3 × 30 sec each leg	3 × 30 sec each leg	2 × 20 sec each leg
Cable hip flexion to hip lock	164	3 × 10 each leg	3 × 10 each leg	3 × 10 each leg	2 × 10 each leg
Block #3					
Weighted crunch with leg lift	159	3 × 10	3 × 10	3 × 10	2 × 10
Weighted single-leg long leg bridge iso	103	2 × 6 (3 sec) each leg	2 × 6 (3 sec) each leg	2 × 6 (3 sec) each leg	2 × 6 (3 sec) each leg
Front foot elevated dumbbell ankle pops	106	3 × 15 sec each leg	3 × 15 sec each leg	3 × 15 sec each leg	2 × 15 sec each leg
Weeks 13-16 (Tuesdays): Power and speed, upper body					
Block #1					
Plyo push-up	125	4 × 5	4 × 4	5 × 3	3 × 5
Bench press	116-117	4 × 5	4 × 4	5 × 3	3 × 5
Box out iso	179	3 × 10 sec each side	3 × 10 sec each side	3 × 10 sec each side	2 × 10 sec each side
Block #2					
Dumbbell single-leg snatch to box	80	3 × 4 each leg	3 × 3 each leg	3 × 3 each leg	2 × 5 each leg
Lat pulldown or pull-up	115 or 122	2 × max reps	2 × max reps	2 × max reps	2 × 5
Stork press	127	3 × 8 each side	3 × 6 each side	3 × 6 each side	2 × 5 each side

Exercise	Page #	Week 13	Week 14	Week 15	Week 16 (deload)
Block #3					
Curl-up	160	3 × 5 (5 sec)	3 × 5 (5 sec)	3 × 5 (5 sec)	2 × 5 (5 sec)
Weighted front plank	171	2 × 45 sec	2 × 45 sec	2 × 45 sec	2 × 45 sec
Wall plate push	134	2 × 10	2 × 10	2 × 10	2 × 10
Weeks 13-16 (Thursdays): Power and speed, lower body					
Block #1					
Rear foot elevated drop catch	77	3 × 4 each leg	3 × 4 each leg	4 × 3 each leg	2 × 5 each leg 1 × 3 each leg
Rear foot elevated split squat	99	3 × 4 each leg	3 × 4 each leg	4 × 3 each leg	2 × 5 each leg 1 × 3 each leg
Resisted lateral drive	92	3 × 4 each side	3 × 4 each side	3 × 3 each side	3 × 3 each side
Block #2					
Trap bar clean pull	75	3 × 4	3 × 3	3 × 3	2 × 5
Supported single-leg RDL	88	3 × 6 each leg	3 × 5 each leg	3 × 5 each leg	2 × 5 each leg
Drop step cable chop	169	3 × 8	3 × 8	3 × 6	2 × 6
Block #3					
Lunge matrix	91	3 × 9 each leg	3 × 9 each leg	3 × 6 each leg	2 × 6 each leg
Dumbbell single-leg wall sit	99	3 × 20 sec each leg	3 × 20 sec each leg	3 × 20 sec each leg	2 × 20 sec each leg
Leg press Achilles iso	107	3 × 5 (5 sec)	3 × 5 (5 sec)	3 × 5 (5 sec)	2 × 5 (5 sec)
Weeks 13-16 (Fridays): Power and speed, upper body					
Block #1					
Push press	78	3 × 6	3 × 5	4 × 4	2 × 5 1 × 3
Barbell bent-over row or single-arm dumbbell row	120 or 121	4 × 6	4 × 5	5 × 4	2 × 5 1 × 3
Cable lift	166	3 × 10 each side	3 × 8 each side	3 × 8 each side	2 × 8 each side

(continued)

Table 5.3 *(continued)*

Exercise	Page #	Week 13	Week 14	Week 15	Week 16 (deload)
Block #2					
Medicine ball rotational chest pass	181	3 × 6 each side	3 × 5 each side	3 × 4 each side	2 × 4 each side
Weighted push-up	123	3 × 6	3 × 5	3 × 5	2 × 5
Split stance cable single-arm high row	111	3 × 8 each arm	3 × 6 each arm	3 × 6 each arm	2 × 6 each arm
Block #3					
Curl-up	160	2 × 5 (5 sec)	2 × 5 (5 sec)	2 × 5 (5 sec)	2 × 5 (5 sec)
Blackburn isometric series	130	2 × 6 (10 sec)	2 × 6 (10 sec)	2 × 6 (10 sec)	2 × 6 (10 sec)
Weighted Copenhagen side plank	178	3 × 20 sec each side	3 × 20 sec each side	3 × 20 sec each side	2 × 20 sec each side

CONCLUSION

As outlined in this chapter, strength is a primary component of a comprehensive basketball performance and injury prevention program. Playing and practicing the game of basketball alone is insufficient to develop all aspects of the body, and therefore external load is needed to create the desired improvements. Resistance training has been shown to improve strength, power, speed, agility, endurance, and body composition, and also reduce the body's risk of injury. However, an optimally designed program also takes into consideration the basketball-specific court work in order to ensure harmonious development of the complete basketball player. Following a properly sequenced strength program will result in more successful basketball athletes and heighten their ability to stay healthy throughout their playing career.

Core Training

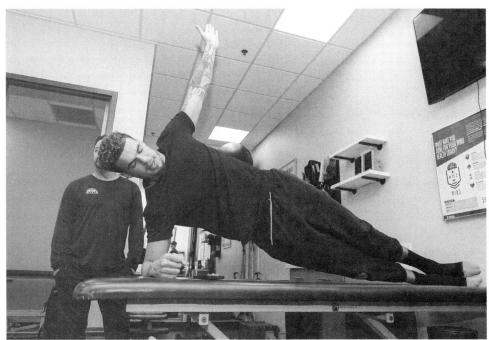

The core is commonly referred to as the powerhouse or the foundation of all limb movements. Core strengthening improves the ability to withstand large forces as the arms and legs move about the body. On the basketball court, improved torso fitness allows for more explosive movements, such as cutting, jumping, and boxing out, and more precise movements like shooting.

A well-conditioned core benefits basketball players' performance by

- enabling them to generate more power in several functional movements, such as running and jumping,
- improving stamina and endurance, and
- reducing the chance of injuries and their severity.

Core development also ensures a solid foundation for the training done in the weight room and contributes to overall athleticism, building a more complete basketball player.

CORE STABILITY DEVELOPMENT

To create core stability the core must be trained in conjunction with the hips, spine, and shoulders. While it is important to train using dynamic core exercises, isometric (nonmoving) exercises are also necessary to prevent movement of the torso during strenuous or explosive basketball movements.

Core training exercises use various types of equipment, including the back extension bench, glute-ham bench, flat bench, pull-up bar, medicine balls, stability balls, Bosu balls, cables, and rubber tubing or bands.

Core stability is a primary component of functional movement, essential in daily living and athletic activities. It is a complex interaction among the core muscles and the specific demands of the task being performed (Bliven 2013). The muscles in the core are classified in two systems: local stabilizers and global mobilizers. Local stabilizers are shorter, deep muscles in the core. Their function is to control movement and steady the body and trunk. Weakness in local stabilizers is related to lower-back pain (Akuthota 2008). The global mobilizers are larger, superficial muscles that are responsible for concentrically producing torque for movements and power (Bliven 2013).

Since basketball is a very explosive sport, training both muscle systems is very important, not only to create the power required to play the game but also to protect and stabilize the trunk. The local stabilizer muscles can be trained with low-grade isometric exercises and the global mobilizers can be trained with powerful exercises, which are described in the next section.

CORE TRAINING EXERCISES

The remainder of this chapter presents 25 core training exercises that are most effective in preparing a basketball player's body for other types of training and on-court performance. Each explanation of the exercises describes correct technique for the best results. It is imperative that the proper technique is followed and mastered prior to advancing the exercise with weight or duration.

Weighted Crunch With Leg Lift

Execution

1. Lie down with your lower back flat against the floor. With both hands hold a 10- to 25-pound (4-11 kg) weight plate or medicine ball with your arms extended overhead so that the weight almost touches the floor (figure 6.1a).
2. Tighten your abdominals and raise your legs straight up while bringing the weight up toward your feet into a V position (figure 6.1b).
3. Slowly return to the starting position.
4. Repeat for the desired number of repetitions.

Figure 6.1   Weighted crunch with leg lift.

Curl-Up

Execution

1. Lie on your back with one knee bent with the foot flat on the floor and the other leg straight. Place your hands under your low back, which will ensure that your spine remains in a neutral, slightly arched position.

Figure 6.2   Curl-up.

2. Lift your head and shoulders an inch off the ground and hold that position for 5 to 10 seconds (figure 6.2).

3. Relax your head back down to the resting position.

4. Repeat for the desired number of repetitions.

Kettlebell Half Dead Bug Press

Execution

1. Begin by lying face up on the floor with both feet in the air (knees are over the hips). The left arm is extended straight up toward the ceiling and the right arm is on the ground in the start of the chest press position. Hold a kettlebell in each hand.

Figure 6.3   Kettlebell half dead bug press.

2. Initiate the movement by simultaneously pressing the right arm up while extending the left leg until it is straight and a couple of inches off the ground (figure 6.3).

3. Return smoothly back to the start position and repeat for the desired number of repetitions, then switch and repeat on the other side.

Cable Dead Bug

Execution

1. Set a cable with a rope attachment to the lowest height with a relatively light weight.
2. Lie face up with your back flat on the floor with your head close to the cable handle and both feet in the air (knees are over the hips). Grab the rope and pull until your arms are fully extended directly over your face (see figure 6.4a).
3. While maintaining this position with the arms extended under load from the cable system, slowly extend one leg straight out, lowering it down toward the floor without contacting it (figure 6.4b).
4. Slowly return your leg to the starting position of 90 degrees of hip and knee flexion and lower the opposite leg toward the floor.
5. Continue repeating the motion with each leg for the desired number of repetitions, making sure to maintain the isometric hold with the arms to help engage the core musculature.

Figure 6.4   Cable dead bug.

Bird Dog

Execution

1. Begin the exercise on your hands and knees. You can use a mat to avoid discomfort.
2. Raise your right hand above your head with your arm parallel to the ground and at the same time raise your left leg straight out behind you while keeping your torso straight (figure 6.5).
3. Slowly return to the starting position.
4. Repeat for the desired number of repetitions, then switch sides and repeat.

Note: For an isometric version, hold each rep for the desired amount of time.

Figure 6.5   Bird dog.

Seated Mini-Band Clamshell

Execution

1. Sit on a bench or box with the mini-band placed directly above your knees.
2. Keep an upright posture and place your feet close to each other.
3. Begin by moving (abducting) the knees away from each other (figure 6.6), then return very slowly to the start position.
4. Repeat for the desired number of repetitions.

Variation

Difficulty can be increased in this exercise by using two mini-bands, one placed directly above the knees and the other placed directly below the knees.

Figure 6.6　Seated mini-band clamshell.

Cable Hip Flexion to Hip Lock

Execution

1. Hook a cable machine attachment to your ankle at ankle height. Stand facing away from the cable (figure 6.7a).
2. Flex your hip and bring your knee up as high as possible and pause briefly (figure 6.7b).
3. Slowly return to the start position.
4. Repeat for the desired number of repetitions, then switch legs.

Figure 6.7   Cable hip flexion to hip lock.

Rotational Plate Lift

Execution

1. Stand tall with your feet shoulder-width apart while holding a 10- to 25-pound (4-11 kg) weight plate by the side of your right hip (figure 6.8a).
2. Lift your arms diagonally upward across your body and rotate your torso to the left (figure 6.8b).
3. Bring the weighted plate back to the starting position and repeat for the desired number of repetitions, then switch to the other side.

Figure 6.8　Rotational plate lift.

Cable Lift

Execution

1. Set a cable machine to a low position (around knee height). Use a handle or straight bar attachment that you can hold with two hands.

2. Stand perpendicular to the cable machine with your feet slightly wider than hip-width apart, with the cable on your left side (figure 6.9a).

3. While holding the handle with both hands and your arms straight, bring the cable upward across your body, slightly turning your torso and finishing with your arms diagonally above your head on the right side (figure 6.9b).

4. Slowly bring the cable back to the starting position and repeat the movement for the desired number of repetitions, then repeat the exercise on the other side.

Figure 6.9 Cable lift.

Landmine Straight-Arm Rotation

Execution

1. Use a landmine exercise device or place a 45-pound (20 kg) bar perpendicular to the bottom corner of a wall, then load the bar or the other end of the landmine device with a weight plate of 25 to 45 pounds (11 to 20 kg).

2. Facing the bar, stand with your feet slightly wider than hip-width apart and hold the loaded end of the bar with both hands with your fingers interlocking (figure 6.10a).

3. Keeping your hips stable and your arms straight, rotate the bar in a big arc to your left side (figure 6.10b), controlling the movement until the arms are at about chest height, then rotate to the right side until the arms are again at about chest height.

4. Repeat back and forth for the desired number of repetitions.

Figure 6.10 Landmine straight-arm rotation.

Cable Rotation

Execution

1. Set up a cable machine at shoulder height.
2. Stand with your feet slightly more than hip-width apart with the cable by your right shoulder.
3. Grab the handle and bring it to the center of your body, then extend your arms and keep them at shoulder level (figure 6.11*a*).
4. Twist your torso to the left, keeping your arms straight out (figure 6.11*b*).
5. Slowly bring the cable back to the center of the body and repeat the movement for the desired number of repetitions before switching to the other side.

Figure 6.11   Cable rotation.

Drop Step Cable Chop

Execution

1. Set a cable with a handle attachment to shoulder height with a relatively light weight. Stand facing the cable with your knees slightly bent and hold the handle attachment with your fingers interlocked (figure 6.12a).

2. Step backward 90 degrees with either leg as you rotate your arms and trunk in the same direction, bringing the handle down toward your thigh (see figure 6.12b).

3. Step back to the starting position and repeat the same motion on the other side.

4. Repeat, alternating each side, for the desired number of repetitions.

Figure 6.12 Drop step cable chop.

Half-Kneeling Cable Chop

1. Kneel on the floor in front of a cable machine, facing perpendicular to the machine.
2. The inside leg closest to the machine is in front with the foot flat on the floor, and the back leg is supported with the back knee and toes.
3. Extend your arms and grab the cable handle that is set to a high position (figure 6.13a).
4. Brace your core, squeeze your glutes, and use your torso to pull the cable down and across your body past your opposite hip (figure 6.13b).
5. Return slowly to the start position and repeat for the desired number of repetitions before switching to the opposite side.

Figure 6.13   Half-kneeling cable chop.

Front Plank

Execution

1. Lie face down on the floor with your body straight and your arms extended forward.
2. Raise your upper body and bring your elbows under your shoulders with your forearms on the floor and angled in. Your hands can be in fists or with palms down on the floor.
3. Raise your body off the floor, keeping it straight and tight. Your forearms, hands, and toes should be touching the floor (figure 6.14a).
4. Hold the straight position without allowing your body to sag downward or your butt to rise upward.

Variation

You can add a single-leg variation to this exercise by holding one leg in the air throughout the set (figure 6.14b).

Figure 6.14   (a) Front plank and (b) single-leg variation.

Front Plank With Alternating Shoulder Taps

Execution

1. Start the exercise in a push-up position with your arms under your shoulders and your feet wider than your body.

2. Keeping your body as straight as possible, take your right hand off the floor and touch your left shoulder (figure 6.15) and slowly return it to the ground.

3. Be sure to maintain your position without twisting your hips or torso.

4. Alternate touching each shoulder for the desired number of repetitions.

Figure 6.15   Front plank with alternating shoulder taps.

Ab Wheel Rollout

Execution

1. Start in a kneeling position with an ab wheel in front of you on the floor. Place a soft pad or mat under your knees for comfort (figure 6.16a).
2. Tighten your core and extend your arms fully.
3. Slowly roll the wheel forward until your body is close to parallel to the floor while keeping your lower back from arching (figure 6.16b).
4. Squeeze your core and roll back to the starting position, hinging at your hips and crunching your abs.
5. Repeat for the desired number of repetitions.

Variations

This exercise can be made easier by using a stability ball or harder with a suspension training device.

Figure 6.16　Ab wheel rollout.

Vertical Core

Execution

1. Set a cable with a rope attachment to about head height with a relatively light weight.
2. Stand tall facing away from the machine in a split stance with one leg in front and the other leg behind. Keep a slight bend in both knees to achieve an athletic position and grab the rope attachment and hold it with both hands over your head with the elbows slightly bent.
3. While maintaining the overhead hold of the rope and the split stance position, slowly extend your torso backward toward the machine, expanding the ribcage (figure 6.17).
4. Flex at the trunk, returning to a tall, upright position.
5. Repeat for the desired number of repetitions before switching legs and repeating on the opposite side.

Figure 6.17   Vertical core.

Paloff Press

Execution

1. Stand in front of a cable machine with the handle attached to the cable at chest height.
2. Turn your body sideways and stand with your feet slightly wider than hip-width apart so that the cable is by the right side of your shoulder.
3. Grab the handle and place it close to your chest. Slowly push the handle out, extending your arms and keeping your hips and torso still (figure 6.18).
4. Bring the handle back to the initial position.
5. Repeat the movement for the desired number of repetitions, then repeat on the other side.

Variation

This exercise can also be done in a split stance position.

Figure 6.18   Paloff press.

Vertical Paloff Press

Execution

1. Set up a cable machine with the handle at chest height.
2. Step away from the machine and stand facing it with your feet shoulder-width apart. Grab the handle and hold it in the center of your chest.
3. Slowly press the handle overhead by extending the arms until they are locked out (figure 6.19). Do not allow any motion in the core throughout.
4. Slowly return to the start position and repeat the movement for the desired number of repetitions.

Variation

You can also perform this exercise in a split stance. Switch which foot is in front after each set.

Figure 6.19   Vertical Paloff press.

Side Plank

Execution

1. Begin on your left side with your feet stacked on top of each other, your body completely straight, and your left elbow under your shoulder with your forearm supporting your body. Your right arm can be pointing toward the ceiling or resting along your right side (figure 6.20).

2. Hold the straight body position and do not let your hips sag down toward the floor.

3. Hold for the desired length of time.

Variation

Lift (abduct) your top leg up in the air to make the side plank more challenging.

Figure 6.20   Side plank.

Copenhagen Side Plank

Execution

1. Begin on your right side with the right elbow on the floor underneath you and your left knee and foot up on a bench or box with the knee bent to 90 degrees. Your left arm can be pointed toward the ceiling or bent with your hand on your waist.
2. Keep your hips and torso in a straight line from shoulders to knee.
3. Lift your right leg off the ground and hold that position for the desired time (figure 6.21).
4. Repeat on the left side.

Figure 6.21   Copenhagen side plank.

Box Out Iso

Execution

1. Stand next to a stable wall and push your forearm against it.
2. Place your opposite foot outside of the hip. Avoid any break in the straight line created by the foot, knee, hip, and shoulder angle.
3. Press as hard as you can into the wall through the forearm without losing the straight line in your body (figure 6.22).
4. Hold for the desired time at maximal effort, then repeat on the other side.

Figure 6.22   Box out iso.

Medicine Ball Rips

Execution

1. Stand in an athletic position with your feet shoulder-width apart while holding a medicine ball.
2. Begin by "ripping" the medicine ball across your body (figure 6.23*a*).
3. Rip back across the body and again to finish on the side opposite to the one on which you started (figure 6.23*b*).
4. The three rips make one repetition. Repeat for the desired number of repetitions.

Figure 6.23   Medicine ball rips.

Medicine Ball Rotational Chest Pass

Execution

1. Stand in an athletic position perpendicular to a wall or solid surface with your knees bent, holding a light, soft medicine ball with both hands at chest level with elbows high.

2. Shift your weight toward the outside leg, loading the hip and rotating your torso toward the outside leg, while continuing to hold the medicine ball at chest height with the outside elbow at shoulder height (figure 6.24a).

3. Quickly drive off the outside foot, rotating your outside hip toward the wall, extending the outside elbow, and driving the palm of your hand into the ball so that you throw the ball toward the wall (figure 6.24b).

4. Let the ball hit the wall and catch it as it returns. You may also allow the ball to bounce before picking it up.

5. Return to the starting position and repeat for the desired number of repetitions before switching sides.

Figure 6.24   Medicine ball rotational chest pass.

Medicine Ball Rotational Throw

Execution

1. Stand sideways several feet away from a wall. Hold a medicine ball with both hands in an athletic stance.

2. Begin by rotating your shoulders away from the wall, winding up in preparation for the throw (figure 6.25a). Immediately reverse direction, turning your shoulders and releasing the ball against the wall explosively (figure 6.25b).

3. Catch the ball off of the rebound from the wall and repeat for the desired number of repetitions before switching sides.

Figure 6.25   Medicine ball rotational throw.

Power Training

Power may be the most important factor in basketball performance because the ability to produce force in a brief moment of time is necessary for key skills, such as the vertical jump (Newton et al. 1999). Power is the ability to exert maximum muscular contraction instantly in an explosive burst of movement. The two components of power are strength and speed.

Power output, although highly related to strength, especially at the higher levels of force, must be developed as a separate component (Kraemer et al. 1995). To gain a better understanding of the various stages of power, look at the force–velocity curve (figure 7.1). This illustration is helpful in determining the effect of certain exercises on power development.

Now that we have established what power is, let's talk specifically about how to train this vital component for success in basketball.

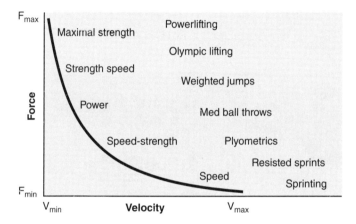

Figure 7.1 Force–velocity curve.

PLYOMETRIC TRAINING

The terms *stretch–shortening cycle exercises* or *plyometrics* describe this type of resistance exercise (Knuttgen and Kraemer 1987). The stretch–shortening cycle refers to a natural part of most movements; the cycle is a sequence of eccentric, isometric, and concentric actions. It is characterized by an eccentric motion leading into a ballistic concentric motion. Plyometric exercises are used to train for speed, power, and starting strength.

The success of plyometric exercises derives from the stretch-reflex properties of the muscle. Loading the muscle during rapid eccentric (lengthening) contractions increases internal muscular tension, which in turn produces stronger dynamic concentric (shortening) contractions during movement. Under these loading conditions, the body is able to produce force with maximum efficiency.

A great way to illustrate this is to take a look at a basketball player going up for a dunk in transition. As the player takes their last step before going up toward the basket, the plant leg, which is still on the floor, is supporting their entire body weight. As the athlete is taking their last step, the muscles undergo an eccentric contraction (lengthening). The nerves in the leg must immediately fire and cause the muscles to concentrically contract (shorten), which allows for the transition of horizontal forces into vertical forces.

This is known as the amortization phase of a plyometric exercise (see figure 7.2). It represents the time it takes to go from an eccentric contraction to a concentric contraction; basically, this is the amount of time spent on the ground. The stronger the athlete becomes, the shorter the amortization phase and the greater the forces developed.

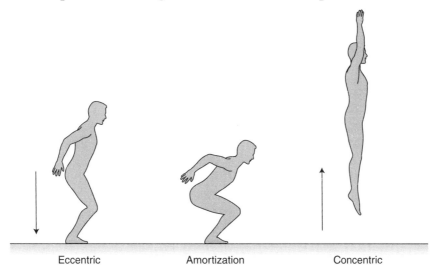

| Eccentric | Amortization | Concentric |

Figure 7.2   Plyometric amortization phase.

Plyometric Safety Considerations

Plyometrics can be performed safely, but as with any exercise there is always the risk of injury. Following is a list of factors that should be considered to ensure safety in plyometric training.

- **Age:** Prepubescent athletes should not engage in higher-intensity plyometric exercises such as depth jumps due to skeletal immaturity. Until open epiphyseal plates are closed, any type of high-intensity explosive exercise should not be prescribed.

- **Body weight:** Because plyometric exercises are high impact, obese (usually more than 30 percent body fat) individuals should be cautioned against plyometrics.

- **Strength:** Strength should be assessed prior to prescribing plyometric exercises, and it has been suggested that an athlete's 1RM squat strength be greater than 1.5 times their body weight to conduct lower-extremity plyometrics. For upper-body extremity plyometrics the athlete's 1RM bench press should be 1.0 to 1.5 times their body weight.

- **Previous injury:** Athletes who have previous injuries such as muscle strains, ligamentous injuries, or spinal injuries (including disk-related disorders) should not be prescribed plyometrics until adequate recovery and strength has been established.

- **Footwear:** Shoes—preferably basketball shoes—should always be worn. They provide good lateral stability, heel cushioning, arch support, and nonslip soles.

- **Jumping surface:** Plyometrics should not be performed on hard surfaces such as concrete and asphalt. However, at the other extreme, soft surfaces that absorb a great amount of shock diminish the effectiveness of the training. A surface with some shock absorption, such as suspended floor, rubber mats, rubber runways, or firm natural grass, may be best.

- **Warm-up:** Warm-up and stretching prior to any plyometric session are extremely important due to the high-intensity eccentric movements. Warm-up increases the sensitivity of the muscle spindle, which activates the stretch reflex to protect the muscle from being overstretched. In addition, activation of the stretch reflex further increases the force of contraction produced with plyometric exercise. Warm-up and stretching also increases the extensibility of muscles and tendons, allowing greater tolerance of the forceful eccentric movement of the stretch-shortening cycle. (See chapter 3, Movement Preparation, and chapter 4, Mobility and Flexibility Training.)

- **Progression:** When beginning plyometrics, one should use low-intensity, higher-volume exercises with a gradual progression of intensity. The principle of slow rate of progression should be followed when any new type of plyometric exercise is introduced.

- **Recovery:** There must be complete recovery between sets to gain maximum benefits from this type of training. Rest intervals should be increased if the athlete is unable to maintain consistent high intensity throughout the training period. Inadequate rest intervals can lead to fatigue and greater risk of injury.

- **Frequency:** Recovery between workouts is extremely important for safe and effective training. Plyometric exercise should never be completed on consecutive days. More is not always better. One or two times per week may be optimal.

Additionally, for advanced depth jump (DJ) training a simple prerequisite can be tested. Compare jump height during a DJ to that of a countermovement jump (CMJ). The athlete is first measured for jump height using a CMJ, then executes a DJ from an 18-inch (45 cm) box. If the DJ height is equal to or greater than the CMJ height, the athlete is ready for DJ plyometric training.

Plyometric Program Development

As you begin to develop and conduct your plyometric program there are several considerations to keep in mind: dynamic warm-up, intensity, exercise categories, volume, rest intervals, and frequency.

Dynamic Warm-Up

A dynamic warm-up is a series of movements performed prior to physical activity. Its purposes are to increase blood flow to the muscles, increase functional mobility, maximize flexibility, and prepare for more vigorous activity. See the movement preparation routines in chapter 3 for examples of dynamic warm-ups.

Intensity

The amount of effort necessary to conduct the exercises prescribed should progressively increase as the athlete continues to develop proficiency. Below are some examples of approximate plyometric exercise progressions from lowest intensity to highest intensity (Jensen and Ebben 2005; NSCA-Lift.org).

1. Submaximal jumps in place (short cone hops, ankle hops, split hops)
2. Submaximal jumps in place (tall cone hops)
3. Squat jumps
4. Weighted jumps
5. Maximum jump and reach without overhead goal
6. Low box and depth jumps
7. Maximum jump and reach to overhead goal
8. Tuck and pike jumps
9. Depth jumps from heights that are similar to the exerciser's actual vertical jump height
10. Single-leg jumps

Exercise Categories

Most plyometric drills fall into one of these five categories.

- **Jumps in place:** Drills involving repeated jumps and landing in the same place, such as multiple vertical jumps while reaching for an overhead object, squat jump, pike jump, or tuck jump.
- **Standing jumps:** Can be performed with either a horizontal or vertical emphasis but typically are performed for one maximal effort. Examples include the single-leg jump, maximal vertical jump, standing long jump, or lateral long jump.

- **Multiple hops and jumps:** Drills involving multiple hops or jumps, including long jumps or cone hops performed in succession, such as five hops in a row.
- **Box drills:** Drills performed using special boxes or other stable elevated surfaces that the athlete attempts to jump onto. Examples of these drills include box jumps, repeated box jumps, and single-leg box jumps.
- **Depth jumps:** Also called drop jumps, these drills are performed by jumping down from a plyometric box or other elevated surface, such as the first row of bleachers. Examples include stepping off the box and landing, stepping off the box and jumping vertically immediately after landing, or stepping off the box, landing, and sprinting (Jensen and Ebben 2005; NSCA-Lift.org).

Volume

Table 7.1 shows three athletic training levels at which athletes begin a plyometric program. Note the various intensity levels and the foot contacts that coincide with those intensities.

Table 7.1   Suggested Plyometric Volume Guidelines

Athletic level	Low intensity (foot contacts)	Moderate intensity (foot contacts)	High intensity (foot contacts)	Sample exercises
Beginner	80-100 contacts	60 contacts (warm-up: low-intensity drills, 40-50 reps)	40 contacts (warm-up: low-intensity drills, 40-50 reps)	Quick feet line drills: side-to-side, up-and-back, foot switches
Intermediate	100-150 contacts	80-100 contacts (warm-up: low-intensity drills, 70-80 reps)	60-80 contacts (warm-up: low-intensity drills, 70-80 reps)	Box jumps, box skips (forward and lateral), power box skips, low hurdle hops
Advanced	140-200 contacts	100-120 contacts (warm-up: low-intensity drills, 80-100 reps)	80-100 contacts (warm-up: low-intensity drills, 80-100 reps)	Depth jumps, series box jumps, high hurdle hops, forward bounds

Rest Intervals

Approximate rest should be 5 to 10 times more than the time required to perform the set of plyometrics. Consequently, if a set of multiple hops takes 4 seconds, you should rest 20 to 40 seconds prior to the next set or exercise. Additionally, limit the number of reps in each set to 10.

Frequency

Training should be performed no more than 3 times per week (once or twice per week is best) on nonconsecutive days. Plyometric training sessions should be scheduled at least 48 to 72 hours apart, allowing adequate time to recover. Always remember that more is not necessarily better. "High quality beats high quantity" is the best rule to follow.

PLYOMETRIC EXERCISES

Performing a series of repeated eccentric and concentric movements can improve many of the movements that are necessary to be successful in basketball. The plyometric exercises that follow are separated into three categories: quick feet, double-leg and single-leg.

QUICK FEET PLYOMETRICS

Quick feet plyometric exercises are a low-impact, high-speed activity, allowing the athlete to develop a base of plyometric training prior to transitioning into more advanced plyometric training.

Side-to-Side

Execution

1. Stand sideways to the line with your left side parallel to the line. Your feet should be hip-width apart, the knees slightly bent, and the arms bent at 90 degrees.
2. Keeping your feet in the starting position, jump sideways over the line and back, as quickly as possible (figure 7.3). Do not jump high; the feet should stay close to the floor.
3. Continue this touch-and-go pattern for the desired number of sets and repetitions.
4. Repeat with your right side.

Variation

This pattern can be completed with a single-leg stance as well. Repeat on both legs.

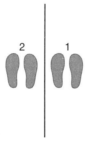

Figure 7.3   Side-to-side drill.

Up-and-Back

Execution

1. Stand facing the line. Your feet should be hip-width apart, the knees slightly bent, and the arms bent at 90 degrees.
2. Keeping your feet in the starting position, jump forward over the line and back, as quickly as possible (figure 7.4). Do not jump high; the feet should stay close to the floor.
3. Continue this touch-and-go pattern for the desired number of sets and repetitions.

Variation

This pattern can be completed with a single-leg stance as well. Repeat on both legs.

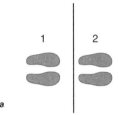

Figure 7.4 Up-and-back drill.

Foot Switches

Execution

1. Stand facing the line. Place one foot over the line and one foot below the line with your knees slightly bent and arms bent at 90 degrees.

2. Switch foot locations from above the line to below the line as quickly as possible (right over the line, left below, right below, left over) (see figure 7.5). A very slight (not high or wide) jump is required to change locations of your feet.

3. Continue this pattern for the desired number of sets and repetitions.

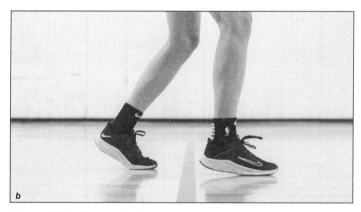

Figure 7.5   Foot switches.

DOUBLE-LEG PLYOMETRICS

In this category are several exercises that can be conducted using various types of equipment such as cones, hurdles, or boxes. These may also be completed with a single cone, box or hurdle, or several in a specific sequence.

Box Jump

Execution

1. Stand facing a box that is 18-48 inches (45-121 cm) high with your feet hip-width apart.
2. Conduct a single CMJ utilizing your arms (figure 7.6a): Jump and land as softly as you can on the top of the box (figure 7.6b).
3. Step back down to the floor.
4. Repeat for the desired number of sets and repetitions.

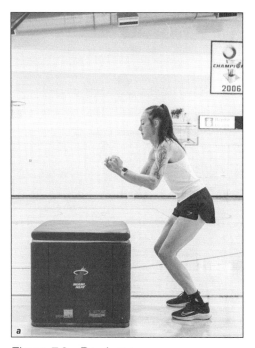 

Figure 7.6　Box jump.

Side-to-Side Box Jump

Execution

1. Stand sideways to a box 6 to 18 inches (15-45 cm) high.
2. Conduct a single CMJ utilizing the arms (figure 7.7*a*): Jump and land on the top (figure 7.7*b*).
3. Immediately jump off and land on the floor on the opposite side (figure 7.7*c*).
4. Immediately jump back up on top of the box
5. Immediately jump off to your original starting point.
6. Repeat this pattern for the desired number of sets and repetitions.

Figure 7.7　Side-to-side box jump

Depth Jump

Execution

1. Stand atop a box 12 to 30 inches (30-76 cm) high (figure 7.8*a*).
2. Jump off the box, landing on the ground.
3. Conduct a single CMJ utilizing the arms, immediately exploding up into a jump for maximal height (figure 7.8*b-c*).
4. Repeat for the desired number of sets and repetitions.

Figure 7.8   Depth jump.

Series Box Jumps

Execution

1. Stand facing a series of two to four aligned boxes, 12 to 24 inches (30-60 cm) high and spaced 2 to 3 feet (60-91 cm) apart, with your feet hip-width apart.

2. Conduct a single CMJ utilizing your arms: Jump and land as softly as you can on the top of the nearest box.

3. Immediately jump down to the floor.

4. As soon as you contact the floor, jump quickly up to the next box in the series (figure 7.9a-b).

5. Repeat for the desired number of boxes, sets, and repetitions.

Figure 7.9 Series box jumps.

Hurdle Hop

Execution

1. Stand facing a hurdle 6 to 30 inches (15-76 cm) high with your feet hip-width apart.
2. Conduct a single CMJ using your arms to jump over the hurdle and land as softly as you can on the opposite side (figure 7.10).
3. Turn around and jump back over the hurdle.
4. Repeat for the desired number of sets and repetitions.

Figure 7.10   Hurdle hop.

Series Hurdle Hops

Execution

1. Stand facing a series of three to six hurdles, 6 to 30 inches (15-76 cm) high, with your feet hip-width apart.
2. Conduct a single CMJ utilizing your arms to jump over the hurdle and land as softly as you can on the opposite side (figure 7.11).
3. Continue jumping over each sequenced hurdle.
4. Repeat for the desired number of hurdles, sets, and repetitions.

Figure 7.11   Series hurdle hops.

SINGLE-LEG PLYOMETRICS

In this category there are several exercises that can be conducted with various types of equipment, such as cones, hurdles, or boxes. These may also be completed utilizing a single cone, box, or hurdle, or several in a specific sequence.

Power Box Skip

Execution

1. Begin with one foot on top of a box that is 12 to 18 inches (30-45 cm) high (figure 7.12a).

2. Driving explosively through the lead foot (the foot on the floor at the start) and utilizing your arms, jump as high as you can and in a skipping motion in midair, switch your feet so that you land with your trailing leg on the top of the box (figure 7.12b).

3. Immediately jump and switch in midair.

4. Repeat this skipping motion, alternating the lead and trail legs, as explosively as possible to achieve maximal height for the desired number of sets and repetitions.

Figure 7.12   Power box skip.

Single-Leg Box Jump

Execution

1. Stand on one leg facing a box 6 to 12 inches (15-30 cm) high with feet shoulder-width apart (figure 7.13*a*).
2. Conduct a single-leg CMJ utilizing your arms and land as softly as you can on the top of the box (figure 7.13*b*).
3. After completing the jump, step down and repeat for the desired number of sets and repetitions on each leg.

Variation

This exercise can also be performed as ricochet box jumps. After landing on top of the box, immediately jump back down to the floor. The second you touch the floor, repeat the jump back up to the top of the box, repeating this pattern as quickly as possible.

 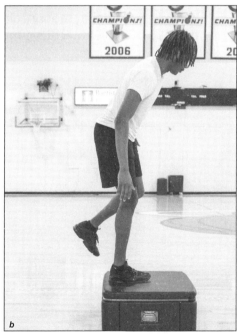

Figure 7.13   Single-leg box jump.

Single-Leg Hurdle Hop

Execution

1. Stand facing a hurdle 6 to 12 inches (15-30 cm) high with feet shoulder-width apart.
2. Conduct a single-leg CMJ utilizing your arms to jump over the hurdle and land as softly as you can on the opposite side (figure 7.14).
3. Turn around and jump back over the hurdle.
4. Repeat for the desired number sets and repetitions.

Figure 7.14   Single-leg hurdle hop.

Single-Leg Hop

Execution

1. Stand on your right leg with your knee slightly bent.
2. Lift your left foot off the ground 4 to 5 inches (10-12 cm) with both arms back and elbows bent (figure 7.15a).
3. Explode up and out, jumping off your right leg and driving both arms up and forward together (figure 7.15b).
4. Land on your right leg under control.
5. Continue this hopping pattern on the right leg for the desired number of repetitions. Then repeat on the left leg.

Figure 7.15   Single-leg hop.

Power Skip

Execution

1. Skip with your left foot by driving your right knee upward and your left arm explosively forward and upward while driving your right arm back (figure 7.16*a*).

2. Next, skip with your right foot by driving your left knee upward and your right arm explosively forward and upward while driving your left arm back in an exaggerated running motion (figure 7.16*b*).

3. Repeat this skipping pattern for maximal height and distance for the desired number of sets and repetitions.

Figure 7.16   Power skips.

Bounding

Essentially bounding is just an exaggerated run with lots of vertical and horizontal displacement. Go for both height and distance with each stride. Try jogging 5 to 10 yards (4-9 m) before starting the drill.

1. Start off as though you were skipping, then push off the ground with one leg and raise high the knee of the other leg (figure 7.17).

2. While you are coming up in your bound, you should have "runner's arm"—that is, the leg with the high knee in conjunction with the opposite arm should come up at a 90-degree angle to shoulder height with the other arm down beside your hip.

3. Repeat this bounding pattern for maximal height and distance for the desired number of sets and repetitions.

Figure 7.17   Bounding.

POWER TRAINING PROGRAM

With the previous information on power in mind and a variety of plyometric exercises to choose from, we can now assemble a power training program. Table 7.2 provides an 8-week off-season power training program employing the plyometrics that have been presented. These plyometric workouts can be integrated into either the 3-day-per-week or 4-day-per-week off-season training calendars in tables 12.1 and 12.2. Please pay very close attention to the rest intervals and the total contacts for the exercises at each intensity. Remember, more is not always better. High quality is more important than high quantity.

Table 7.2 Sample 8-Week Plyometric Training Program

Exercise (low intensity)	Week 1: Plyo #1 and #2*	Week 2: Plyo #3 and #4
Up-and-back drill (p. 191)	2 × 10	3 × 10
Side-to-side drill (p. 190)	2 × 10	3 × 10
Foot switches (p. 192)	2 × 10	3 × 10
	Total contacts: 60	**Total contacts:** 90
	Rest between sets: 60 sec	**Rest between sets:** 60 sec
	Rest between exercises: 60 sec	**Rest between exercises:** 60 sec
Exercise (moderate intensity)	**Weeks 3-4: Plyo #5-#8**	**Weeks 5-6: Plyo #9-#12**
Box jump (p. 193)	3 × 10	3 × 10
Power box skip (p. 199)	3 × 10	4 × 10
Side-to-side box jump (p. 194)	3 × 10	4 × 10
Hurdle hop (p. 197)	3 × 10	4 × 10
	Total contacts: 120	**Total contacts:** 150
	Rest between sets: 60-90 sec	**Rest between sets:** 60-90 sec
	Rest between exercises: 60-90 sec	**Rest between exercises:** 60-90 sec
Exercise (high intensity)	**Week 7: Plyo #13 and #14**	**Week 8: Plyo #15 and #16**
Series box jumps (p. 196)	3 × 8 *(1 set is down and back 2 times)* (2 boxes/forward 18 inches)	3 × 6 *(1 set is down and back 1 time)* (advance to 3 boxes/forward 24 inches)
Hurdle hop (p. 197)	3 × 8 *(1 set is down and back 2 times)* (2 hurdles/forward 24 inches)	3 × 6 *(1 set is down and back 1 time)* (advance to 3 hurdles/forward 30 inches)
Depth jump (p. 195)	5 × 5 (1 box, 18 inches high)	5 × 5 (advance to 1 box, 24-30 inches high)
Power skip (p. 203)	5 × 20 yards or meters; this equals 4 reps)	6 × 20 yards or meters; this equals 4 reps)
	Total contacts: 93	**Total contacts:** 85
	Rest between sets: 60-90 sec	**Rest between sets:** 60-90 sec
	Rest between exercises: 60-90 sec	**Rest between exercises:** 60-90 sec

* These numbered plyometric workouts correspond to the plyometric workouts in the sample 16-week off-season training calendars in tables 12.1 and 12.2.

ADVANCED POWER TRAINING

When athletes have mastered the previously presented power training drills and developed a good power base, more advanced power training is an option. Maximal power can be achieved through weighted jump drills and resisted sprints.

These are not plyometric drills. However, they are additional ways for athletes to add to their power profile. The descriptions in each area help to calculate an accurate prescribed load for each individual athlete.

Turner and colleagues (2012) showed maximal power output in a weighted hex bar jump to be at loads of 10 to 20 percent of the one-repetition maximum (1RM) back squat. Additionally, Harris and colleagues (2000), in another study of the power and maximum-strength relationship in dynamic and static weighted jumps, found maximal power output to be at an external load of 10 percent of 1RM back squat.

For many athletes, especially younger athletes, a standard trap bar is too heavy to fall within 10 to 20 percent of their 1RM squat max. Using dumbbells or a weight vest instead of a trap bar is a good solution.

Weighted Jump

Execution

1. Determine 1RM back squat for the athlete (can be estimated).
2. Load the athlete with total weight of 10 to 20 percent of 1RM.
3. Instruct the athlete to jump maximally while maintaining good form (figure 7.18).
4. Reset and repeat 3 to 5 jumps for 2 or 3 sets with full recovery (2 to 5 minutes) between each set.

Figure 7.18   Weighted jump.

For resisted sprints, Cross and colleagues (2017) found that load that produced a 48 to 52 percent decrease in sprint time at a given distance versus an unweighted maximal effort sprint at the same distance produced maximal power output throughout the sprint. Sprint distances of 11 to 21 yards (10-20 m) should be used to train for maximal power.

Resisted Sprint

Execution

1. Set up cones 11 to 21 yards (10-20 m) apart.
2. Time the athlete in an unweighted maximal-effort sprint at the given distance and record the time.
3. After full recovery, repeat the unweighted sprint two or three times and average the times.
4. Add weight to the sled or implement (around 25 percent of body weight is a good place to start), and time the resisted sprint (figure 7.19).
5. Record time and adjust weight up or down based on how close the athlete was to 50 percent of their unweighted sprint at the same distance.
6. Reset and repeat 3 to 12 resisted sprints at 50 percent with full recovery between each rep.
7. End session with one or two unresisted sprints at same distance.

Figure 7.19   Resisted sprint.

CONCLUSION

Power training typically involves exercises that apply the maximum amount of force as fast as possible. Throughout this chapter we have discussed examples of various exercises and drills that allow players to engage in these training activities. By employing the drills and exercises systematically and performing them correctly, athletes are sure to become more efficient and powerful in their movements, thus giving them a greater opportunity to excel on the court.

Speed and Agility Training

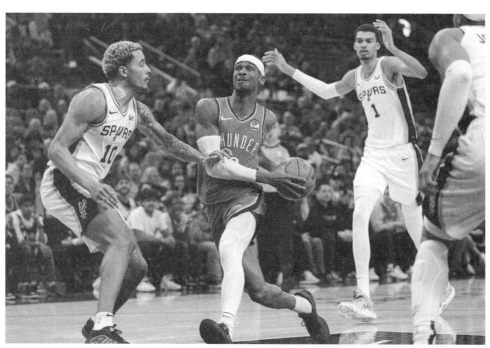

One defining feature of almost any successful athlete in a team sport is the ability to simply move fast. In sports that are dominated by size, such as American football, speed becomes an equalizer for players of smaller stature like Kyler Murray. In sports that require great skill, such as soccer, players like Kylian Mbappé can separate themselves by covering a lot of ground very quickly. In sports that reward fast-paced play, like basketball, athletes like Russell Westbrook can wow spectators by blowing by their opponents. In the Summer Olympic Games, the 100-meter sprint is perhaps one of the most watched events worldwide. There is just something special about watching an athlete who possesses the gift of great speed.

In this chapter we discuss two different types of speed: linear and lateral. In the first section we discuss linear speed, which is the ability to express speed in a straight line. In the second section, we discuss lateral speed, which is the ability to move at an angle and change directions quickly and efficiently. In each section we begin by defining and describing the most important aspects of the types of speed and then explain simple drills to help improve those qualities in athletes of any age or skill level.

LINEAR SPEED

In most team sports, the faster athlete has a significant advantage over their opponent. Basketball is no different. While most people are drawn to the changes of direction and agility in basketball, the fact is athletes spend about 40 percent of their court time running in a straight line or semi-straight line. Driving toward the basket, chasing a loose ball, and running in transition during a fast break are all examples of moments when an athlete is accessing linear speed abilities on the basketball court.

Linear speed may also be the defining characteristic of the word *athlete*. Very often, the world's best athletes are described as fast. This is with good reason. Many athletic feats can be related to sprinting ability. This includes jumping from a dead stop, as in the vertical jump, jumping from a moving start, as in a high jump or long jump, and even the ability to change direction abruptly. It can be argued that sprinting forms a strong part of the foundation for most, if not all, athletic qualities. Therefore, we should pay special attention to sprinting or "linear speed" in our training program for the basketball athlete.

Before beginning our discussion on speed, it is important to note that linear speed or linear running is one of the most studied topics in sports. We could easily write an entire book on the science and biomechanics of linear speed. But in this chapter, we discuss the nuts and bolts of running fast and provide some simple drills that can be implemented immediately.

Linear speed is defined as maximal velocity demonstrated in a straight line. In this chapter we discuss two kinds of linear speed, acceleration and top-end speed running. We also introduce what is called "curvilinear" speed. Curvilinear running is defined in a number of different ways.

Generally speaking, curvilinear running is when the running is not performed in a straight line; however, the mechanics of the movement do not significantly diverge from those of linear speed. Examples of curvilinear running are rounding the bases in baseball or running the curve in track and field. This is usually seen on the basketball court when players drive and wind past and through defenders when attacking the rim on offense.

Linear speed is usually defined using the following formula:

$$\text{Stride Length} \times \text{Stride Frequency} = \text{Speed}$$

The concept of stride length is fairly simple yet can be misdefined at times. Stride length is not simply the distance from foot strike to foot strike, though that is easy to measure and to see. Stride length is actually the distance that the athlete's center of gravity is projected with each ground contact. While this definition of stride length is more difficult to measure, it accounts for a problem in sprinting called *overstriding*. Overstriding is a common running error in which the athlete reaches too far forward with their lead leg, causing their foot to contact the ground too far in front of their center of gravity. In this case, the athlete's foot actually creates braking forces, causing the athlete to lose speed rather than gain speed. A common cause of overstriding is a misunderstanding of the definition of stride length. True stride length is determined not by how far the athlete reaches with their lead leg but rather by the impulse the athlete creates as their foot contacts the ground to propel them forward. When sprinting full speed, the foot is in contact with the ground for a very short period of time, in some cases less than 0.1 second. The major determinant of an athlete's stride length is the amount of force they can put into the ground in that very short period of time. This quality can be improved with proper training through some of the drills we present in this chapter.

The concept of stride frequency is generally defined as how quickly a stride can be completed. Higher stride frequency means the athlete is able to get more foot contacts in a given amount of time. One of the primary characteristics of stride frequency is the speed at which an athlete can perform a cycling action of the lower extremity. This characteristic can be honed by improving an athlete's stride mechanics. In this chapter, we provide simple drills that can be implemented to improve stride frequency.

Now that we've defined these concepts, it is easy to see the interplay between stride length and stride frequency that creates speed. The goal when training an athlete should be to optimize both stride length and stride frequency. Emphasizing one over the other can very easily cause problems, and the athlete's speed will suffer. One example would be to overemphasize stride frequency by asking an athlete to get in as many steps as possible in a given distance. What would likely happen is that in an attempt to speed up their stride frequency, the athlete would no longer project their center of gravity forward, thereby shortening their stride length and losing overall speed. Always keep in mind that both of these qualities are highly important when developing speed.

As mentioned earlier, we can divide linear speed into two categories, acceleration and top-end speed. These two types of linear speed are distinguished by some key features in their mechanics. They also require different drill sets in order to improve stride length and stride frequency. In the coming sections, we discuss the key differences between acceleration and top-end speed as well as provide some simple drills to help your athletes improve stride length and stride frequency in each.

Acceleration

Acceleration is defined in physics as the rate of change of speed. In sprinting, it is defined as the phase in running when an athlete builds up to maximal running speed. The mechanics of acceleration are fundamentally different from running at maximal velocity. Figure 8.1 points out the key features of what is called the acceleration posture.

Acceleration is characterized by three key points. First is the forward lean of the torso. This allows the center of gravity to be displaced forward, in front of the base of support, which creates the appropriate vectors for driving the body forward. Second, the drive knee leads the way. This creates what is typically called a positive shin angle in the front leg, which creates appropriate angles to drive the body forward. Finally, when accelerating, the athlete needs to create what can be referred to as a power line. A power line is the direct line of force from the angle at which the drive leg contacts the ground straight through the center of gravity, thereby creating efficient energy use. A common mistake with the power line is the assumption that the athlete always needs to reach full triple extension to create a strong power line. While full triple extension may be beneficial in some circumstances, it may not be in others and therefore is not a requirement in all drills. Here are drills that address acceleration by targeting stride length and stride frequency.

Figure 8.1   Acceleration posture.

ACCELERATION DRILLS THAT TARGET STRIDE LENGTH

A-Skip

In this drill, the athlete is performing a simple skipping movement while abiding by the rules of acceleration. When skipping, it is important to maintain an upright posture and not create the forward lean that was discussed earlier. The reason is that the speed of linear motion during this drill is not fast enough to necessitate a forward lean.

Execution

1. A good skipping posture begins with a straight line from the drive leg through the center of gravity (figure 8.2a).
2. The knee of the swing leg drives you in the direction of motion with a crisp tempo, maximizing time in the air and minimizing time on the ground.
3. Perform this drill in sets of 10 to 20 yards (9-18 m).

Variation

Difficulty can be increased in this drill by using band resistance around the hips (figure 8.2b).

Figure 8.2   (a) A-skip and (b) A-skip with resistance.

Horizontal Bound

Bounding is a more intense form of skipping in which the athlete does not perform a double contact on each leg; they simply alternate foot contacts, which makes this drill much closer to running.

Execution

1. Because this drill creates faster linear motion, you will have more forward lean than in the A-skip drill (figure 8.3a).
2. Continue to display a good power line, with the knee of the drive leg leading the way.
3. Perform this drill in sets of 15 to 30 yards (13-27 m).

Variation

This drill can be made progressively more difficult using band resistance around the hips (figure 8.3b).

Figure 8.3 *(a)* Horizontal bound and *(b)* horizontal bound with resistance.

ACCELERATION DRILL THAT TARGETS STRIDE FREQUENCY

High Knees

In this drill, the athlete has an upright posture since the goal is not to create fast linear motion. Instead, the drill focuses on stride frequency, not stride length.

Execution

1. Perform high knees as fast as you can for a given distance. The fast high knees should coincide with fast arm action from the shoulder (figure 8.4a).

2. A common mistake in this drill is taking steps that are too long. Steps in this drill should be short so you can get as many reps in for the given distance as possible while focusing on making each stride as fast as possible.

3. Perform the drill for 5 to 10 yards (4-9 m).

Variation

This drill can be made progressively more difficult using band resistance around the hips (figure 8.4b).

Figure 8.4   (a) High knees and (b) high knees with resistance.

ACCELERATION DRILLS: PUTTING IT ALL TOGETHER

Chase Drill

Athletes typically run faster in competitive situations. There is no better way to create competition than to do chase drills in which one athlete is trying to escape another. Chase drills also provide a lot of fun in your training sessions, which makes them highly valuable. While there are a lot of different chase drill variations, here is a common variation for acceleration.

Execution

1. Athlete 1 begins standing up, while athlete 2 is 3 to 4 yards (2-3 m) in front of them in the push-up position.
2. On the "Go!" call, both athletes explode into a sprint.
3. Athlete 1 attempts to tag athlete 2 from behind.
4. This drill should be 10 to 20 yards (9-18 m) in distance. Repeat for the desired number of repetitions.

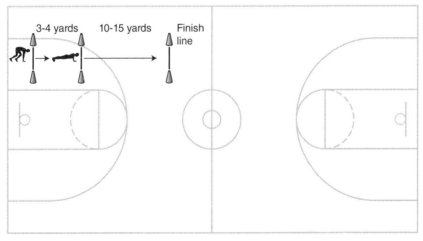

Figure 8.5   Chase drill.

Resisted-Sprint Start

Resisted-sprint starts are a very common way to make athletes faster. Several forms of resistance can be used, including band resistance and weighted sleds. When performing weighted sprints, the coach should ensure that the athlete's technique does not begin to break down. This is an indication that too much resistance is being used. A general rule for dictating how much resistance to use is the "truck test." The truck test simply states that if the athlete begins to look like they are pulling a truck behind them, the amount of resistance needs to be reduced.

Execution

1. Attach a weighted sled with a harness or belt. Stand in a split stance start position.

2. The athlete explodes into a sprint and pulls the sled the desired distance. Resisted-sprint starts can be performed for a variety of distances but most commonly are 10 to 20 yards (9-18 m). Repeat for the desired number of repetitions.

Figure 8.6   Resisted-sprint start.

Top-End Speed

What is meant by top-end speed mechanics? We have defined acceleration as the phase of running in which the athlete is gaining speed and momentum. *Top-end speed* is a term describing the mechanics an athlete displays once they have reached a speed they would like to maintain. This can look different depending on the event. In the 100-meter dash in track and field, the athletes reach top-end speed mechanics once they have achieved maximal velocity, and they hold that speed for a very short duration, maybe just a couple of seconds. However, in a marathon, athletes want to maintain a submaximal speed for a much longer duration. In both cases, the mechanics of these athletes attempting to maintain a specific velocity look fairly similar.

Figure 8.7 shows the similarity between a sprinter and long-distance runner. Both athletes use similar mechanics once they have reached a speed they want to maintain.

EMMANUEL DUNAND/Getty Images

PIERRE VERDY/Getty Images

Figure 8.7   Comparison of the running mechanics of *(a)* a sprinter and *(b)* a long-distance runner.

An important question to consider is why basketball players would need to perform top-end speed drills, especially since basketball players rarely reach top running speeds. This is primarily because the length of the court acts as a constraint. Nevertheless, an argument can be made that this is a valuable skill for all athletes because it is the fastest movement the human body can perform. As such, when athletes improve their maximal sprint velocity, many other movement qualities tend to improve as well, such as acceleration and lateral speed, both very important for basketball players. This makes top-end speed a generally undertrained but highly valuable quality, especially in younger, developing athletes.

Figure 8.8 shows good top-end speed body positioning. In contrast to the acceleration posture, the top-end speed posture is characterized by an upright torso (figure 8.8a). While the acceleration phase is dominated by high horizontal ground reaction forces in order to gain velocity and momentum, the upright torso of the top-end speed posture allows better transmission of vertical ground reaction forces as the athlete maintains velocity.

Another big difference between acceleration and top-end speed mechanics is in the swing leg. While acceleration is characterized by the knee driving forward in a piston-type action, in top-end speed mechanics, the athlete first brings their heel as close as possible to their hip (figure 8.8b). In doing so, the athlete has created a mechanical advantage to drive their knee forward and carry their body in that direction.

As we did with acceleration, we can divide top-end speed drills into two buckets: drills targeting an improvement in stride length and drills targeting improvements in stride frequency.

Tim Clayton/Corbis/Getty Images

HASLIN Frederic/Getty Images

Figure 8.8   Good top-end speed body position: *(a)* upright torso and *(b)* heel close to hip.

TOP-END SPEED DRILLS THAT TARGET STRIDE LENGTH

B-Skip

The primary difference between the B-skip drill and the A-skip drill, described in the acceleration section, is that the B-skip motion consists of more knee extension during the downward phase of the swing leg to better mimic top-end speed mechanics.

Execution

1. Begin with a straight line from your drive leg through the center of gravity (figure 8.9*a*).
2. Drive the knee of your swing leg in the direction of motion.
3. After your knee reaches the highest point, drive the foot back down to the ground to prepare for contact. You should extend your knee as the swing leg is moving into hip extension, during the downward phase of the swing (figure 8.9*b*). Aim to time the moment you reach maximal knee extension with the moment the foot reaches just under, or slightly in front of, the center of gravity. You should not reach maximal knee extension before the foot hits the ground.
4. Perform this drill for 15 to 30 yards (13-27 m) for the desired number of repetitions.

Note: A common mistake in doing this drill is when the knee extension of the swing leg is performed during the upward motion of the swing leg, creating an inappropriate pattern. This complicated timing sequence makes a seemingly simple drill difficult for the athlete to master. But if done well, this drill can give the athlete a good feel for appropriate timing and ground contact positioning that can improve their ability to propel themselves forward when sprinting.

Variation

To progress with this drill, the athlete can hold light dumbbells of 10 to 15 pounds (4-6 kg) at their side (figure 8.9*c*). This weight placement helps develop the vertical ground reaction forces that characterize top-end speed.

Figure 8.9 *(a, b)* B-skip and *(c)* weighted B-skip.

Vertical Bound

Vertical bounding is similar to the horizontal bounding drill discussed in the acceleration section but with a few key differences.

Execution

1. To begin, assume a more upright posture to better mimic top-end speed mechanics.

2. Instead of driving the knee forward, drive the knee in a more vertical direction. This combination of an upright torso and a vertical knee drive will result in gaining more height than linear distance, hence the term vertical bounding (figure 8.10).

3. Perform this drill for 15 to 30 yards (13-27 m) for the desired number of repetitions.

Note: This drill is much easier to perform properly by jogging into the starting line instead of starting from a dead stop.

Figure 8.10   Vertical bound.

TOP-END SPEED DRILLS THAT TARGET STRIDE FREQUENCY

Butt Kicks

As discussed earlier, one of the defining characteristics of top-end speed mechanics is that the heel is raised to the hip before the athlete drives the knee forward. The butt kick exercise is meant to get the athlete comfortable with that motion, since this position allows the athlete to have a mechanical advantage for a more effective swing phase.

Execution

1. In this exercise, demonstrate an upright posture and quickly bring your heels up to the buttocks (figure 8.11). A subtle amount of forward knee motion is allowed while this action occurs.

2. If you remain in the proper torso position, each step will be only 6 to 8 inches (15-20 cm) in distance. A common mistake with this drill is losing the upright torso position, which causes the strides to become much longer.

3. Practice this drill only for very short distances such as 5 to 10 yards (4-9 m), but complete as many reps as possible in that distance.

Figure 8.11   Butt kicks.

Dead Leg Drill

This drill is another very difficult one to perform correctly. You again assume and maintain an upright posture. One leg is locked in extension for the entirety of the drill. This leg is the dead leg. The live leg will perform a fast cycling action.

Execution

1. Remember the proper sequencing of actions in the swing leg during top-end speed. You begin the swing action by bringing the heel to the hip, then drive forward with the knee (figure 8.12*a*).

2. On the way down, the hip and knee extend simultaneously reaching maximal extension at ground contact (figure 8.12*b*). Don't skip the heel-to-hip phase of the swing to move directly into a knee drive. Doing this might be appropriate for improving acceleration mechanics, but it is not appropriate if the goal is to improve top-end speed.

3. Practice this drill only for very short distances such as 5 to 10 yards (4-9 m), but complete as many reps as possible in that distance.

Variation

This drill can also be done by providing 12-inch (30 cm) cones or mini hurdles for the athlete to cycle over each step. The cones or hurdles can act as cues that make it easier for the athlete to visualize the motion for the drill.

Figure 8.12 Dead leg drill. The left leg is the dead leg, and fast cycles are performed with the live right leg.

TOP-END SPEED DRILL: PUTTING IT ALL TOGETHER

Build-Up Runs

In this drill we are trying to isolate the athlete's top-end speed by eliminating the acceleration portion of the sprint.

Execution

1. Establish a 15- to 20-yard (13-18 m) zone in which to build up speed.
2. Place cones at the end of the build-up zone to indicate the start of the sprint zone, and also cones 10 to 20 yards (9-18 m) after that to mark the end of the sprint zone (figure 8.13). (It is advisable to start with shorter distances and work toward longer ones.)
3. Reach your top speed by the time you hit the sprint zone, and maintain that speed through the entirety of the sprint zone.
4. Once through the sprint zone, slowly bring yourself to a stop.
5. Repeat for the desired number of repetitions.

Note: Hold proper technique when running through the sprint zone.

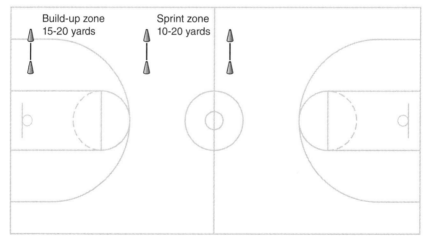

Figure 8.13   Build-up runs.

Curvilinear Sprinting

Curvilinear sprinting is a very important topic to discuss when it comes to almost any team sport. Rarely in team competition is running performed in a direct straight line. When the athlete is sprinting, but instead of running linearly (i.e., in a straight line) they are moving at angles or around turns, the term used to describe this action is *curvilinear*. In the sport of basketball, this action can be seen on almost every possession. Whether they are handling the ball or not, athletes move quickly to create space from defenders. Because of the number of players in a small space, the athletes are constantly turning corners, moving around picks, or attempting to create an advantageous angle to the rim. These are all examples of athletes using their sprinting abilities while moving in a curvilinear fashion. Figure 8.14 provides an example of this motion.

As shown in the photo, as the athlete attempts to turn a corner, his torso leans in the direction he is turning. This creates some interesting mechanics in the lower limbs. The athlete's inside leg requires much more foot and ankle mobility to undertake a motion called eversion (the athlete's right foot in figure 8.14). This motion of the inside leg is very important for balance. The more mobility the athlete has available in the ankle, the stronger angles they are likely to make with their torso, giving them an advantage in these scenarios.

Another key feature of the inside leg position is the amount of adduction present at the hip. In order to counterbalance the lean of the torso, the inside leg actually crosses the midline during each stride. The more extreme the angle the athlete is taking, the more extreme the crossover step is (see right leg in figure 8.14).

As you can see, the mobility and mechanics of the inside leg are key to how effectively the athlete can perform curvilinear sprints. In fact, during curvilinear running, the inside and outside legs perform distinctly differ-

Christian Petersen/Getty Images

Figure 8.14 Curvilinear running: Steve Nash leans his torso to the right in order to turn at an angle to the right. This lean puts his right hip in an adducted position and his right ankle in an everted position.

ent functions. Because of the hip adduction and eversion of the ankle, the inside leg has much longer ground contact times than the outside leg. This is advantageous for pushing the body forward. Therefore, the inside leg becomes the acceleration and balance leg that generates speed for the athlete. The outside leg, however, has a different role. While it is less involved in balance and acceleration, its job is to maintain the momentum that is created by the inside leg. Therefore, the outside leg tends to follow the rules of top-end speed.

Because of the interplay between acceleration, top-end speed, and curvilinear sprinting, drills designed to target curvilinear running make a perfect add-on to just about any linear speed training session. Following are a few drills you can use to challenge your athletes' abilities to move and sprint at angles or around curves.

Three-Point Line Run

On the basketball court, the three-point line provides a natural curve for us to utilize for curvilinear runs.

Execution

1. To set up this drill, place a line of cones about 4 feet (1 m) inside and outside of the three-point line to create two running lanes.
2. Starting on the inside lane, sprint the inside of the three-point line, circle around a cone, and sprint back in the outside lane (figure 8.15). This provides experience running at angles in both directions.

Variation

This drill can be made more intense by allowing one athlete to chase another through the drill.

Figure 8.15 Three-point line run.

Figure 8 Drill

Execution

1. Set up cones in a figure 8 pattern (figure 8.16).
2. You can start in either direction, but the goal is to run the figure 8 as quickly as possible.

Variation

You can make the drill harder by making the figure 8 more narrow, forcing you to move at sharper angles.

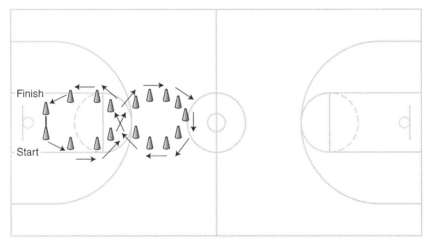

Figure 8.16   Figure 8 drill.

Linear Speed: Putting It All Together

After reading this section on linear speed, you now have an arsenal of drills and skills that you can do with basketball players of any age. It's time we briefly discuss putting all of these concepts into a single linear speed training session.

Every training session should begin with a dynamic warm-up (see chapter 3, Movement Preparation). After the general warm-up, we can begin to do specific drills based on the goal of that training session. In this case, the skill is linear speed. The session should begin with slower-moving drills and progress to faster and more complex drills. Table 8.1 shows an example of a linear speed training session using drills discussed in this chapter.

Table 8.1 Sample Linear Speed Training Session

Drill	Skill	Intensity
General dynamic warm-up	Not applicable	Low to moderate
A-skip (p. 213): 2-4 reps × width of court	Acceleration: stride length	Low to moderate
High knees (p. 215): 2-4 reps × half width of court	Acceleration: stride frequency	Low to moderate
Butt kicks (p. 222): 2-4 reps × half width of court	Top-end speed: stride frequency	Low to moderate
Horizontal bound (p. 214): 4-6 reps × width of court	Acceleration: stride length	Moderate to high
Resisted-sprint start (p. 217): 4-6 reps × width of court	Acceleration	High
Figure 8 (p. 227): 2 reps in each direction	Curvilinear sprinting	High
Chase drills (p. 216): 2-4 reps × half- or full-court length	Acceleration	Very high

LATERAL SPEED

When discussing lateral speed, it's important to break it down into its individual components. It's also important to understand the terminology used in the literature. The terms *agility, change of direction,* and *lateral speed,* among others, are all used somewhat synonymously, yet with very small differences that create somewhat semantic-driven discussions. To keep things simple for the purposes of this book, we put all of these concepts into the category of lateral speed. Simply put, lateral speed includes the ability to accelerate in one direction, decelerate, and reaccelerate in another direction. On the basketball court, this is usually done in response to an external stimulus such as the movement of an opponent, so our training should take those environmental dynamics into account.

In this chapter we break down the individual skills that are most commonly used in basketball to quickly and efficiently accelerate, decelerate, and reaccelerate. Each skill is accompanied by simple drills to improve that individual skill. We then show some common reactive drills that combine multiple skills to make the training much more gamelike.

The individual skills for lateral speed can be broken down into three separate categories: initiation, movement, and direction. Initiation is characterized by how we prepare our body to move. Movement denotes the common ways in which we move laterally, or in a nonlinear direction. Direction includes the skills we use to create angles or change our direction of movement. Let's look at each of these categories individually.

Initiation

When we talk about how we initiate lateral movement, three things must be discussed. First, we need to discuss stance, or the athletic position, because this sets the stage for all lateral movements. Second, we discuss what is called the split step, and finally, we address the POP step.

Stance

The athletic position is widely regarded as one of the foundational aspects of movement in all sports. In the athletic position, the feet are slightly wider than the athlete's shoulders, and the athlete's weight is on the inside edges of their feet. In order to load the hips, the athlete's hips need to be hinged backward so that their shoulders are in front of their knees. This forms the base for all lateral movements (figure 8.17).

When discussing the proper stance, it's important to discuss stance depth, or how much the athlete should be bending at the knee. A key understanding of depth is that different depths are suitable for different scenarios on the court. Low stances are ideal for situations in which the athlete may be taking contact because low stances allow for greater balance and stability. An example of this scenario may be an athlete preparing their body to get through a screen from another player. A low stance is a good choice in that instance. The downside of choosing a low stance is that we can't move as quickly in that position, putting us at risk of losing out to a faster opponent. A higher stance is more suitable for gaining speed. In a scenario in which the athlete is guarding someone in the open court, a higher stance is a better option. The key takeaway from the discussion surrounding stance depth is that we should prepare our athletes to adapt to different circumstances.

Hannah Foslien/Getty Images

Figure 8.17 Steph Curry in an athletic position.

Split Step

In basketball, specifically on the defensive end of the floor, it is important that athletes preload their body for an explosive reactive movement while at the same time creating a balanced base. This is achieved by a quick rise and drop of the center of gravity, coupled with a fast split of the athlete's feet (figure 8.18). This motion allows the athlete to find the inside edge of their feet while at the same time preloading their body, in much the same way as a countermovement is used in a vertical jump to improve power production. The split step can be seen in almost any sport, from a tennis player preparing to respond to a serve to a baseball infielder preparing to respond to a batted ball. This movement is considered global and is critical to prepare the body to move in a reactive manner. As such, we should take this action into account when coaching athletes through lateral speed drills.

Drills for the split step are fairly simple and can be used in any warm-up routine. Following are a few drills that teach the athlete to quickly load themselves into a balanced base.

Figure 8.18　Lu Dort executes a split step on defense.

Katelyn Mulcahy/Getty Images

Speed Ladder Split Steps

Execution

1. Start at one end of a ladder with both feet inside the first square (figure 8.19a).

2. Hop on two feet through the ladder, alternating from having both feet inside the ladder in one square to both feet outside the ladder in the next (figure 8.19b-c).

3. When both feet are inside the ladder, stand as tall as possible. When both feet are outside the ladder, land in a good athletic position, as discussed previously. This allows you to feel what it means to load and split, changing from high to low.

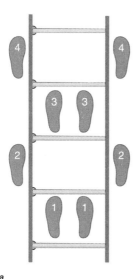

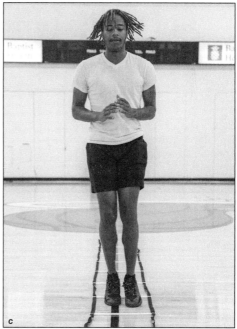

Figure 8.19   Speed ladder split steps.

Low Box Straddle Hop

This drill teaches the athlete to quickly split their feet and create appropriate stiffness in their feet and ankles, which is required for reactive and explosive movement.

Execution

1. Start by standing with the feet hip-width apart on top of a box 3 to 4 inches (7-10 cm) high (figure 8.20a).
2. Hop off the box, landing so that you straddle it (figure 8.20b), then hop back on top of the box as quickly as possible.
3. You can easily make this drill into a game by seeing how many touches you can get in a specific time period.

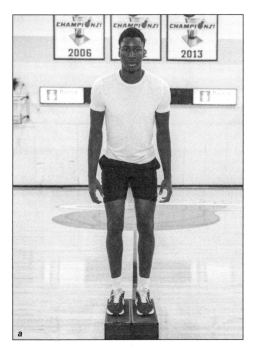

Figure 8.20   Low box straddle hop.

POP Step

The POP step is an idea coined by the famous coach Lee Taft. POP stands for push-open-push. These terms describe the motions any athlete goes through when initiating lateral movement. Whether the athlete is shuffling, performing a crossover step, or turning and sprinting, they always start with the POP action. In figure 8.21, the athlete is making their first movement to the right in an attempt to cut off their opponent. The athlete begins that motion with a strong push off the trailing leg (the left leg in the picture). After pushing off the left leg, the athlete then opens their lead hip, knee, and foot to point them in the intended direction (the right side in the picture). The final action would be a strong push (or pull) off the lead leg (the right leg in the photo). This action, while simple, is extremely important to master in order to display a quick and explosive lateral first step.

POP step drills are usually simple to incorporate into a warm-up routine. The most important concept to remember about this movement is not what drills to do but what *not* to do. Many athletes are taught that they should keep all their toes square while moving laterally. This is a well-intended but misguided coaching decision. Staying square while moving laterally rarely happens in any sport, especially when athletes are moving at high speeds. Here are two easy drills that can be used to teach an athlete proper body positioning for a POP step. Doing these simple drills leads to more efficient execution of the more complex drills presented later in this chapter.

Figure 8.21   Lu Dort performing a POP step on his left leg moving to the right.

Jonathan Bachman/Getty Images

POP Iso Hold on Wall

Execution

1. Stand about 6 to 10 inches (15-25 cm) from a wall with the feet a little more than shoulder-width apart.

2. Move into a deep defensive stance, then lean your elbow into the wall and lift the inside leg, keeping the inside knee pointed at an angle toward the wall (figure 8.22). By pushing the elbow into the wall, you are recreating the position and actions of the POP step, or the push–open–push position.

3. Hold this position for 10 to 20 seconds on each side.

Figure 8.22   POP iso hold on wall.

POP Load and Lift on Wall

Execution

1. Stand just beyond a full arm's length from a wall and place one hand on the wall at shoulder height, creating a slight body lean into the wall (figure 8.23*a*).
2. Slightly bend the outside leg and reach your inside leg back and across the body (figure 8.23*b*).
3. Finally, push off the outside leg while driving the inside leg up, turning the knee and foot toward the wall (figure 8.23*c*), thereby recreating the POP step position.
4. Perform this drill for 6 to 10 reps on each side.

Figure 8.23   POP load and lift on wall.

The concepts of athletic position, stance, split step, and POP step, and their associated drills, conclude our summary of the initiation phase of lateral speed. They may seem elementary, but these positions and drills are essential in building the athlete's foundation for more explosive and efficient lateral movement, which is covered in our next section.

Movement

We just discussed the initiation of lateral movements. We can now discuss the movements themselves. In basketball there are really two foundational movements we use to move laterally: the shuffle step and the crossover run. Any other lateral movement used during competition is usually a variation of these two movements.

Shuffle Step

The first movement is a shuffle step or a defensive slide. In this motion, the athlete is moving laterally while keeping their chest and pelvis both facing relatively perpendicular to the direction of motion. This is a commonly recognized movement, but just to be sure we are all using the same terminology, see figure 8.24 for an example of the shuffle step.

Cameron Pollack / Getty Images

Figure 8.24 DeMar DeRozan shuffling and displaying a good POP step position. His chest and pelvis are facing the same direction, which categorizes this movement as a shuffle step.

Lane Shuffles for Speed

Execution

1. Start on one side of the lane and shuffle as quickly as possible to the opposite side of the lane. Initiate the movement with a POP step by starting with a strong push off the outside foot, then drive the lead knee in the direction you need to go (figure 8.25).

2. Move back and forth across the lane for a given number of reps.

Figure 8.25   Lane shuffle for speed.

Band-Resisted Shuffle Steps

Execution

1. Start on one side of the lane and perform one to three explosive shuffle steps with a long resistance band around your waist (figure 8.26a).
2. Initiate the shuffle step using the POP step motion.
3. Repeat for the desired number of repetitions and then switch sides.

Variation

Progressions of this drill include moving the band to the athlete's upper chest to add a further challenge to the athlete's core strength (figure 8.26b).

Figure 8.26 Band-resisted shuffle steps: (a) band around waist and (b) band around upper chest.

Crossover Run

The second lateral movement used in basketball is the crossover step. The crossover step movement is more complex than the shuffling movement. In the crossover step, the athlete's chest remains perpendicular to the direction of motion (as in the shuffle step), but the hips, knees, and feet face in the direction of motion (as they do in sprinting). In this position, the athlete is essentially shuffling with their upper body and sprinting with their lower body (figure 8.27). This body position is generally referred to as hip–shoulder dissociation because the hips face one direction while the shoulders are facing another. This movement is used in situations that demand more speed than that with which the athlete is capable of shuffling. While this may seem complex and difficult to perform, we actually see this motion a lot during competition because it can be performed at much higher speeds than shuffling and enables the athlete to cover more ground. Because of this, athletes who perform this movement well have a distinct advantage on the basketball court, especially on the defensive end of the floor.

Drills for crossover running usually start by teaching the athlete the concept of hip–shoulder disassociation, allowing them to feel what turning the hips while the shoulders stay square should feel like.

David Berding/Getty Images

Figure 8.27 Shai Gilgeous-Alexander performing a crossover step while guarding the ball handler. His eyes and chest remain square to the ball handler while his hips and feet turn in the direction of movement.

Backward Carioca

Execution

This is a warm-up drill that allows the athlete to feel the hips turn while the chest stays still. This drill does a great job of making the athlete aware of their feet moving under their center of gravity and can set the stage for more complex drills ahead.

1. Begin in a defensive stance and start moving backward while performing alternating crossover steps (figure 8.28a-b).
2. Keep your eyes and chest facing straight ahead while the hips rotate underneath you.
3. Practice this drill for 10 to 20 yards (9-18 m) for the desired number of repetitions.

Variation

This drill can be progressed by alternating directions every two or three steps instead of every step.

Figure 8.28   Backward carioca.

Step and Cross Drill

This drill is a fantastic way to introduce the crossover run as it appears in competition. When doing the step and cross drill, the athlete is responding to verbal cues from the coach.

Execution

1. Begin in a defensive stance. When the coach says "Step!", perform a POP step in the desired direction and hold that position (figure 8.29*a*).

2. The coach will then say "Cross!". Drive off of the lead leg and quickly drive the trail knee across the body (figure 8.29*b*). Then square back up as quickly as possible (figure 8.29*c*).

3. Turn your hips, knees, and feet in the desired direction, all while keeping the eyes and chest facing straight ahead.

4. Repeat for the desired number of repetitions.

Variations

- This drill can be progressed by removing the pause between the step and the cross phase of the movement.

- It can also be progressed by having the athlete move in one direction using the crossover step, then quickly reverse direction and return to the original starting position using either a shuffle step or a crossover step.

Figure 8.29   Step and cross drill.

Direction

The skills of shuffling and crossover running underlie the ability to move laterally on the basketball floor. We discussed how to initiate motion through the proper stance, split steps, and POP steps. We also discussed how to move through space using the movement skills of shuffling and crossover running. Now let's discuss how to create good angles using skills that determine the body's direction as we move laterally.

In basketball it's obviously advantageous to be able to move laterally as quickly as possible. However, the best athletes also know how to take good angles and change those angles as quickly as possible. In most team sports, movement is reactive and can take place in any direction at any time. In order to be efficient with these constantly changing dynamics, athletes must be able to use two main skill sets to establish their direction of movement and change direction of movement. These two skills are called foot repositioning and the change of direction step.

Foot Repositioning

In order to understand the concept of foot repositioning, we have to discuss the relationship between our center of gravity (usually around the pelvis area) and our base of support (our feet, in this case). When our center of gravity is directly over our base of support and we push into the ground, we move our center of gravity straight up, as in a vertical jump. If our center of gravity is in front of our base of support and we push into the ground, we move forward as in a sprint start. We can repeat each possible scenario, but you get the idea. If an athlete wants to move quickly at an angle backward, they must know how to quickly arrange their center of gravity and their base of support in a position that is mechanically efficient to move in that direction. They are left with two options: First, they can move their center of gravity to the appropriate position relative to their base of support. Second, they can move their base of support to create the appropriate angle relative to their center of gravity. As it turns out, it is much faster and more efficient for the human body to move its base of support (the feet) than it is to shift the entire center of gravity, so the best option is to perform a quick foot repositioning movement to give ourselves the best possible angle.

Quarter Eagle

This is a common drill to teach athletes to reposition their feet under their center of gravity.

Execution

1. Begin the drill by assuming a defensive stance (figure 8.30*a*).
2. On the coach's cue, perform a quarter turn with the feet and hips while keeping the eyes and chest facing forward (figure 8.30*b*).
3. Don't pop up out of your stance; rather, stay in a low position and quickly move your feet without raising the center of gravity.
4. Perform by holding the foot position after performing the quarter eagle, or perform the quarter eagle and quickly return to the starting position.
5. Repeat for the desired number of repetitions on each side.

Figure 8.30   Quarter eagle.

Speed Ladder Foot Repositioning

Much has been written about the use of speed ladders for speed and agility development. A speed ladder's role in agility development lies mostly in teaching athletes to quickly reposition their feet under their center of gravity. This makes speed ladders a valuable tool to use when foot repositioning is the goal. The drill that follows is only one example of a speed ladder concept that can be used to work on basketball-specific foot repositioning.

Execution

1. Start by facing the long side of the ladder.

2. As you begin to move your feet quickly, only your trail leg will touch in and out of each square while they work their way down the full length of the ladder (figure 8.31a). Use a hip–shoulder dissociation strategy to move the foot in and out of each square (figure 8.31b). Keep your eyes and chest facing forward while the hips quickly turn to move the feet.

3. Repeat for the desired number of repetitions in both directions.

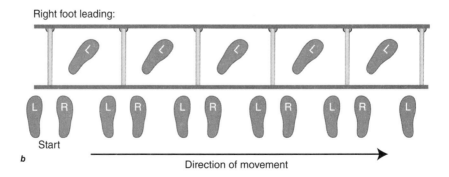

Figure 8.31 Speed ladder foot repositioning.

Change of Direction Step

The second direction skill is the change of direction step. The change of direction step is really two movements combined into one. This movement combines both deceleration and reacceleration into a single action. Imagine an athlete shuffling quickly to their left while guarding an opponent. As their opponent stops and reverses direction, the defender must follow suit by decelerating their momentum to the left and reaccelerating their body to the right. In this example, the change of direction is accomplished by a hard change of direction step on the defender's left foot.

The general rules of efficiently changing direction are twofold. The first rule is that the athlete should use the inside edge of a flat foot to halt their momentum. This foot position takes advantage of surface friction of the whole foot and the anatomy of the ankle to provide a firm surface by which to stop and restart. A common error with this movement is attempting to stop too far up on the toes, leaving the ankle vulnerable to a sprain or an ankle roll. This position is called a toe fault (see figure 8.32).

The second rule is that the athlete should display great control of their center of mass when changing directions. This can best be seen by watching the athlete's shoulders and hips. Both shoulders and hips should remain somewhat parallel to the ground during the change of direction action. Figure 8.33 shows a common fault in which the athlete loses control of their center of gravity, usually due to a lack of core strength. This fault creates a delay in reaccelerating in the opposite direction, giving the opponent a considerable advantage. This error is called a shoulder fault.

Figure 8.32 Athlete displaying a toe fault while attempting to perform a change of direction step on his right leg. This position leaves the athlete vulnerable to ankle sprains.

Figure 8.33 Athlete displaying a shoulder fault while attempting a change of direction step on his left leg. This position leaves the athlete vulnerable to injury and causes a delay when changing direction.

Numerous drills can challenge the change of direction step. As long as the drill follows these two rules, it can be an effective strategy to use to improve the change of direction step. Here are examples of change of direction step drills.

Speed Ladder Ickey Shuffle

Execution

1. Start the drill facing the short edge of the ladder.
2. Start on one side of the ladder and move to the other side by touching both feet in a square and one foot to the outside of the square (figure 8.34a).
3. The change of direction step is challenged when the foot hits the ground outside the ladder. At that moment, follow the rules of the change of direction step by staying on the inside edge of a flat foot and keeping the shoulders and pelvis parallel to the ground (figure 8.36b).
4. Repeat for the desired number of repetitions.

Variation

To make this drill more challenging, get farther from the ladder with the outside foot on each side.

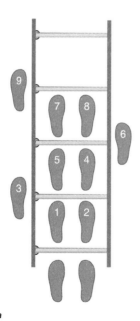

Figure 8.34 Speed ladder Ickey shuffle.

Dowel Shuffle

Execution

1. Start by holding a dowel on your upper back in a back squat position.

2. When the coach cues you, begin shuffling in one direction (figure 8.35a). The coach will then give a verbal or visual cue to change direction. You must then plant your outside foot to decelerate and reaccelerate in the opposite direction (figure 8.35b). The two rules of the change of direction step must be followed during this action.

3. Repeat for the desired number of repetitions.

Figure 8.35   Dowel shuffle.

Reactive Drills

Since we have discussed the concepts of initiation, movement, and direction, we should now discuss how to combine all these individual skills into more gamelike conditions using reactive agility drills. In reactive agility drills, the athlete is responding to their environment reflexively. During these drills, there should be less structure and cueing to encourage the athlete to respond in a more reflexive manner. In the next section we give three examples of reactive agility drills, but it's important to mention that the creativity of the coach is the only limitation to reactive drills. The more gamelike and competitive these drills are, the better.

Four-Cone Drill

Execution

1. Place four cones or markers in a 30- by 15-foot (9 by 4 m) rectangle.
2. Stand even with and in the middle of the two front cones (figure 8.36).
3. On the coach's cue, move to a cone and then back to the starting position as quickly as possible, using either a shuffle step or crossover run. Display proper foot repositioning and change of direction steps when moving to the cone and back to the starting position.
4. The concepts of initiation, movement, and direction should all be used. This means initiating the drill with a good stance, split step, and POP step action.
5. Once you are back in the starting position, the coach can cue to move to another cone.
6. Repeat for 1 to 5 reps.

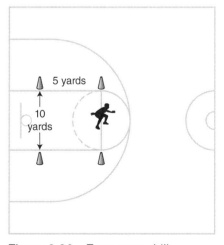

Figure 8.36   Four-cone drill.

Mirroring

Execution

1. In this drill, one athlete mirrors another athlete or coach.
2. Set two cones as boundaries approximately 30 feet (9 m) apart.
3. On the coach's cue, one player moves as quickly as possible, staying within the boundaries, and the mirroring player attempts to stay with them (figure 8.37).
4. The coach should pay close attention to how the mirroring athlete changes direction to ensure they are following the rules of proper lateral movement.
5. This is a short drill, usually lasting less than 10 seconds.

Figure 8.37   Mirroring.

Tennis Ball Catch

Execution

This drill can add some fun to any training session.
1. Start in an athletic stance facing the coach.
2. The coach throws tennis balls from side to side, forcing you to shuffle or crossover run quickly to catch the ball and immediately return back to the starting position (figure 8.38).
3. Make sure you are using proper footwork throughout the drill.
4. Repeat for 6 to 10 catches.

Figure 8.38　Tennis ball catch.

Lateral Speed Training Session

After reading this section on lateral speed, you now have an arsenal of drills and skills that you can do with basketball players of any age. It's time we briefly discuss putting these concepts into a single lateral speed training session.

Every training session should begin with a dynamic warm-up (see chapter 3, Movement Preparation). After a general warm-up, we can begin more specific drills based on the goal of that training session. In this case, it is lateral speed and agility. The session should begin with slower-moving drills and progress to faster and more complex drills. Table 8.2 shows an example of a lateral speed training session using drills from this chapter.

Table 8.2 Sample Lateral Speed Training Session

Drill	Skill	Intensity
General dynamic warm-up	Not applicable	Low to moderate
POP iso hold on wall (p. 234): 2 × 20 each side	POP step	Low
Backward carioca (p. 240): 4 reps × width of court	Crossover run	Low to moderate
Speed ladder split steps (p. 231): 4 reps	Split step	Moderate
Speed ladder foot repositioning (p. 244): 4 reps	Foot repositioning	Moderate
Speed ladder Ickey shuffle (p. 246): 4 reps	Change of direction step	Moderate
Band-resisted shuffle steps (p. 238): 3 sets × 3-5 reps	Shuffle step	High
Mirroring (p. 249): 4 reps × 10 seconds	Multiple	Very high

SAMPLE SPEED AND AGILITY PROGRAM

Table 8.3 will take you through 8-week sample programs for acceleration, lateral speed, top-end speed, and lateral change of direction. These programs can be integrated into either the 3-day-per-week or 4-day-per-week off-season training calendars in tables 12.1 and 12.2. These drills should be done after, or blended into, a dynamic warm-up and before the lifting program for the day.

Table 8.3 Sample 8-Week Speed and Agility Program

	Monday: Acceleration, Weeks 1-4			
Drill	Week 1: Speed/agility #1*	Week 2: Speed/agility #5	Week 3: Speed/agility #9	Week 4: Speed/agility #13
A-skip (p. 213)	4 × 15 yards	6 × 15 yards	6 × 20 yards	4 × 15 yards
High knees (p. 215)	4 × 10 yards	6 × 10 yards	6 × 10 yards	4 × 10 yards
Horizontal bound (p. 214)	4 × 15 yards	6 × 15 yards	6 × 20 yards	4 × 20 yards
Resisted-sprint start (p. 217)	6 × 10 yards	8 × 15 yards	8 × 15 yards	6 × 10 yards
Chase drill (p. 216)	× 4	× 6-8	× 6-8	× 4

(continued)

Table 8.3 *(continued)*

Monday: Acceleration, Weeks 5-8			
Drill	**Week 5:** Speed/agility #17	**Week 6:** Speed/agility #21	**Week 7:** Speed/agility #25	**Week 8:** Speed/agility #29
Resisted A-skip (p. 213)	4 × 10 yards	6 × 10 yards	6 × 10 yards	4 × 10 yards
Resisted high knees (p. 215)	4 × 10 yards	6 × 10 yards	6 × 10 yards	4 × 10 yards
Resisted horizontal bound (p. 214)	4 × 15 yards	6 × 15 yards	6 × 15 yards	4 × 15 yards
Resisted-sprint start (p. 217)	6 × 10 yards	8 × 15 yards	8 × 15 yards	6 × 10 yards
Chase drill (p. 216)	× 4	× 6-8	× 6-8	× 4

Tuesday: Lateral Speed, Weeks 1-4			
Drill	**Week 1:** Speed/agility #2	**Week 2:** Speed/agility #6	**Week 3:** Speed/agility #10	**Week 4:** Speed/agility #14
POP iso hold on wall (p. 234)	2 × 15 sec each leg	3 × 20 sec each leg	3 × 20 sec each leg	2 × 15 sec each leg
Speed ladder split steps (p. 231)	× 2 rounds	× 2 rounds	× 2 rounds	× 2 rounds
Speed ladder foot repositioning (p. 244)	× 2 rounds	× 2 rounds	× 2 rounds	× 2 rounds
Speed ladder Ickey shuffle (p. 246)	× 2 rounds	× 2 rounds	× 2 rounds	× 2 rounds
Dowel shuffle (p. 247)	× 2 each way	× 3 each way	× 3 each way	× 2 each way
Tennis ball catch (p. 250)	× 4-6 reps	× 4-6 reps	× 4-6 reps	× 4-6 reps

Tuesday: Lateral Speed, Weeks 5-8			
Drill	**Week 5:** Speed/agility #18	**Week 6:** Speed/agility #22	**Week 7:** Speed/agility #26	**Week 8:** Speed/agility #30
POP load and lift on wall (p. 235)	2 × 8 each leg	3 × 8 each leg	3 × each leg	2 × 8 each leg
Backward carioca (p. 240)	4 × width of court	4 × width of court	4 × width of court	4 × width of court
Low box straddle hop (p. 232)	2 × 10 sec	3 × 10 sec	3 × 10 sec	2 × 10 sec
Quarter eagle (p. 243)	2 × 6-8 reps	3 × 8-10 reps	3 × 8-10 reps	2 × 6-8 reps

Drill	Week 5: Speed/agility #18	Week 6: Speed/agility #22	Week 7: Speed/agility #26	Week 8: Speed/agility #30
Band-resisted shuffle steps (p. 238)	× 2 each way	× 3 each way	× 3 each way	× 2 each way
Tennis ball catch (p. 250)	× 4-6 reps	× 4-6 reps	× 4-6 reps	× 4-6 reps

Thursday: Top-End Speed, Weeks 1-4

Drill	Week 1: Speed/agility #3	Week 2: Speed/agility #7	Week 3: Speed/agility #11	Week 4: Speed/agility #15
Butt kicks (p. 222)	4 × 10 yards	6 × 10 yards	6 × 15 yards	4 × 10 yards
B-skip (p. 220)	4 × 15 yards	6 × 15 yards	6 × 15 yards	4 × 15 yards
Dead leg drill (p. 223)	2 × 15 yards each leg	3 × 20 yards each leg	3 × 20 yards each leg	2 × 20 yards each leg
Build-up runs (p. 224)	6 × 10 yards	8 × 15 yards	8 × 15 yards	6 × 10 yards
Three-point line run (p. 226)	× 3 each way	× 4 each way	× 4 each way	× 2 each way

Thursday: Top-End Speed, Weeks 5-8

Drill	Week 5: Speed/agility #19	Week 6: Speed/agility #23	Week 7: Speed/agility #27	Week 8: Speed/agility #31
Butt kicks (p. 222)	4 × 10 yards	6 × 10 yards	6 × 15 yards	4 × 10 yards
B-skip with dumbbells (p. 220)	4 × 15 yards	6 × 15 yards	6 × 15 yards	4 × 15 yards
Vertical bound (p. 221)	4 × 15 yards	6 × 20 yards	6 × 20 yards	4 × 15 yards
Build-up runs (p. 224)	6 × 15 yards	8 × 20 yards	8 × 20 yards	6 × 15 yards
Figure 8 drill (p. 227)	× 2 each way	× 3 each way	× 3 each way	× 2 each way

Friday: Lateral Change of Direction, Weeks 1-4

Drill	Week 1: Speed/agility #4	Week 2: Speed/agility #8	Week 3: Speed/agility #12	Week 4: Speed/agility #16
POP iso hold on wall (p. 234)	2 × 15 sec each leg	3 × 20 sec each leg	3 × 20 sec each leg	2 × 15 sec each leg
Speed ladder split steps (p. 231)	× 2 rounds	× 2 rounds	× 2 rounds	× 2 rounds
Speed ladder foot repositioning (p. 244)	× 2 rounds	× 2 rounds	× 2 rounds	× 2 rounds

(continued)

Table 8.3 *(continued)*

Friday: Lateral Change of Direction, Weeks 1-4 *(continued)*				
Drill	**Week 1: Speed/agility #4**	**Week 2: Speed/agility #8**	**Week 3: Speed/agility #12**	**Week 4: Speed/agility #16**
Speed ladder Ickey shuffle (p. 246)	× 2 rounds	× 2 rounds	× 2 rounds	× 2 rounds
Dowel shuffle (p. 247)	× 3 each way	× 4 each way	× 4 each way	× 3 each way
Mirroring (p. 249)	× 4-6 reps	× 4-6 reps	× 4-6 reps	× 4-6 reps
Friday: Lateral Change of Direction, Weeks 5-8				
Drill	**Week 5: Speed/agility #20**	**Week 6: Speed/agility #24**	**Week 7: Speed/agility #28**	**Week 8: Speed/agility #32**
POP load and lift on wall (p. 235)	2 × 8 each leg	3 × 8 each leg	3 × each leg	2 × 8 each leg
Backward carioca (p. 240)	4 × width of court	4 × width of court	4 × width of court	4 × width of court
Low box straddle hop (p. 232)	2 × 10 sec	3 × 10 sec	3 × 10 sec	2 × 10 sec
Quarter eagle (p. 243)	2 × 6-8 reps	3 × 8-10 reps	3 × 8-10 reps	2 × 6-8 reps
Band-resisted dowel shuffle (p. 247)	× 3 each way	× 4 each way	× 4 each way	× 3 each way
Four-cone drill (p. 248)	× 4-6 reps	× 4-6 reps	× 4-6 reps	× 4-6 reps

Full rest between each rep to maximize speed.

* These numbered speed/agility workouts correspond to the speed/agility workouts in the sample 16-week off-season training calendars in tables 12.1 and 12.2.

CONCLUSION

Speed is often what we think of when defining athleticism. While other characteristics could be argued, speed is the skill that stands out and creates advantages in most sports. Basketball is no different. Whether the athlete is sprinting down court to get to the basket or quickly changing directions as a defender, speed finds its way into the game. Although genetics to a large extent dictates the ceiling of an athlete's speed potential, the skill of speed is a trainable and often overlooked aspect of athletic development for sports like basketball. Armed with the basic principles and scalable drills from this chapter, you will be able to build foundational skills to improve both linear and lateral speed in basketball players at any level.

Chapter 9

On-Court Conditioning

Issac Baldizon/Getty Images

Playing basketball at a high level demands that players be in great condition. In order to compete for an entire game and season, players must be prepared to play with minimum fatigue. Games are often decided in the final minutes, and the players and teams that resist fatigue and keep their composure have a huge advantage over their lesser-conditioned opponents. High-level conditioning is more than just playing basketball. Ideally, conditioning begins on the track and progresses to on-court conditioning drills that build the stamina needed to endure the rigors of the basketball season. The conditioning outlined in this chapter is meant to supplement speed and agility training and all other basketball-specific training that players participate in throughout the year. Conditioning needs to be more than just court work and basketball drills. Adding sprint workouts and a specific conditioning plan will take athletes' conditioning to the next level.

In an ideal off-season, conditioning begins at the track with general conditioning and progresses toward more specificity as the season approaches. Running 200- and 400-meter repeats is a great way to build stamina and endurance before transitioning toward on-court conditioning designed specifically for basketball. Track conditioning has been omitted from the 4- and 6-week programs at the end of this chapter, since the short time frame necessitates a quick ramp up to on-court conditioning. The 8-week program includes 2 weeks of track conditioning, and if you are fortunate enough to have more than 8 weeks for an off-season conditioning program, you may prolong the track conditioning phase before moving to on-court conditioning for the 6 weeks leading up to the season.

Before beginning sprints or any other intense activity, make sure to properly warm up. (See chapter 3, Movement Preparation, for a great guideline on how to build up to more intense activity.)

ON-COURT CONDITIONING DRILLS

The following on-court conditioning exercises comprise linear and curvilinear sprinting, speed and agility, and basketball-specific drills.

In basketball, sprints will rarely be perfectly linear. Players are often moving at angles, turning corners, moving around picks, and getting an angle on the opposing players. Curvilinear sprinting is sprinting forward around a curved path. Curvilinear sprinting complements linear sprinting in training for the demands of basketball and helps players maintain speed, agility, and quickness under fatigue.

Speed and agility drills are primarily used to train athletes to be more explosive and reactive. Doing these drills toward the beginning of training sessions and taking longer rest intervals helps maximize muscular and nervous system recovery, allowing the athlete to focus on the quality of these movements and drills. Depending on the intent of the training session, these drills may be done in different work-to-rest ratios and under more fatigue in order to shift the focus toward conditioning.

Refer to chapter 8 for more specifics on this type of training and chapter 12 for how to integrate it into your overall plan. Many speed and agility drills can be used for conditioning, but the curvilinear sprints (three-point line runs and figure 8 drills) are especially appropriate for conditioning workouts.

In addition to on-court running workouts for conditioning, basketball conditioning drills such as full-court shooting may be done as a part of court workouts to increase basketball-specific conditioning and work on maintaining skill through fatigue.

10s

Execution

1. Starting at one baseline, sprint to the far baseline, touching it with one foot, then quickly turn around and sprint back to the starting point (figure 9.1).

2. When turning at each baseline, alternate the plant foot to avoid developing asymmetries from always turning on the same side.

3. Repeat for a total of 10 court lengths.

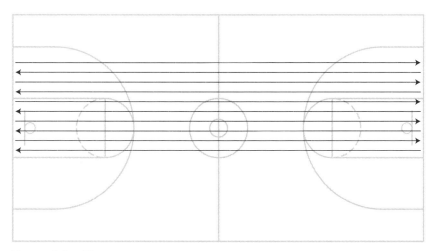

Figure 9.1   10s.

Quick 4s

Execution

1. Starting at one baseline, sprint to the far baseline, touching it with one foot, then quickly turn around and sprint back to the starting point. When turning at each baseline, alternate the plant foot to avoid developing asymmetries from always turning on the same side. Repeat one more trip for a total of 4 court lengths.
2. Rest 20 seconds, then repeat the 4 court lengths.
3. Rest again for 20 seconds and repeat for one final set of 4 court lengths (figure 9.2).
4. One set is a total of 3 repetitions of 4 court lengths.

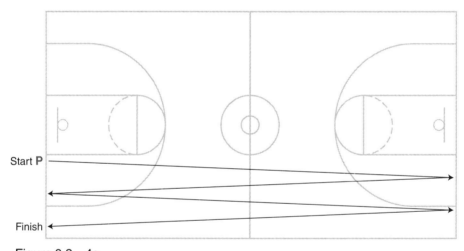

Figure 9.2   4s.

17s

Execution

1. Starting at one baseline, sprint to the far baseline, touching it with one foot, then quickly turn around and sprint back to the starting point (figure 9.3). When turning at each sideline, alternate the plant foot to avoid developing asymmetries from always turning on the same side.

2. Repeat for a total of 17 court widths.

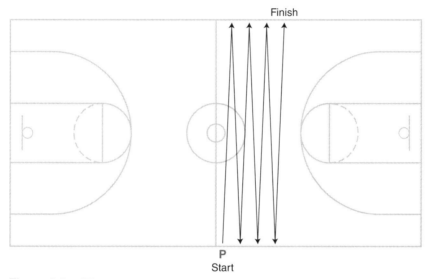

Figure 9.3　17s.

Line Drill

Execution

1. Start at one baseline. Sprint to the near free throw line and back to the starting point, then sprint to the half-court line and back to the starting point, then sprint to the far free throw line and back to the starting point, then sprint to the far baseline and back to the starting point (figure 9.4).

2. Repeat for the prescribed number of repetitions.

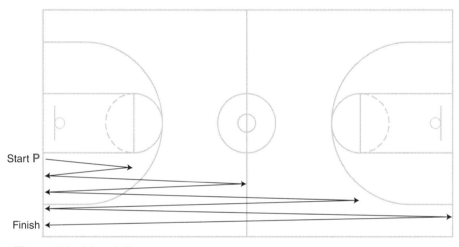

Figure 9.4   Line drill.

X Drill

The X drill includes both sprints and defensive slides.

Execution

1. Start in one corner and sprint to the opposite corner.
2. Immediately slide laterally along the baseline to the other corner, turn toward the court, and repeat to the opposite side (figure 9.5).
3. Repeat for the prescribed number of repetitions.

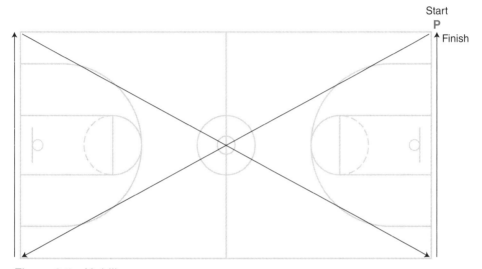

Figure 9.5   X drill.

Three-Point Line Runs

Execution

1. Start in one corner of the court on the baseline and sprint around the three-point arc to the other corner of the same baseline, touching it and then sprinting back to the starting point (figure 9.6).

2. Repeat for the prescribed number of repetitions.

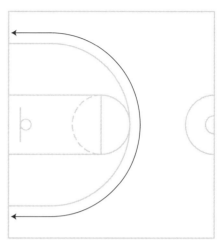

Figure 9.6   Three-point line runs.

Figure 8s

Execution

1. Set up two cones, as seen in figure 9.7. The cones may be widely spaced to get more running in or more tightly to allow you to work on turning at sharper angles.

2. The goal is to perform a figure 8 around both cones as quickly as possible. This may be done as a curvilinear sprint or facing in one direction the entire time to work on multidirectional movement.

3. Continue for the prescribed number of repetitions.

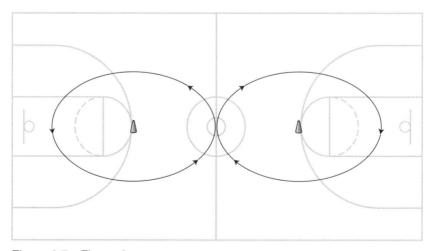

Figure 9.7   Figure 8s.

Full-Court Layups

Execution

1. Start at one baseline, facing the court, holding a basketball.
2. Dribble to the opposite basket and shoot a layup.
3. Get your own rebound, dribble back to the first basket, and shoot another layup (figure 9.8).
4. Continue for the prescribed number of repetitions.

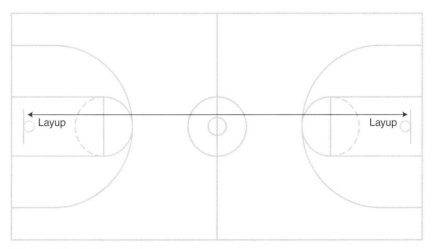

Figure 9.8   Full-court layups.

Full-Court Corner 3s

Execution

1. This drill is ideally done with two rebounders/passers to assist the sprinter/shooter. The shooter starts in one corner of the court; the first rebounder or passer passes the ball to the shooter, who shoots a corner 3.

2. The passer gets the rebound while the shooter sprints to the opposite end of the court, where the other rebounder or passer passes the ball to the shooter, who shoots another corner 3. The passer gets the rebound while the shooter sprints back to the starting point.

3. Continue for the prescribed number of repetitions.

Note: This drill may also be done solo, where you get your own rebound and dribble to the opposite end of the court for the next shot.

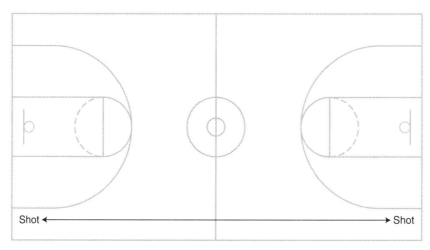

Figure 9.9   Full-court corner 3s.

Full-Court Star Drill

Execution

1. This drill is ideally done with two rebounders/passers to assist the sprinter/shooter. The shooter starts in one corner of the court; the first rebounder passes the ball to the shooter, who shoots a corner 3 (1).

2. The passer gets the rebound while the shooter sprints to the opposite end of the court, where the other rebounder passes the ball to the shooter, who shoots another corner 3 (2).

3. The passer gets the rebound while the shooter sprints to the other corner on the first end of the court, where the other rebounder passes the ball to the shooter, who shoots another corner 3 (3).

4. The passer gets the rebound while the shooter sprints to the opposite end of the court, where the other rebounder passes the ball to the shooter, who shoots another corner 3 (4).

5. The passer gets the rebound while the shooter sprints to the wing on the first end of the court, where the rebounder passes the ball to the shooter, who shoots a wing 3 (5).

6. The passer gets the rebound while the shooter sprints to the wing on the other end of the court, where the rebounder passes the ball to the shooter, who shoots a wing 3 (6).

7. The passer gets the rebound while the shooter sprints across the court to the other wing on the first end of the court, where the rebounder passes the ball to the shooter, who shoots a wing 3 (7).

8. The passer gets the rebound while the shooter sprints to the wing on the other end of the court, where the rebounder passes the ball to the shooter, who shoots a wing 3 (8).

9. The passer gets the rebound while the shooter sprints to the top of the key on the first end of the court, where the rebounder passes the ball to the shooter, who shoots a straight-on 3 (9).

10. The passer gets the rebound while the shooter sprints to the top of the key on the other end of the court, where the rebounder passes the ball to the shooter, who shoots another straight-on 3 (10).

11. Continue for the prescribed number of repetitions.

Note: This drill may also be done solo, where you get your own rebound and dribble to the opposite end of the court for the next shot.

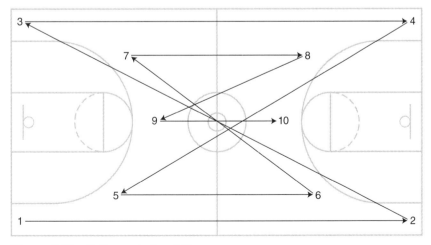

Figure 9.10   Full-court star drill.

Sideline Sprint Layup

Execution

1. This drill is ideally performed with one rebounder/passer to assist the sprinter/shooter. The shooter starts in one corner of the court on the left sideline near the baseline, facing the basket. The rebounder/ passer is in the lane near the basket, in position to pass the ball and then quickly grab the rebound after the layup and get out of the shooter's way.

Start
Finish P

Figure 9.11   Sideline sprint layup.

2. The shooter sprints toward the basket. The rebounder delivers a pass in stride to the shooter, who goes for a left-handed layup, then continues to the far sideline.

3. The rebounder gets the rebound and gets back into position. The shooter touches the sideline and immediately sprints back toward the basket as the rebounder delivers another bounce pass to the shooter, who goes for a right-handed layup, then continues sprinting to the original sideline.

4. Continue this pattern for 3 to 5 repetitions.

Full-Court Sprint With Chest Pass

Execution

1. Start with two players on the baseline on each side of the lane, facing the court, with one athlete starting with the ball.

2. Both athletes sprint full court, maintaining lane width between them, while continuously chest passing the ball back and forth.

3. Both athletes touch the far baseline and immediately turn around and sprint back, continuing to pass the ball.

4. Continue this pattern for 4 to 6 court lengths.

Note: Make sure to focus on quality passes, and do not travel.

Full-Court Sprint With Bounce Pass

Execution

1. Start with two players on the baseline on each side of the lane, facing the court, with one athlete starting with the ball.
2. Both athletes sprint full court, maintaining lane width between them, while continuously bounce passing the ball back and forth.
3. Both athletes touch the far baseline and immediately turn around and sprint back, continuing to pass the ball.
4. Continue this pattern for 4 to 6 court lengths.

Note: Make sure to focus on quality passes, and do not travel.

CARDIO EQUIPMENT

Traditional cardio equipment such as treadmills, stationary bikes, elliptical trainers, and the like can complement on-court conditioning. For example, getting off the court periodically to log some cardio miles can help to reduce stress on joints while maintaining or even improving conditioning level. Cardio conditioning can also bridge the gap when players are dealing with a specific injury that takes them off the court for a period of time. As with the on-court conditioning, anaerobic intervals will be most transferable to basketball, but there is a place for slower, steady aerobic work, especially on lighter recovery days.

SEASONAL CONDITIONING PHASES

There are four conditioning phases throughout the season:

- **Off-season:** The off-season is when players prepare physically for the demands of the season. Following a progressive conditioning plan ensures that players are prepared before the season begins. Furthermore, it can improve performance and reduce injury risk during the season. The best way to prepare is to begin with the end in mind. Find out when training camp or the first day of practice begins, then plan backward from there to ensure that the athlete is on track to be in great shape to start the season. These workouts should be done to supplement on-court basketball workouts, where players will be developing skills as well as conditioning their body to the specific demands of basketball movements and energy systems. The program also must have flexibility based on court work. Each workout should not be considered a requirement or followed rigidly regardless of how court work goes on a given day. If the on-court workout goes long, or if players continue playing 3v3 or 5v5 for much longer than planned, adjustments must be made to the volume.

- **Preseason:** Preseason is the period between the first practice and the first regular season game. This period typically includes "training camp" and may include exhibition games that do not count toward the team record. The focus is on the court, and the load of practices and games should provide enough conditioning for players to maintain or improve conditioning level going into the regular season.

- **In-season:** During the season, the majority of conditioning comes from games and practices. Depending on practice and game loads, extra conditioning may be needed, especially for players not playing big minutes or not in the rotation during games. The off-season conditioning workouts, cardio equipment intervals, and increased court work, including full-court drills or extra 2v2 or 3v3 games, help simulate the load of playing bigger minutes in order to keep these players ready to step in and not fatigued when they are called upon. Coaches may consider load data or minutes played to inform decision making when planning conditioning workouts. For example, if a player is averaging only 10 minutes per game, they likely need extra conditioning to stay ready to play bigger minutes if there is a favorable matchup or an injury to a teammate that alters playing time. Coaches may use time or interval units to make up the difference based on the player's current on-court load.

- **Postseason:** The period immediately after the season, but before off-season training begins for the next season, should consist of rest and active rest. Initially, players should recover physically and mentally from the long season. This period should not consist of formal workouts, but athletes should be encouraged to do general fitness activities such as swimming, hiking, biking, or playing other sports. Some athletes may go right into a spring sport such as tennis or track and field, so they will have to find a balance between recovery and preparation initially to prevent overtraining. Chapter 10 includes more on this topic.

OFF-SEASON CONDITIONING PROGRAM

This chapter includes options for an 8-week program, 6-week program, and 4-week program depending on your time constraints (see tables 9.1-9.3). The 8-week program is ideal to prepare for the coming season, but since not every team or athlete realistically has an 8-week block to devote to training, the 6-week or 4-week programs allow athletes to build a solid base, maximizing whatever time they have before the season. These conditioning workouts can be integrated into either the 3-day-per-week or 4-day-per-week off-season training calendars in tables 12.1 and 12.2.

Many coaches and programs institute a conditioning test prior to or during training camp to ensure that players are prepared to handle the increased demands of training camp and the coming season. A conditioning test serves two important purposes: (1) assessing players' conditioning level and (2) ensuring that players are properly training in the weeks leading up to the conditioning test and training camp, so that players understand expectations and train to pass the test, rather than leaving it up to chance. (Conditioning tests and assessments are laid out in chapter 2.)

Table 9.1 Sample 8-Week Off-Season Conditioning Program

Week	Day 1	Day 2
1	**Conditioning #1*** Stride 4 × 400 m 2:30 recovery	**Conditioning #2** Stationary bike × 30 min Moderate intensity
2	**Conditioning #3** Stride 6 × 400 m 2:30 recovery	**Conditioning #4** Stationary bike × 30 min Moderate intensity
3	**Conditioning #5** 2 × 10s on court 2:00 recovery	**Conditioning #6** 4 × 90 sec on treadmill 3:00 recovery
4	**Conditioning #7** 3 × 10s on court 2:00 recovery	**Conditioning #8** 6 × 60 sec on treadmill 2:00 recovery
5	**Conditioning #9** 3 × 10s on court 2:00 recovery	**Conditioning #10** X drill 2 × 3 2:00 recovery Three-point run 6s × 6 1:30 recovery
6	**Conditioning #11** 4 × 10s on court 2:00 recovery	**Conditioning #12** X drill 2 × 3 1:30 recovery Three-point run 6s × 6 1:00 recovery
7	**Conditioning #13** 4 × 10s on court 2:00 recovery	**Conditioning #14** Figure 8s 3 × 5 laps of 10 yards (9 m) 1:00 recovery Quick 4s 2 × 3 :20/2:00 recovery
8	**Conditioning #15** 5 × 10s on court 2:00 recovery	**Conditioning #16** Figure 8s 4 × 5 laps of 10 yards (9 m) 1:00 recovery Quick 4s 3 × 3 :20/2:00 recovery

* These numbered conditioning workouts are integrated into the sample 16-week off-season training calendars in tables 12.1 and 12.2.

Table 9.2 Sample 6-Week Off-Season Conditioning Program

Week	Day 1	Day 2
1	**Conditioning #1*** 2 × 10s on court 2:00 recovery	**Conditioning #2** 4 × 90 sec on treadmill 3:00 recovery
2	**Conditioning #3** 3 × 10s on court 2:00 recovery	**Conditioning #4** 6 × 60 sec on treadmill 2:00 recovery
3	**Conditioning #5** 3 × 10s on court 2:00 recovery	**Conditioning #6** X drill 2 × 3 2:00 recovery Three-point run 6s × 6 1:30 recovery
4	**Conditioning #7** 4 × 10s on court 2:00 recovery	**Conditioning #8** X drill 2 × 3 1:30 recovery Three-point run 6s × 6 1:00 recovery
5	**Conditioning #9** 4 × 10s on court 2:00 recovery	**Conditioning #10** Figure 8s 3 × 5 laps of 10 yards (9 m) 1:00 recovery Quick 4s 2 × 3 :20/2:00 recovery
6	**Conditioning #11** 5 × 10s on court 2:00 recovery	**Conditioning #12** Figure 8s 4 × 5 laps of 10 yards (9 m) 1:00 recovery Quick 4s 3 × 3 :20/2:00 recovery

* These numbered conditioning workouts are integrated into the sample 16-week off-season training calendars in tables 12.1 and 12.2.

Table 9.3   Sample 4-Week Off-Season Conditioning Program

Week	Day 1	Day 2
1	**Conditioning #1*** 2 × 10s on court 2:00 recovery	**Conditioning #2** 4 × 60 sec on treadmill 2:00 recovery
2	**Conditioning #3** 3 × 10s on court 2:00 recovery	**Conditioning #4** X drill 2 × 3 2:00 recovery Three-point run 6s × 6 1:30 recovery
3	**Conditioning #5** 3 × 10s on court 2:00 recovery	**Conditioning #6** X drill 2 × 3 2:00 recovery Three-point run 6s × 6 1:30 recovery
4	**Conditioning #7** 4 × 10s on court 2:00 recovery	**Conditioning #8** Figure 8s 3 × 5 laps of 10 yards (9 m) 1:00 recovery Quick 4s 2 × 3 :20/2:00 recovery

* These numbered conditioning workouts are integrated into the sample 16-week off-season training calendars in tables 12.1 and 12.2.

Recovering and Resting

Physical recovery from an athletic performance perspective can range from relatively easy intervention strategies to very complex intervention strategies. These are the three main goals of this chapter:

1. Simplify these strategies and help to create an understanding of the different forms of recovery
2. Gain a better understanding of how to implement those specific recovery strategies
3. Discuss modalities related to recovery

The *Oxford English Dictionary* defines recovery as both "A return to a normal state of health, mind or strength" and "An action or process of regaining possession or control of something stolen or lost." When you apply these two definitions to the human body and more specifically the game of basketball, you begin to understand why athletes need to recover. Basketball and its physical and mental stressors are quite demanding and can reduce an athlete's ability to perform at a high level day in and day out.

The first definition links recovery to the concept of "normal," and the second definition frames it in terms of something "stolen or lost." If you examine those terms more closely, you begin to understand how basketball affects not only the physical health but also the mind of the athlete. The demands of the game take a toll on the athlete's ability to physically play the game as well as the mental capacity to contemplate the game.

MVPs OF RECOVERY

In this chapter we discuss methodologies and practical applications for recovery strategies that can help the basketball athlete return to normal. But first, we discuss the MVPs (most valuable players) of recovery: *sleep, nutrition,* and *work capacity.*

Sleep

Sleep is the most important factor in athletic performance and recovery. If there is no other takeaway from this chapter, remember that sleep is king! An athlete can hydrate, stretch, and consume fruits and vegetables, but if their sleep is not optimal, athletic performance and recovery will suffer. A study by Fullagar and colleagues (2015) examined the effects of sleep on athletic performance as well as physiological and cognitive performance. Improved sleep can help to not only increase your athletic performance, such as sprinting, jumping, and skills, but also improve your ability to recover (physiology) and your reaction time and mental acuity (cognition). Unfortunately, there is no one-size-fits-all approach here, but in general, it is recommended for athletes to achieve a minimum of 8 to 10 hours of uninterrupted sleep during the night.

Proper sleep affects everything about the human body: metabolism, dietary choices, relationships, ability to handle physical and mental stress, and brain function, among many others. Sleep hygiene means following the habits and practices that are conducive to sleeping well on a regular basis. Williamson and Feyer (2000) have shown that going without sleep for 24 hours is the equivalent of being legally drunk!

In a sleep study conducted at Stanford University (Mah et al. 2011), subjects were asked to increase their sleep as much as possible, with a minimum of 10 hours in bed each night, for a duration of 5 to 7 weeks. During this time, such measures as sprint timing, reaction timing, shooting accuracy from both the free throw line and the three-point line, perceived fatigue, and physical and mental well-being were recorded. All such measures improved, including more than 9 percent in shooting accuracy from both the free throw and three-point lines, sprint scores, reaction timing, physical and mental well-being during practices and games, and perceived fatigue subscales.

Sleep deprivation has been shown to have a significant impact on athletic performance, namely submaximal, prolonged exercise. A study by Halson (2014) demonstrated the impacts of diet and nutrition on sleep. Some of the findings from the study are listed below.

- Diets higher in carbohydrates resulted in shorter time (latency) to fall asleep.
- Diets higher in protein resulted in better sleep quality.
- Diets higher in fat negatively affected total sleep time.
- Diets with decreased total caloric intake resulted in a disruption of sleep quality.

Sleep is even more critical to athletes when factoring in training load, practices, games, and travel. These habits must be addressed as an athlete would address any other weakness in their game.

Following is a list of factors that affect sleep and ways to correct them.

- **Poor dietary choices:** Avoid or minimize the consumption of alcohol and processed food.
- **Room temperature:** Maintain a room temperature between 65 and 67 degrees Fahrenheit (18-19 degrees Celsius).
- **Blue light:** Utilize blue-light-blocking glasses or put away the television, cellular phones, and video games at least two hours prior to bedtime.
- **Stress:** Apply breathing and relaxation techniques to get your mind ready to sleep.

- **Environment:** Use blackout shades and turn off lights or any distractions that can keep you from falling asleep or that may wake you up too early (such as morning sunlight).
- **Dehydration:** Maintain proper hydration throughout the day. Avoid drinking excess water prior to bed to avoid waking up to urinate.
- **Time zone changes:** Athletes traveling over several time zones experience disrupted sleep-wake cycles. Traveling west to east is very different from traveling east to west. Read current literature on best practices to avoid sleep disturbances.

These intervention strategies aim to improve sleep and can help an athlete to get a good night's rest.

Nutrition

Nutrition is not only a key component to getting a great night's sleep—it's also a key component of recovery. The reason nutrition is so important to sleep is that food contains essential vitamins and minerals needed for recovery, and those vitamins and minerals create the chemistry required for getting a great night's sleep. Here is a list of some vitamins and minerals that can promote sleep hygiene and where they can be found in food.

- **Iron** is a mineral in our blood that provides oxygen to our cells and tissues. Iron deficiency has been associated with sleep disorders, ADHD, and restless legs syndrome, to name just a few. Iron is found in dark-green leafy vegetables, beef, veal, chicken, broccoli, fortified cereals, and nuts. Iron is best absorbed in the presence of vitamin C. Vitamin C can be found in oranges, strawberries, and broccoli.
- **Magnesium** is a mineral that assists in nerve and muscle function, may reduce blood pressure, and can help maintain strong bones. Magnesium can affect sleep quality as well and serves as an alternative to melatonin supplementation. Magnesium is found in spinach as well as most seeds and nuts, including almonds and pumpkin seeds.
- **Calcium** is most known for its role in helping to maintain strong bones. Adequate dietary calcium intake is also crucial to maintain and assist proper brain and muscle function. Calcium has the ability to lower blood pressure, which is important for recovery and a good night's sleep. Calcium requires vitamin D for absorption. Direct sunlight on the skin—as little as 15 minutes per day—creates vitamin D. Dietary sources of calcium and vitamin D include nuts, milk, cheese, salmon, and fortified foods such as orange juice.
- **Potassium** is another mineral required for sleep and recovery. It lowers blood pressure, improves muscle and brain function, and assists in fluid balance in the body as a key electrolyte. Some of the many food sources high in potassium are bananas, beans, potatoes, dark leafy greens, avocados, and nuts.

- **B vitamins** are vital for converting food into energy and improving red blood cells, which carry oxygen molecules. There are numerous B vitamins (B1, B2, B3, B5, B6, B7, B9, and B12), each with a specific name and function. Food sources rich in B vitamins include lean meats and fish, citrus fruits such as oranges and lemons, avocados, beans, eggs, and fortified cereals.

- **Vitamin E** is a strong antioxidant and helps the body maintain a strong immune system against damage from free radicals, viruses, and bacteria. Vitamin E also plays a role in the formation of red blood cells, which carry oxygen. Vitamin E is found in foods such as nuts, seeds, and green leafy vegetables.

Nutrition is critical to sleep hygiene. In short, an athlete must eat a balanced diet containing lean proteins, dark leafy vegetables, nuts, fish, and a variety of fruits and other vegetables. It's best to eat dinner a minimum of two hours prior to bedtime to avoid disrupting a good night's sleep, and hydration should be maintained throughout the day since dehydration also affects sleep.

Work Capacity

Work capacity is the athlete's ability to perform repetitive and technically proficient sports skills and exercise without the onset of fatigue. In a practical application, it is the ability to handle the load of a single practice, game, training week, or cycle. Work capacity is vital to understanding the athlete's need for recovery. The greater capacity an athlete has to handle volume and intensity, the less dependent they become on recovery strategies. Many factors contribute to work capacity, among them relative strength, training status, nutrition, hydration, sleep, and genetics.

For instance, Athlete A comes into training camp in the fall having completed an off-season of periodized training and conditioning, and thus is in optimal shape for handling the demands of training camp. Athlete B comes into training camp out of shape but is looking to "play into shape" in preparation for the upcoming season. Both athletes complete the same training load during training camp. Which athlete will need the greatest intervention of recovery strategies in order to handle the next day's training load? Athlete B, based on the fact that their given work capacity is much less than Athlete A's. Athlete B is operating at a much higher relative intensity than Athlete A, requiring a greater mechanical and physiological demand to complete the same training load.

Work capacity can be achieved or even improved in a variety of ways:

- Improved nutrition
- Strength training
- Conditioning
- Shooting workouts

- Biking and metabolic circuit training
- Improved sleep
- Mindset training

An athlete must be able to handle not only the demands of a single bout of training but also the cumulative demands of the day-to-day and week-to-week training loads of a basketball season. In short, the better physically and mentally prepared the athlete is to handle the demands of basketball, the fewer intervention strategies are required to help that athlete return to normal.

SECONDARY INTERVENTIONS

The MVPs of recovery—sleep, nutrition, and work capacity—are the primary intervention strategies. They are considered primary because the secondary recovery interventions are ineffective in helping the body to recover unless the athlete's sleep hygiene, nutritional intake, and physical and mental preparedness have been previously addressed.

These five secondary interventions begin at the cessation of an in-season training session, practice, or game and require active participation. It is important to note that these strategies do not apply to off-season training because the primary goal of off-season training is adaptation. Off-season recovery is a topic for another discussion.

Secondary Recovery Strategy 1: Stop the Insult

The first recovery strategy is to "stop the insult"—in other words, remove the stressor or stressors that are contributing to the athlete's need to recover. If you're in the kitchen cooking dinner and cut yourself with a kitchen knife, the answer to recovery isn't to switch to a butter knife and continue to cook. The answer is to stop, clean the wound, and bandage it up. Though this strategy isn't a true intervention, it is often the most important first step in recovery.

Stopping the insult could mean taking your shoes off after a three-hour practice. Extra shots, extra weights, extra goofing around on the court offsets the time and physiology required for the athlete to make a meaningful recovery. These are examples of diminishing returns: The more you do, the worse off you are. There is a sweet spot in training that author Timothy Ferriss refers to as minimum effective dose (MED) or "the smallest dose that will produce the desired outcome."

> *"To boil water, the MED is 212°F (100°C) at standard air pressure. Boiled is boiled. Higher temperatures will not make it 'more boiled.' Higher temperatures just consume more resources that could be used for something else more productive."*
>
> *Timothy Ferriss*

For example, if an athlete spends an extra 15 minutes "getting up shots" after practice, compounded for every practice that week, that adds up to 1 hour per week, 4 hours per month and 20 to 30 hours per season, depending on the length of the season and assuming the team plays two or three games per week! Those 20 to 30 hours are crucial, especially in the postseason, when athletes should be at a peak level of conditioning and not running on fumes. This is not to imply that an athlete should not stay after practice and work on their individual skills but to understand the situation that will lead to the best transfer of that skill.

Secondary Recovery Strategy 2: Rehydrate

Rehydration is a key component of nutrition that cannot be overlooked. It has been demonstrated that even a 2 percent reduction in body weight from loss of sweat can have detrimental effects on performance and cognition. A simple weigh-in before practice and weigh-out after practice can quantify how much water or sports drink to consume after that training session.

Here is a simple formula to follow:

- For every 2.2 pounds (0.9 kg) of sweat loss, consume 1 quart (1 l) of water.
- To make it even more simple, consume 4 cups of water for every 2.2 pounds lost.

Water is generally the best hydration intervention, assuming athletes typically consume sufficient sodium and electrolytes in their daily diets. Consuming too many high-sugar/high-sodium sports drinks can lead to upset stomach and even weight gain if the duration and intensity of the session doesn't require such forms of hydration.

When addressing the anaerobic energy system utilized in basketball, alkaline water may be worth looking into. Alkaline water has been shown to have a positive impact on pH balance versus table water alone (Harris et al. 2019). This suggests that water content is important, and other studies have demonstrated similar findings. Scientists studied deep-ocean water and found it has a greater hydration effect than sports drinks or typical drinking-water alone (Harris et al. 2019; Chycki et al. 2017).

The amount of water an athlete is recommended to consume has not been generally agreed upon because sweat rates and body types and sizes vary. An easy equation for maintaining proper hydration, minus water consumed during exercise, is 50 percent of an athlete's body weight in fluid ounces of water. For example, a 200-pound (90 kg) athlete should consume 100 fluid ounces of water throughout the day.

Secondary Recovery Strategy 3: Refuel

Refueling is key, especially immediately following a training session. Make sure you refuel with a smoothie, piece of fruit, protein bar, or protein shake that has a sufficient balance of carbohydrate and protein within 20 to 30 minutes of the cessation of that training session for optimal uptake of nutrients. A guideline for finding a smoothie or protein shake that is designed for recovery is a 3:1 carbohydrate-to-protein ratio. For example, for every 30 grams of carbohydrates a smoothie or protein shake contains, ensure it has at least 10 grams of protein. Furthermore, if the training session was not sufficient for this intervention due to short duration or low intensity, eating a meal is probably the best strategy in this situation. Overfeeding can cause a loss of performance in the form of weight gain from consuming excess calories.

Secondary Recovery Strategy 4: Reflect

Taking 5 or 10 minutes to reflect on a training session as the body starts to cool down can help start the mental and emotional recovery process. As previously stated, the mind is connected to the body. Athletes can use this strategy to help shift from the sympathetic nervous system (fight or flight/survival/cortisol) to the parasympathetic nervous system (rest/digest).

Reflection is your mind's way of processing the training session—of finding ways to comprehend that session. Reflect on what positives occurred during the session. What did you do well? What could you have done better? Did you miss some shots or defensive assignments that you should have made? Positive self-talk can be used during reflection to help develop mental resiliency.

A sample reflection session could look like this:

1. Take off your shoes.
2. Grab a smoothie and a foam roller.
3. Find a quiet place in the gym or weight room.
4. Use the foam roller to get to "open book" breathing (see figure 10.1). Open book breathing is performed by lying flat on your back with knees bent and feet flat on the ground. Rock your entire body to one side, preferably with a foam roll or block between your knees. Open your upper chest to the opposite side with your head following your moving arm to the same side. Perform deep abdominal breathing while taking slow, deep breaths and trying to relax.
5. Slow your breath using deep belly or nasal breathing.
6. Find any tension in your muscles and try to relax.
7. Reflect on the training session: what went well, what didn't go so well, what you could do next time to make the session better, and what you learned.

Figure 10.1 Open book breathing.

Secondary Recovery Strategy 5: Ice or a Cold Tub

There are many studies demonstrating the advantages of cold water immersion (CWI, see figure 10.2) and contrast water immersion therapy (CWIT). Benefits include physiological improvement, such as the removal of waste by-products, and reducing pain, swelling, and muscle soreness. Psychological improvements have also been reported in athletes, such as the perception of recovery and overall improvements in well-being (Sánchez-Ureña et al. 2015, Machado et al. 2016).

Recommendations range from 10 to 15 minutes of continuous CWI to 2- to 3-minute bouts of cold alternating with warm showers or baths CWIT. Water temperature recommendations are 52 to 60 degrees Fahrenheit (11-15 °C). As with any training recommendation, start warmer, start shorter (5 to 10 minutes), and pace yourself as you adapt to the cold water. You can always increase your time, up to 20 minutes.

South Florida Sun-Sentinel/Getty Images

Figure 10.2   Cold water immersion can reduce pain, swelling, and muscle soreness.

PLAYER TRAINING LOAD

Most of the attention that NBA sport science receives from the public is centered on the controversial phrase "load management" as teams try to mitigate injury risk and keep their stars fresh for deep playoff runs, which can include an additional 28 games in the postseason (on top of the 82-game regular season, which is played in approximately 175 days). Many factors go into how each team makes informed decisions using insights based on data for how to best use their players. Training load is an important piece of recovery due to the rate and frequency of load that dictate to what extent an athlete needs to recover.

To comprehend load management, we must examine the different components of sport science and how you can use various technologies and scientific principles to make data-informed decisions that allow your athletes to perform and recover at the highest level.

Collecting data on athletes' external and internal load can be done with different techniques, products, and technologies. It is important to note that it is easy to get lost in the vast amount of data generated by wearables and other technologies, which makes it important to keep things simple. Decide what metrics are most important to track for basketball: Which ones will provide meaningful and actionable data? Additionally, it is important to monitor athletes both individually and as a team to properly identify significant changes in their data and then make appropriate adjustments or interventions.

External load is simply the physical work being performed on the court or in the weight room. It is associated with volume, intensity, and density. Traditionally, strength and conditioning coaches have tracked load or volume in the weight room by multiplying sets by reps (for example, 3 × 5) and then multiplying weight on the bar during each set (150 pounds [68 kg]) to understand total load lifted (2,250 pounds [1,020 kg]) for a particular exercise. This method can be used for every exercise performed to gain an understanding of total load of the session. Although there are several ways coaches can calculate load and break it down even further, by sets and reps at certain percentages of the athlete's 1 rep maximum, there is a need to understand external load during work performed on the basketball court.

Measuring external load during games and practices is most typically done by using a sensor that the player wears on the body to track position (coordinates) on the court using radiofrequency, inertial sensors, or Global Positioning System. To accurately measure motion and training load metrics, wearable devices house an accelerometer, gyroscope, and magnetometer.

Measuring the external load on the body allows the coach to safely progress or regress training activities based on the athlete's status, time of year, sleep, and internal load response.

Internal load represents the athlete's neurological, physiological, and psychological response to the external load from training. The internal response to external load can cause neurological disruptions to the autonomic nervous system, affecting things like breathing rate, heart rate, and digestion, which can lead to a physiological response of the energy systems and tissues within the body. Measuring external load is important, but how an athlete responds to the same load may vary daily due to a variety of different circumstances, such as a lack of sleep, illness, and so on. Measuring an athlete's' readiness is one of the key indicators of how much external load they can tolerate.

Performance monitoring can straddle the line between internal and external load monitoring because certain devices can measure how the body is reacting to both types of loads. For example, a force plate can be used to monitor fatigue and how the athlete is responding to the physical stressor imposed on the body. For the discussion of performance monitoring, we simplify the message and discuss tools that are used to measure the response to a training stimulus without diving into the nuance of whether it is used for external or internal load. The methods and devices are tools that are traditionally used in the weight room.

DOES LOAD MANAGEMENT WORK?

As NBA salaries have skyrocketed over the past two decades, teams have increasingly attempted to protect their most significant investments—players earning the most money and those who are deemed most important in the team's success—from injury by resting them more. Seldom do star players play on consecutive nights, much to the disappointment of ticket-buying fans and to the concern of the league office. As a result, a new Player Participation Policy was instituted beginning with the 2023-2024 NBA season in an effort to stem the number of rest or "load managed" games a player would sit out over the 82-game regular season schedule.

Somewhat bolstering the league's position was a 57-page report shared with each team in January 2024, summarizing a study based on a 10-year analysis of the number of games played and the incidence of player injuries. In the report summary, the researchers concluded that the data did not show an association between missing games for rest or load management and lower injury risk even after accounting for age, injury history, and minutes played.

NBA officials and others who evaluated the results of the study were quick to say that the data are by no means conclusive due to the type of analysis and the number of factors involved. For example, the study offers no insight as to how rest affected player performance. Furthermore, the study includes only NBA players and not players at the high school or college levels who play fewer games that are more spaced out over the course of their seasons.

This will, no doubt, be a subject of further investigation and debate in the years ahead. In the meantime, individual player differences must always be taken into account in determining when rest is beneficial and prudent for their well-being and performance.

Source: https://www.cbssports.com/nba/news/what-the-nbas-load-management-report-didnt-say-about-rest-and-injuries/

Radio Frequency Identification (RFID)

Radio frequency identification (RFID) has seen a steady rise to prominence in basketball to measure external loads because it does not require a clear view to the sky like GPS units do. A "chip" (transponder) is worn by the athlete and electromagnetic fields transmit a signal to a radio receiver and transmitter, giving locations on the court, distance, and speed of movement.

RFID is commonly used to measure distance, distance spent in different velocity bands or speed zones, maximum velocity, acceleration, and deceleration. Additionally, RFID systems allow you to track an athlete's training and competition volume, intensity, and density. Common volume metrics include total distance, mechanical load, and total duration. Common intensity metrics include high-speed distance, distance per minute (i.e., meters per minute), load per minute, maximum velocity, jumps per minute, accelerations/decelerations per minute, and others. Common density metrics include average speed and average mechanical load over the course of a practice or game. These metrics can provide insight when comparing athlete loads and intensities to one another in different positions, drills, practices, and competitions.

Data collected through these metrics allow you to assess the physical demands of your athletes in their sport, which in turn allows you to make informed decisions regarding practice and training plans to optimize performance, improve recovery and aid in return to play after injuries, and reduce fatigue. In addition, understanding the demands of the game means you can decide which drills are most gamelike, prepare for the most difficult aspects of the game, and choose which drills to avoid depending on the focus of the practice session.

Global Positioning Unit

GPS devices are another common external-load monitoring tool used among strength and conditioning coaches and sport scientists. Most GPS wearables also contain an accelerometer, gyroscope, and magnetometer. GPS is commonly used to measure distance, distance spent in different velocity and speed zones, maximum velocity, acceleration, and deceleration. GPS has been shown to collect valuable and reliable external load data utilizing a variety of metrics to get a clear representation of what each athlete is experiencing in regard to their performance and prescribed recovery methods.

Player training load is measured both externally and internally. It is vital to not only understand the difference between the two but also to understand how each athlete is adapting. Sport science gives us tools to understand these metrics and make more accurate recommendations about performance, recovery, and future training loads.

MENTAL AND EMOTIONAL RECOVERY

Mental and emotional recovery are often overlooked and neglected. The stigma behind mental and emotional health, especially in sports, can leave athletes feeling they must hide feelings of being overwhelmed, anxious, helpless, or depressed, but mental and emotional recovery have importance and connectedness to actual recovery. The mind is connected to the body and the body, as we know, cannot function without the brain.

The mental demands of sports in general are very high. Basketball is no different. Athletes want to perform at their highest level. They want to play well. Developing mental capacity and resiliency is another form of work capacity and is a trait that can be trained and developed.

Here are some examples of mental stressors:

- Remembering the playbook
- Remembering defensive coverages
- Keeping the opponent from scoring
- Remembering how many points they have scored
- Missing shots
- Getting little playing time
- Handling a verbally abusive coach
- Playing in front of a crowd
- Playing in front of someone they are trying to impress or someone highly regarded
- Playing a nationally televised game
- Procrastinating, such as putting off a homework assignment that is due next week

Cortisol, one of the primary stress hormones, plays a crucial role in the nervous system's "fight or flight" response. It is important during times of stress, including participating in sports. Cortisol also can be harmful if stress becomes chronic. Cortisol can affect mood, sleep, and even thought patterns. If stress is not managed properly, over time an athlete can overtrain, underperform, become sick, and even get injured.

Cortisol can also be created through thought and self-speak. When an athlete has persistent negative thoughts and emotions, the body's sympathetic nervous system is on constant alert, which makes it literally impossible to start the recovery process. What you speak comes back into your own head. In terms of mental and emotional recovery, your body physically reacts to stress. This cyclical pattern should be addressed early in the preseason. Speaking and thinking positively can augment a physical recovery session and lead to greater improvements physiologically.

Some mental and emotional interventions could look like this:

- Breathing exercises or utilization of a breathing app
- Taking a night walk
- Meditation—working to quiet the mind
- Prayer
- Connecting with a trusted friend or loved one
- Listening to relaxing music
- Working with a psychologist or psychiatrist
- Steam room, sauna, cold tub, or shower to improve resiliency

PASSIVE RECOVERY MODALITIES

Passive recovery is a time of little to no effort that allows the body to heal. Massage, foam rolling, compression, and cryotherapy are examples of passive recovery modalities that athletes can use to recover.

Massage

Massage has been argued over for decades as to its direct role in recovery. The argument against massage is that the scientific community cannot prove it works. The argument *for* massage is the topic of this chapter—improvements in mental and emotional recovery.

In sport science, we use rating of perceived exertion (RPE), which has had significant impacts on quantifying and qualifying training loads. When an athlete perceives their exertion levels or their sense of well-being, it is exactly that, *their* perception. In separate studies, athletes reported psychological benefits, feelings of well-being, increases in perceived recovery, and decreases in perceived muscle soreness after massage (Hemmings et al. 2000; Kargarfard et al. 2016).

The following are other benefits of massage (Hemmings et al. 2000):

- Increases circulation and widens blood vessels
- Increases vital capacity and expiratory volume
- Increases skin temperature and lymphatic circulation
- Decreases anxiety, stress, beta waves, and cortisol
- Decreases lymphedema (swelling in the skin and around the joints)
- Decreases keloids or scar tissue formation
- Improves relaxation, motor skill, and muscle length
- Decreases muscle tension

- Increases urine production and elimination of nitrogen and sodium chloride
- Improves sleep, mood, and mental health
- Promotes healing through human touch

Foam Rolling

Foam rolling has become mainstream for athletes of all levels and for good reason. Studies have continued to show it as an effective tool to combat delayed-onset muscle soreness as well as alleviate muscle tenderness (Pearcey et al. 2015). Reducing recovery time makes athletes better prepared for their next workout session, thus resulting in better long-term training outcomes.

Compression

A new tool in the world of recovery modalities is air compression devices. Although they have seen use in clinical settings for circulation-related disorders for some time, they are only recently being used to boost performance and recovery in athletes. Studies debate the physiological effects of air compression, but as with massage, athletes in recovery have a perception that it is effective. There is a strong relationship between the body and mind, and an athlete's perception of successful recovery is just as important to recovery as a physiological response.

Cryotherapy

Cryotherapy has been a favorite of athletes for many years. Localized ice, whole-body water immersion, and the most recent addition, whole-body cryotherapy, are the most common. The most widely cited benefit of cryotherapy is reduced inflammation of muscle tissue. Reducing muscle inflammation after training shortens recovery time and results in the following training session being more productive. Whole-body cryotherapy is still in its infancy and its effectiveness is to be determined, but there is no denying the psychological effect it has on athletes. It is often more tolerable than cold-water immersion, and thus more athletes can reap its potential benefits.

Many of the studies pertaining to the use of cryotherapy resulted in mixed results from a physiological perspective. Some of the findings recommend the use of cryotherapy for recovery interventions but not for immediate performance gains. In other words, cryotherapy does not elicit immediate improvements on jumping or sprinting (Vieira et al. 2015), but it is believed to effect immediate improvements in the body's ability to start the recovery process (Pournot et al. 2011).

Reconditioning and Returning to Play

Basketball is a physically demanding sport, not only in taxing the body's energy systems, muscles, joints, and connective tissues, but also in the sometimes punishing contact with opponents in games, teammates in practice, the gym floor, and even the basketball goal. All too often, this physical toll is paid in the form of injury. Rarely does a player make it through the entire season without incurring some type of injury that requires days, weeks, and even months of healing rest, medically prescribed rehab, and a reconditioning protocol that prepares the player to return to game action.

This chapter addresses the last stage of that postinjury process: the training an athlete needs to return to competition after a successful rehabilitation program. We refer to this reconditioning period as the return-to-play (RTP) process. It must be taken seriously by players coming back from an injury and their coaches. Missteps or shortcuts can result in reinjury and at the very least are likely to diminish the athlete's fitness and performance for weeks.

Patience is the key here. When an athlete attempts to rush the process, more harm than good results, including even more time missed than would otherwise have been the case if the RTP process had been allowed to take its full course.

While the RTP timeline can differ based on the nature and seriousness of the injury, the steps toward recovery often share similarities. This process can include several phases, starting after the athlete has been medically cleared and rehabbed to the point where appropriate physical activity and retraining can begin. Each phase has specific goals and activities that are monitored regularly to ensure the athlete progresses appropriately.

Although the details are beyond the scope of this book, it's important to understand what must happen before medical clearance can be granted. Following the injury diagnosis, treatment, and sufficient healing, the athlete begins the early stages of the rehabilitation process, guided by a certified athletic trainer or physical therapist to ensure the healing process of damaged tissues continues and to prevent further damage to the affected area. This rehab phase is focused on improving the athlete's isolated strength, mobility, stability, and joint function, while also addressing any underlying weaknesses or imbalances that could have contributed to the initial injury. During this phase the athlete is monitored and advanced based on their progress and the goals that were established in the initial assessment. These can include

- reduction in symptoms,
- improvement in joint function, and
- achievements in strength and stability testing.

It's important to note that later in the rehabilitation process, depending on the injury, it is possible for the athlete to engage in some skill development activities and low-impact conditioning if it does not interfere with tissue healing.

Setting objective targets at the beginning of RTP is important in determining how to progress an athlete for a safe return to competition. This should involve consulting appropriate medical professionals and collecting baseline targets of strength, range of motion, and cardiorespiratory fitness to gauge how the athlete is progressing. Goals can be adjusted depending on the athlete's response and commitment to retraining.

RESUMING STRENGTH TRAINING AND CONDITIONING

Following medical clearance by an athletic trainer, the athlete may begin strength training and conditioning, preferably under the supervision of a certified strength and conditioning specialist. This postrehabilitation phase of RTP shares many of the goals set out in the previous rehab phase but with a more specific focus on developing functional strength and movement patterns to start preparing the athlete for the physical demands of basketball. During this phase there is a gradual progression of

- multijoint strength training,
- cardiorespiratory fitness training,
- balance and proprioception training, and
- introduction of agility and plyometric training.

Monitoring by qualified professionals and coaching staff and honest reporting by the athlete during the retraining process are essential to a successful RTP process. When an athlete reports any discomfort, pain, or unusual feelings, it's important to listen. This feedback helps adjust the retraining plan to best suit the athlete and foster continued progress. Regular meetings with athletic trainers, physical therapists, strength coaches, and sport coaches can also be helpful in tracking progress and addressing any concerns. Using tools and tests to check the athlete's strength, range of motion, and ability to function helps ensure that the athlete is on the right track and not doing damage or regressing.

Recovery is a fundamental component of the RTP process. Monitoring recovery throughout reconditioning is essential to the athlete's successful return to play because the response of the body is unique to every individual and injury. Some red flags to look for that may indicate insufficient monitoring and recovery include

- significant swelling,
- sharp pain,
- prolonged recovery, and
- decreased performance.

SIGNS OF AN ATHLETE FAVORING THE OLD INJURY

It is common for athletes returning to play after an injury to consciously or subconsciously exhibit compensatory behaviors to protect the previously injured area. This can not only adversely affect their RTP progress and their performance on the court when they do return but can also lead to new injuries if unchecked. Here's what to watch for:

- **Hesitation:** There might be a noticeable pause or reluctance before making moves, such as cutting or jumping, that involve the previously injured area.
- **Altered mechanics:** An athlete might change their movement patterns. For example, they might land more heavily on one leg after a jump or pivot differently.
- **Reduced performance:** Jumping heights might be lower or strides might be shorter on one side.
- **Avoidance of contact:** Athletes might shy away from situations where the injured area could be harmed, like going for a contested rebound.
- **Vocal or facial cues:** Signs of discomfort, pain, or frustration can often be discerned from an athlete's facial expressions or vocal reactions.

It is expected and normal for athletes to feel soreness at the old injury site when they start moving again. However, there is a difference between "good" and "bad" soreness.

- *Good soreness* is a general muscle discomfort that comes after new or hard activity and fades with rest and light stretching or movement.
- *Bad soreness* is a sharp pain, especially at the injury spot. If it changes how an athlete moves, like causing a limp, it's a warning sign.

If the soreness gets worse or doesn't get better after three days, the training might be too much for the athlete, and intensity, load, or frequency—or all three—should be adjusted. Sharp pain, especially where the old injury was, means the athlete should stop and be examined by a medical professional. This also applies if the pain is consistently at a level 5 or higher out of 10 during any activities.

BASKETBALL-SPECIFIC TRAINING

As the athlete progresses through the final stages of rehabilitation and approaches on-court activities, the training should begin to mirror the unique demands of basketball. This phase is a bridge between general strength and conditioning to more functional sport-specific training. Once players have built a solid foundation of fitness and strength, the focus shifts to basketball-specific training. This is aimed at

- developing power,
- increasing agility and jumping ability, and
- improving cardiorespiratory fitness.

The aims at this point are to restore, if not improve upon, the athlete's preinjury level of athleticism and prevent reinjury. As the athlete reintegrates into full practices, this type of training and its physical benefits should make the player feel more resilient and confident to perform to their full potential without hesitation.

Power Development

Basketball requires athletes to be powerful in actions such as jumping for a rebound or accelerating in a fast break. Athletes can develop power and boost their ability to quickly generate force by incorporating the following training approaches to their program.

- **Olympic lifts (with variations):** These bolster the athlete's ability to generate force quickly. For example, performing trap bar clean pulls, push presses, and kettlebell snatches.
- **Nonspecific plyometric drills:** These improve the athlete's jumping and landing capacity and performance with exercises such as hurdle hops, depth jumps, and repeat pogo jumps.

Agility and Jumping Ability

In reacting to their opponents, basketball athletes need to be able to change directions quickly or jump up to block a shot or secure a rebound. Training these elements and specific basketball patterns can enable athletes to perform at a high level on the court.

- **Change of direction drills:** These develop the athlete's ability to rapidly change directions quickly to react to an opponent's movements.
- **Basketball-specific jump and plyometric training**: This training improves the athlete's jumping and landing skills in ways that mimic movements during play.

Cardio Conditioning

Basketball has periods of low to moderate activity with bursts of high-intensity play. Choosing conditioning drills that replicate those patterns is the best way to prepare the athlete.

- **Timed-interval running:** This can be utilized to mimic the stop-and-start nature of basketball. These drills incorporate designated work:rest ratios that replicate what the athletes may experience during a game.
- **On-court (position-specific) drills:** These drills are similar to timed-interval running but emphasize specialized elements and movement patterns for the various positions. For example, a center might focus on short, intense actions like running up to set a screen and then rolling to sprint to the paint.

PREPARING FOR RETURN TO PLAY

The final phase of RTP is a gradual reintroduction to basketball and court-based activities with the coach, preferably monitored by an athletic trainer or a strength and conditioning specialist. While the sport-specific strength activities will continue in the weight room, this is also a time for basketball-specific skill work to begin on the court, which is essential to help athletes regain their on-court abilities and confidence. A variety of drills and exercises can be incorporated to improve sport-specific skills:

- Dribbling, passing, and defensive drills
- Noncontact basketball-specific via 5v0 offense running plays
- Progress through controlled settings of contact via 1v1, 2v2, and 3v3 drills until full contact during 5v5 practices

An example of the entire RTP process is provided in table 11.1. Obviously, the time frames and some of the goals may have to be adjusted depending on the injury and the response of the athlete to the reconditioning program.

On-Court Drills

The return to on-court drills after rehab must be approached carefully. The athlete must be physically prepared and the drills introduced gradually. Here are a variety of on-court drills with guidelines for introducing them into the RTP process and modifying them for varying intensities as the athlete progresses.

Table 11.1 Sample 12-Week Return-to-Play Program

Phase	Weeks	Goal
Postrehabilitation resumption of activity	1-2	• Tissue repair • Restore range of movement (ROM) and joint function • Improve isolated strength
Resume strength training and conditioning	3-6	• Multijoint strength • Cardiorespiratory fitness • Balance and proprioception • Introduce low-level agility and plyometrics
Basketball-specific training	7-9	• Improve strength and power • Increase agility and jumping ability • Improve cardiorespiratory fitness
Lead-up to return to competition	10-12+	• Practice (5v0) • Gradual progress to contact practice starting at 1v1 and progressing to 5v5 • Return to competition

Dribbling Drills

Start with stationary dribbling in place.

Progressions

Initiate moving dribbling drills, first in a straight line, then with changes in direction. Increase the speed and complexity of the dribbling patterns over time.

Shooting Drills

Begin with free throw shooting or spot shooting, ensuring the player is using proper mechanics.

Progressions

Incorporate movement, such as catch-and-shoot drills or pull-up jump shots. Later, add defense simulations.

Passing Drills

Start with stationary two-hand chest passes to a partner.

Progressions

Introduce bounce passes, overhead passes, and one-handed passes. Progress to passing on the move and incorporate defensive pressure.

Cutting and Change of Direction Drills

Begin with slow, deliberate cuts and pivots without a ball.

Progressions

Introduce the ball and increase the speed. Incorporate sudden stops and direction changes.

Rebounding Drills

Start with simple box out drills without jumping.

Progressions

Progress to actual rebounding, first without opposition and then with mock defenders.

Defensive Drills

Initiate with defensive slides within short distances, focusing on form.

Progressions

Extend the sliding distance, incorporate closeouts, and then simulate on-ball defense scenarios.

RETURNING TO BASKETBALL COMPETITION

Reintegrating a previously injured athlete into full-contact basketball activities, from 1v1 play to full 5v5 scrimmages, requires both physical readiness and sport-specific conditioning. As an athlete progresses from individual drills to team dynamics, it's important to carefully monitor the athlete through each stage.

- **1v1:** Begins when the athlete can complete all on-court drills without pain or discomfort. There should be no swelling or signs of inflammation after a training session. The athlete can exhibit stable, controlled movements, especially those that mimic game situations (cuts, pivots, jumps).

  » Begin with half-court 1v1 to limit the running distance.
  » Start with controlled offensive and defensive scenarios, such as post-up moves or closeout situations.

- **2v2:** The athlete has comfortably engaged in several 1v1 sessions without issues. They can handle quick decision-making scenarios without hesitation. The athlete exhibits confidence in their movement and has regained agility.

» Use half-court settings initially to reduce running time and quick changes in direction.

» Introduce pick-and-roll or off-ball movement scenarios to simulate game situations but with fewer players.

- **5v5:** The athlete has been able to engage in multiple 2v2 sessions without any sign of discomfort or reduced performance. Cardiorespiratory endurance is near preinjury levels, allowing for longer durations of play. The athlete shows a regained sense of game-readiness and confidence.

» Start with short-duration scrimmages, focusing on specific game situations.

» Monitor for fatigue: Tired players can resort to poor mechanics, increasing the risk of injury.

» Initially, limit aggressive defensive plays, such as full-court presses, to reduce unpredictable scenarios.

ADDRESSING COMPENSATION BEHAVIORS

When an athlete exhibits reluctance to engage fully in training or competition, or the athlete makes a notable change in mechanics after returning to play, these measures may help address the problem.

- **Open communication:** Encourage athletes to communicate any fears, pain, or discomfort. Understanding their mental state can provide insight into their physical actions.

- **Targeted rehab and strengthening:** Even after returning to play, continue with exercises that target the previously injured area to build strength and confidence.

- **Sport-specific drills:** Repetitive, sport-specific drills can help retrain the body in proper mechanics. For instance, for a player hesitant to jump, plyometric drills might be reintroduced. These not only help the athlete regain an expected performance level but may also boost the athlete's confidence.

Return-to-Play Restrictions

As athletes return to competitive play after an injury, a cautious and systematic approach is crucial to ensure their safety and reduce the risk of reinjury. Restricting play in certain aspects can help transition the player back into full competition more safely.

- **Minimize consecutive minutes:** Start by limiting the number of continuous minutes an athlete plays. For example, they might play in 5-minute spurts with breaks, even if they feel they could go longer.
- **Reduce total game minutes:** Initially, the athlete might participate for only a fraction of the game, such as playing 10 out of 40 minutes. This can be gradually increased in subsequent games as their stamina and comfort level improve.
- **Avoid back-to-back games:** If possible, avoid having the athlete play in consecutive games without rest days in between. This allows time to monitor how their body responds postgame and ensure there's no delayed inflammation or soreness.

RTP Protocols for Specific Injuries

RTP protocols can serve as a road map to help make decisions and guide the athlete toward a successful reintegration back to the court. These protocols include different strategies for various types of injuries that are intended to prepare athletes for the demands of basketball and minimize the risk of reinjury after they have made a safe return.

It is important to consider each athlete's individual needs and position-specific demands when using these protocols. RTP timelines can vary based on each athlete and the severity of injury, as detailed in the following time frames, goals, and strategies for each stage of the RTP protocol.

Illness

Illness, regardless of severity, can leave athletes compromised in multiple areas, including

- cardiorespiratory fitness,
- muscle strength,
- coordination, and
- cognitive function.

Ignoring illness-related factors and allowing athletes to compete while sick may put at risk other athletes, worsen their own symptoms, and increase their risk of sports-related injuries.

Muscle Strain and Contusion

- **Assessments**
  - » Determine grade of muscle injury (I, II, III)
  - » Functional testing

- **RTP criteria**

  » Tissue healing

  » Pain-free full range of motion

  » Restoration of baseline strength

  » Pain-free completion of basketball-specific drills and activities

- **Sample timeline and retraining steps**

  » Weeks 1-2

    - Goals: reduce swelling and pain at injury site

    - Activities: rest and soft tissue work to promote tissue healing

  » Weeks 3-4

    - Goals: restore motion and functional strength at injury site

    - Activities: isometrics until isotonic exercises can be performed around injury site

  » Weeks 5-6

    - Goals: improve strength, introduce power exercises, introduce sport-specific exercises and drills

    - Activities: increase loading of isotonic exercise, incorporate power exercises at low intensity, begin noncontact basketball with coach and return to 5v0 practices

  » Weeks 7-8

    - Goals: return to sport-specific activities and progress from 1v1 controlled contact to 5v5 practice or scrimmage

    - Activities: continue strength and power training activities and begin practicing with team until full return to play

Ankle Sprain

- **Assessments**

  » Determine grade of sprain (I, II, III)

- **RTP criteria**

  » Ankle stability

  » Full range of motion and strength around the ankle joint

  » Performance of sport-specific activities without pain or instability

- **Sample timeline and retraining steps**

  » Weeks 1-2

    - Goals: reduce swelling and pain at injury site
    - Activities: compression and mobility exercises to promote tissue healing

  » Weeks 3-4

    - Goals: restore ROM and incorporate low-weight-bearing exercises
    - Activities: band ABCs (loop a band around the front of your foot and hold each end with your hands, then move your foot to draw out each letter of the alphabet), light walking, assisted calf raises

  » Weeks 5-6

    - Goals: restore strength and stability
    - Activities: calf raises, balance and proprioception exercises, light plyometrics or court drills at reduced volume and intensity

  » Weeks 7-8

    - Goals: regain strength and power
    - Activities: moderate to high plyometrics, increased volume of court drills, progressively loaded calf raises

Patellar Tendon Injury

- **Assessment**

  » Pain estimation during loaded activities
  » Functional strength testing
  » Evaluate pain again 24 hours after loaded activities

- **RTP criteria**

  » Tissue healing and pain management
  » Recovery of functional strength and loading capacity
  » Ability to resume normal activities without pain the following day

- **Sample timeline and retraining steps**

  » Weeks 1-2

    - Goals: reduce pain at injury site
    - Activities: isometric quadriceps exercises (Spanish squats, quad extensions 5 × 45-second holds)

» Weeks 3-4

- Goals: increase tissue-loading capacity via isometric exercise without pain
- Activities: loaded isometric quad extensions (5 × 45-second with 2 minutes rest)

» Weeks 5-6

- Goals: restore strength and ability to perform isotonic exercises
- Activities: eccentric leg press, squats, leg extensions (3-4 sets of 15 repetitions max)

» Weeks 7-8

- Goals: improve elasticity of tendon by introducing plyometric and energy-storage exercises
- Activities: introduce vertical jumps (box jumps, squat jumps, countermovement jumps) and horizontal jumps (broad jumps, bounds), continue strength exercises from previous weeks

» Weeks 9-10

- Goals: moderate to high plyometrics, increased volume of court drills
- Activities: increase intensity of isotonic and isometric exercises as well as vertical and horizontal jumping, return to court for 5v0 practice with the team

» Weeks 11-12

- Goals: gradual return to sport activities with the team, monitor volume and intensity to avoid setbacks from court activities
- Activities: begin full-contact practices, maintain strength training to prevent future setbacks

Knee Ligament Injury

- **Assessment**

  » Evaluate joint stability
  » Ensure ligament integrity via imaging

- **RTP criteria**

  » Tissue healing and joint integrity and stability
  » Full range of motion and baseline functional strength
  » Ability to perform cutting, pivots, and jumps without pain or instability

• **Sample timeline and retraining steps**

» Months 1-2

- Goals: tissue healing, gradual restoration of ROM
- Activities: non-load-bearing exercises while braced, gradual return to weight-bearing walking in pool

» Months 3-4

- Goal: open-chain strength exercises, low-intensity conditioning activities
- Activities: isometric quad extensions, glute bridges, upper-body conditioning, pool workouts

» Months 5-6

- Goals: closed-chain functional strength exercises, balance and proprioception, low-intensity plyometric and conditioning activities
- Activities: split squat lunges, squats, light jumping and plyometric exercises, anti-gravity treadmill running

» Months 7-9 (and onward)

- Goals: increase strength and power, introduce sport-specific drills on court
- Activities: walking lunges, box jumps, plyometrics, jumping and cutting drills, court workouts

Concussion

A concussion is a traumatic brain injury that can have serious short- or long-term consequences. Naturally, this requires careful consideration when it comes to RTP. Basketball athletes who have been diagnosed with a concussion must prioritize their health and well-being and be removed from participation until medically cleared by a professional.

Even after symptoms have subsided, athletes should enter a gradual RTP protocol to ensure a safe return to competition. Concussion symptoms can include

- headache,
- dizziness,
- loss of memory,
- poor coordination and balance, and
- blurred vision.

The concussion RTP protocol can begin once the athlete no longer shows concussion symptoms at rest. Athletes should follow a step-by-step protocol, monitored by a medical professional, until they are cleared for participation. If symptoms return at any stage during the RTP protocol, the athlete should cease exercise and repeat the stage the next day until they are symptom free.

- **Stage 1:** Light aerobic activity (stretching, balance training, walking, stationary bike)
- **Stage 2:** Sport-specific exercise (dribbling, free throws, spot shots)
- **Stage 3:** Noncontact drills (triggers into shots, 5v0 practice)
- **Stage 4:** Full-contact practice once medically cleared
- **Stage 5:** Return to competition

Complete Conditioning Program

To this point in the book, we've presented information, recommendations, and training protocols for players to gain strength, power, and speed; improve their conditioning and mobility; and ensure they are getting proper recovery and rest to reap the most benefits from their training regimens. Each element. contributes to the athlete's overall conditioning, performance, and health.

In this chapter we synthesize all the scientific knowledge, training techniques, and workouts already presented into a year-long program for players' optimal physical development and performance during the season and postseason competition. In the strength and conditioning community, we consider this synthesizing process to be an art, because there are so many variables to take into account in designing the very best plan for each athlete on the team.

The athlete assessments described in chapter 2 are vital in determining your physical training road map. Assessment results gauge the team's overall conditioning level and reveal key insights into each player's strengths and weaknesses. The assessments also help to establish training goals, which are crucial when it comes to creating a comprehensive program and prescribing individual training plans.

Including movement preparation, mobility, and flexibility ensures a proper warm-up for workouts and can decrease the risk of injury. Mobility and flexibility training also improves a player's joint range of motion, allowing them to get the maximum benefit from their strength, power, speed, and agility training.

Strength is the foundational element of basketball fitness—it helps to increase power, speed, and agility and makes the body more durable to meet the demands of the sport. Power helps the athlete become more explosive and faster. Speed and agility training improves reaction time, changes of direction, speed, and heightens the ability to change speed and movement patterns. Finally, on-court basketball conditioning maximizes a player's ability and capacity to run, defend, shoot, and compete on the court at a high intensity for extended periods of time.

Training all these athletic attributes must be done strategically so players do not overtrain and possibly injure themselves in the process. Allowing the body to recover is just as important as the training. Recovery is more than just resting between sets; it also entails giving the body a break while eating and hydrating properly to reenergize it for the next workout or game.

With all those factors in mind, let's look at how to design and implement an annual basketball conditioning program. In addition to a master plan, we will also present options and possible considerations in the quest to provide the best basketball performance training prescription.

TRAINING CYCLES

Specific team and individual training goals can be accomplished only through an organized plan that applies the proper progression of conditioning. For most players and teams, this starts early in the off-season, following a proper rest interval after the preceding competitive season. This year-round schedule of training is often referred to as a *macrocycle*.

Within that macrocycle are distinct periods of training (i.e., preseason, in-season, postseason, and off-season), also called *mesocycles*. During each of these mesocycles, the goals and therefore what is emphasized in that training period may, and really should, differ, but also have some overlapping features. For example, the first mesocycle might focus on hypertrophy (gaining muscle size). The second mesocycle might emphasize strength gains. The third mesocycle might focus on increasing speed and power. Finally, the fourth mesocycle might aim at maintaining improvements in muscle size, strength, speed, and power while increasing on-court conditioning.

To ensure proper selection, sequencing, and progression of training activities within each mesocycle, the plan is organized into even smaller periods (weeks and days) called *microcycles*. These microcycles not only serve to properly progress training but also help the coach to monitor players' development, make specific adjustments as needed, and provide an opportunity to set more immediate goals that will keep athletes highly motivated throughout the process. In the sample programs provided later in this chapter, we present 3-day and 4-day off-season, 3-day preseason, and 2-day in-season examples.

In this chapter we provide different ways to design your off-season program and obtain the desired goals using information presented in the previous chapters. It's important to develop a program with progressive phases and stay with it. Be consistent! Consistency gives you a better chance of seeing and measuring improvement. Don't hesitate to step back and take the time to analyze your program and the team's gains every few weeks. This is the time to make any necessary changes or modifications to the program that could help athletes achieve their individual goals. For instance, you could change from a 3-day-per-week program to a 4-day-per-week program, making appropriate nutritional changes, increasing conditioning if you notice athletes getting winded, and increasing recovery time and sleep.

When you get down to actually designing a program, there are many factors to consider. How many days per week to train? Which days of the week to train? What part of the day to train? What type of training (strength, power, agility, speed, conditioning, mobility) to emphasize on what days? In what sequence should these various types of training be performed? These are just a few considerations. The information and options we provide give you plenty of guidance to form the best strength and conditioning program for your needs and goals.

OFF-SEASON TRAINING

The first mesocycle, the off-season, is the most important training phase because this is where the majority of strength, hypertrophy, power, speed, mobility, and flexibility gains can be made. However, before off-season training begins, athletes need time, typically 2 or 3 weeks, following the final game of the prior season to allow their bodies to rest and recover. All players, but especially those who played the most minutes competitively in-season, need time to refresh mentally and physically and prepare for the next physical challenge.

Off-season training can last 4 to 6 months, depending on when postseason play ends and the next preseason period begins. However, to be consistent with the training protocols in previous chapters, we will make this off-season mesocycle example 16 weeks long.

This is the most progressive cycle of training. It's the longest uninterrupted period of training and also has more opportunity for periods of recovery, which is when many of the physiological gains occur. During the first 4 to 8 weeks of off-season training, the type of conditioning presented in chapter 9 should be minimal, occurring only during limited scrimmaging and any organized basketball games athletes may participate in. There will be plenty of time for on-court conditioning during the preseason training period. Plus, we recommend a progressive 4-week, 6-week, or 8-week conditioning training block to be inserted beginning at week 8, 10, or 12 of the off-season. Not only is the off-season the time to make the biggest strides in the athletic characteristics, but it's also the time to make big gains in improving athletes' basketball skills as well.

When planning for a 16-week off-season training program, you want to schedule in the appropriate active rest and recovery weeks using the guidelines presented in chapter 5, Strength Training. For example, you might opt for this protocol:

Week	Training Focus
1-2	Muscular endurance and general physical preparation
3-6	Hypertrophy
7	Active rest and deload
8-11	Base strength
12	Active rest and deload
13-15	Power and speed
16	Active rest (just prior to the start of preseason training)

You need to determine how many days per week you will train and on what days. Everyone's schedule differs, but here are a couple of examples of how a weekly off-season training plan might be organized.

Training 3 Days per Week

Training 3 days per week can look different depending on your schedule. One option is three total-body sessions with a minimum of 1 day between lifting workouts. This could be a Monday/Wednesday/Friday or Tuesday/Thursday/Saturday or even a Monday/Wednesday/Saturday training schedule. We provide an example of this program in table 12.1.

Alternatively, you can schedule upper-body and lower-body days, with a total-body workout on the third day. This method allows for a higher volume of work on both the upper-body days and the lower-body days. This way, you can train different body areas, such as Monday/Tuesday/Thursday or Friday, or even a Monday/Wednesday/Friday.

Table 12.1 Sample 16-Week Basketball Off-Season Training Calendar: 3 Total-Body Workouts per Week

Week # Training phase	Monday	Tuesday	Wednesday	Thursday	Friday
Week 1 General physical preparation 1	TB lift: GPP 1/1 (2 × 15 circuit style)		TB lift: GPP 1/2 (2 × 15 circuit style)		TB lift: GPP 1/3 (1 × 15, 2 × 12 circuit style)
Week 2 General physical preparation 2	TB lift: GPP 2/1 (3 × 12 circuit style)		TB lift: GPP 2/2 (2 × 12, 1 × 10 circuit style)		TB lift: GPP 2/3 (1 × 12, 2 × 10 circuit style)
Week 3 Hypertrophy 1	TB lift: HYP 1/1 (3 × 10)		TB lift: HYP 1/2 (2 × 10, 1 × 8)		TB lift: HYP 1/3 (1 × 10, 2 × 8)
Week 4 Hypertrophy 2	TB lift: HYP 2/1 (3 × 8)		TB lift: HYP 2/2 (2 × 8, 1 × 7)		TB lift: HYP 2/3 (3 × 7)
Week 5 Hypertrophy 3	TB lift: HYP 3/1 (4 × 8)		TB lift: HYP 3/2 (3 × 8, 1 × 7)		TB lift: HYP 3/3 (2 × 8, 2 × 7)
Week 6 Hypertrophy 4	TB lift: HYP 4/1 (1 × 8, 3 × 7)		TB lift: HYP 4/2 (4 × 7)		TB lift: HYP 4/3 (4 × 7)
Week 7 Active rest/ deload	TB lift (2 × 6)		TB lift (2 × 12)		TB lift (2 × 8)
Week 8 Base strength 1	Spd/Agil #1 TB lift: BS 1/1 (2 × 7, 1 × 6) Plyo #1	Spd/Agil #2 Conditioning #1 (8 wk)	TB lift: BS 1/2 (1 × 7, 2 × 6)	Spd/Agil #3 Conditioning #2 (8 wk)	Spd/Agil #4 TB lift: BS 1/3 (3 × 6) Plyo #2

(continued)

Table 12.1 *(continued)*

Week # Training phase	Monday	Tuesday	Wednesday	Thursday	Friday
Week 9 Base strength 2	Spd/Agil #5 TB lift: BS 2/1 (3 × 5) Plyo #3	Spd/Agil #6 Conditioning #3 (8 wk)	TB lift: BS 2/2 (3 × 5)	Spd/Agil #7 Conditioning #4 (8 wk)	Spd/Agil #8 TB lift: BS 2/3 (3 × 5) Plyo #4
Week 10 Base strength 3	Spd/Agil #9 TB lift: BS 3/1 (4 × 4) Plyo #5	Spd/Agil #10 Conditioning #5 (8 wk) or #1 (6 wk)	TB lift: BS 3/2 (4 × 4)	Spd/Agil #11 Conditioning #6 (8 wk) or #2 (6 wk)	Spd/Agil #12 TB lift: BS 3/3 (4 × 4) Plyo #6
Week 11 Base strength 4	Spd/Agil #13 TB lift: BS 4/1 (5 × 3) Plyo #7	Spd/Agil #14 Conditioning #7 (8 wk) or #3 (6 wk)	TB lift: BS 4/2 (5 × 3)	Spd/Agil #15 Conditioning #8 (8 wk) or #4 (6 wk)	Spd/Agil #16 TB lift: BS 4/3 (5 × 3) Plyo #8
Week 12 Active rest/ deload	Spd/Agil #17 TB lift (1 × 10, 1 × 8) Plyo #9	Spd/Agil #18 Conditioning #9 (8 wk), #5 (6 wk), or #1 (4 wk)	TB lift (2 × 6)	Spd/Agil #19 Conditioning #10 (8 wk), #6 (6 wk), or #2 (4 wk)	Spd/Agil #20 TB lift (2 × 6) Plyo #10
Week 13 Power and speed 1	Spd/Agil #21 TB lift: P&S 1/1 (3 × 5) Plyo #11	Spd/Agil #22 Conditioning #11 (8 wk), #7 (6 wk), or #3 (4 wk)	TB lift: P&S 1/2 (3 × 5)	Spd/Agil #23 Conditioning #12 (8 wk), #8 (6 wk), or #4 (4 wk)	Spd/Agil #24 TB lift: P&S 1/3 (3 × 5) Plyo #12
Week 14 Power and speed 2	Spd/Agil #25 TB lift: P&S 2/1 (4 × 4) Plyo #13	Spd/Agil #26 Conditioning #13 (8 wk), #9 (6 wk), or #5 (4 wk)	TB lift: P&S 2/2 (4 × 4)	Spd/Agil #27 Conditioning #14 (8 wk), #10 (6 wk), or #6 (4 wk)	Spd/Agil #28 TB lift: P&S 2/3 (4 × 4) Plyo #14
Week 15 Power and speed 3	Spd/Agil #29 TB lift: P&S 3/1 (4 × 3) Plyo #15	Spd/Agil #30 Conditioning #15 (8 wk), #11 (6 wk), or #7 (4 wk)	TB lift: P&S 3/2 (4 × 3)	Spd/Agil #31 Conditioning #16 (8 wk), #12 (6 wk), or #8 (4 wk)	Spd/Agil #32 TB lift: P&S 3/3 (4 × 3) Plyo #16
Week 16 Active rest/ deload *Week before practice begins*	TB lift (3 × 5)		TB lift (3 × 5)		TB lift (2 × 5, 1 × 3)

Week # Training phase	Monday	Tuesday	Wednesday	Thursday	Friday
How to read a block	Sample calendar block: TB lift: HYP 2/3 (3 × 7)	How to interpret: Lift type: phase, week #/ workout # (sets × repetitions)		Interpretation: Total-body lift: hypertrophy phase, week 2/workout 3 (3 sets × 7 repetitions)	

Note: This example shows a Monday/Wednesday/Friday schedule, but training days can also fall on Tuesday/Thursday/Saturday or Monday/Wednesday/Saturday.

The lifting workouts can be found in table 5.2. The plyometric workouts can be found in table 7.2. The speed and agility workouts can be found in table 8.3. The conditioning workouts can be found in tables 9.1 through 9.3.

BS = base strength; GPP = general physical preparation; HYP = hypertrophy; P&S = power and speed; Plyo = plyometrics; Spd/Agil = speed/agility; TB = total body.

The **8-week** conditioning program is for athletes needing more conditioning playing only 1 or 2 times per week. The **6-week** conditioning program is for athletes needing some extra conditioning. The **4-week** conditioning program is for better-conditioned athletes playing 3 or 4 times per week.

Training 4 Days per Week

Training 4 days per week can be advantageous for athletes who need to concentrate on increasing muscle size and strength. With this approach the athlete will gain more training exposures each week and accumulate more volume as well. Similar to the 3-day plan, you can design a 4-day lifting schedule in different ways. One way is to designate upper-body and lower-body days (see table 12.2 for an example of this type of program).

Another option is to split the workouts into movement groups. For example, day 1 and day 3 might focus on upper-body pull and lower-body push exercises, and day 2 and day 4 might swap the focus, with upper-body push and lower-body pull exercises. These 4 lift days can be accomplished on a Monday/Tuesday/Thursday/Friday schedule, allowing Wednesday to be a recovery day from lifting, or on a Tuesday/Wednesday/Friday/Saturday schedule, with Thursday as a recovery day, although athletes can also train 4 consecutive days if needed.

Table 12.2 Sample 16-Week Basketball Off-Season Training Calendar: 4 Workouts per Week, Upper-Body/Lower-Body Split Routine

Week # Training phase	Monday	Tuesday	Wednesday	Thursday	Friday
Week 1 General physical preparation 1	**LB lift: GPP 1/1** (2 × 15 circuit style)	**UB lift: GPP 1/2** (2 × 15 circuit style)		**LB lift: GPP 1/3** (1 × 15, 2 × 12 circuit style)	**UB lift: GPP 1/4** (1 × 15, 2 × 12 circuit style)
Week 2 General physical preparation 2	**LB lift: GPP 2/1** (3 × 12 circuit style)	**UB lift: GPP 2/2** (3 × 12 circuit style)		**LB lift: GPP 2/3** (3 × 12, 1 × 10 circuit style)	**UB lift: GPP 2/4** (3 × 12, 1 × 10 circuit style)
Week 3 Hypertrophy 1	**LB lift: HYP 1/1** (3 × 10)	**UB lift: HYP 1/2** (3 × 10)		**LB lift: HYP 1/3** (2 × 10, 1 × 8)	**UB lift: HYP 1/4** (2 × 10, 1 × 8)
Week 4 Hypertrophy 2	**LB lift: HYP 2/1** (3 × 8)	**UB lift: HYP 2/2** (3 × 8)		**LB lift: HYP 2/3** (2 × 8, 1 × 7)	**UB lift: HYP 2/4** (2 × 8, 1 × 7)
Week 5 Hypertrophy 3	**LB lift: HYP 3/1** (4 × 8)	**UB lift: HYP 3/2** (4 × 8)		**LB lift: HYP 3/3** (2 × 8, 2 × 7)	**UB lift: HYP 3/4** (2 × 8, 2 × 7)
Week 6 Hypertrophy 4	**LB lift: HYP 4/1** (1 × 8, 3 × 7)	**UB lift: HYP 4/2** (1 × 8, 3 × 7)		**LB lift: HYP 4/3** (4 × 7)	**UB lift: HYP 4/4** (4 × 7)
Week 7 Active rest/ deload	**LB lift** (2 × 12)	**UB lift** (2 × 12)		**LB lift** (2 × 12)	**UB lift** (2 × 12)
Week 8 Base strength 1	**Spd/Agil #1** **LB lift: BS 1/1** (1 × 7, 2 × 6) **Conditioning #1 (8 wk)**	**Spd/Agil #2** **UB lift: BS 1/2** (1 × 7, 2 × 6) **Plyo #1**		**Spd/Agil #3** **LB lift: BS 1/3** (3 × 6) **Conditioning #2 (8 wk)**	**Spd/Agil #4** **UB lift: BS 1/4** (3 × 6) **Plyo #2**
Week 9 Base strength 2	**Spd/Agil #5** **LB lift: BS 2/1** (3 × 5) **Conditioning #3 (8 wk)**	**Spd/Agil #6** **UB lift: BS 2/2** (3 × 5) **Plyo #3**		**Spd/Agil #7** **LB lift: BS 2/3** (3 × 5) **Conditioning #4 (8 wk)**	**Spd/Agil #8** **UB lift: BS 2/4** (3 × 5) **Plyo #4**
Week 10 Base strength 3	**Spd/Agil #9** **LB lift: BS 3/1** (4 × 4) **Conditioning #5 (8 wk)** or **#1 (6 wk)**	**Spd/Agil #10** **UB lift: BS 3/2** (4 × 4) **Plyo #5**		**Spd/Agil #11** **LB lift: BS 3/3** (4 × 4) **Conditioning #6 (8 wk)** or **#2 (6 wk)**	**Spd/Agil #12** **UB lift: BS 3/4** (4 × 4) **Plyo #6**

Week # Training phase	Monday	Tuesday	Wednesday	Thursday	Friday
Week 11 Base strength 4	Spd/Agil #13 LB lift: BS 4/1 (5 × 3) Conditioning #7 (8 wk) or #3 (6 wk)	Spd/Agil #14 UB lift: BS 4/2 (5 × 3) Plyo #7		Spd/Agil #15 LB lift: BS 4/3 (5 × 3) Conditioning #8 (8 wk) or #4 (6 wk)	Spd/Agil #16 UB lift: BS 4/4 (5 × 3) Plyo #8
Week 12 Active rest/ deload	Spd/Agil #17 LB lift (1 × 10, 1 × 8) Conditioning #9 (8 wk), #5 (6 wk), or #1 (4 wk)	Spd/Agil #18 UB lift (1 × 10, 1 × 8) Plyo #9		Spd/Agil #19 LB lift (1 × 10, 1 × 8) Conditioning #10 (8 wk), #6 (6 wk), or #2 (4 wk)	Spd/Agil #20 UB lift (1 × 10, 1 × 8) Plyo #10
Week 13 Power and speed 1	Spd/Agil #21 LB lift: P&S 1/1 (3 × 5) Conditioning #11 (8 wk), #7 (6 wk), or #3 (4 wk)	Spd/Agil #22 UB lift: P&S 1/2 (3 × 5) Plyo #11		Spd/Agil #23 LB lift: P&S 1/3 (3 × 5) Conditioning #12 (8 wk), #8 (6 wk), or #4 (4 wk)	Spd/Agil #24 UB lift: P&S 1/4 (3 × 5) Plyo #12
Week 14 Power and speed 2	Spd/Agil #25 LB lift: P&S 2/1 (4 × 4) Conditioning #13 (8 wk), #9 (6 wk), or #5 (4 wk)	Spd/Agil #26 UB lift: P&S 2/2 (4 × 4) Plyo #13		Spd/Agil #27 LB lift: P&S 2/3 (4 × 4) Conditioning #14 (8 wk), #10 (6 wk), or #6 (4 wk)	Spd/Agil #28 UB lift: P&S 2/4 (4 × 4) Plyo #14
Week 15 Power and speed 3	Spd/Agil #29 LB lift: P&S 3/1 (4 × 3) Conditioning #15 (8 wk), #11 (6 wk), or #7 (4 wk)	Spd/Agil #30 UB lift: P&S 3/2 (4 × 3) Plyo #15		Spd/Agil #31 LB lift: P&S 3/3 (4 × 3) Conditioning #16 (8 wk), #12 (6 wk), or #8 (4 wk)	Spd/Agil #32 UB lift: P&S 3/4 (4 × 3) Plyo #16

(continued)

Table 12.2 *(continued)*

Week # Training phase	Monday	Tuesday	Wednesday	Thursday	Friday
Week 16 Active rest/ deload *Week before practice begins*	LB lift (3 × 5)	UB lift (3 × 5)		LB lift (2 × 5, 1 × 3)	UB lift (2 × 5, 1 × 3)
How to read a block	Sample cal- endar block: LB lift: BS 1/3 (3 × 6)	How to interpret: Lift type: phase, week #/ workout # (sets × repetitions)		Interpretation: Lower-body lift: base strength phase, week 1/ workout 1 (3 sets × 6 repetitions)	

Note: The lifting workouts can be found in table 5.3. The plyometric workouts can be found in table 7.2. The speed and agility workouts can be found in table 8.3. The conditioning workouts can be found in tables 9.1 through 9.3.

BS = base strength; GPP = general physical preparation; HYP = hypertrophy; LB = lower body; P&S = power and speed; Plyo = plyometrics; Spd/Agil = speed/agility; UP = upper body.

The **8-week** conditioning program is for athletes needing more conditioning playing only 1 or 2 times per week. The **6-week** conditioning program is for athletes needing some extra conditioning. The **4-week** conditioning program is for better-conditioned athletes playing 3 or 4 times per week.

Along with your strength training, you'll also need to schedule other training throughout the week, including conditioning, speed and agility, and plyometrics. Tables 5.2 and 5.3 include the sample strength training workouts that are part of the training calendars in tables 12.1 and 12.2. You will find the plyometric workouts in table 7.2, the speed and agility workouts in table 8.3, and the conditioning workouts in tables 9.1 through 9.3. If you lift 3 or 4 days per week, supplement your week with four speed and agility workouts, two plyometric training sessions, and two conditioning workouts during the last 4 to 8 weeks of the 16-week program. It is more beneficial to add the increased load later in the off-season, approaching the preseason, as opposed to earlier on in the off-season, when you are just coming out of your competition season.

Whether you're training 3 or 4 days per week, we strongly recommend you *always leave 1 day per week for full recovery*. This means no lifting, no conditioning, no playing, no agilities, and no plyometrics—just let your body recover. Below are examples of how to strategically organize other training around strength training sessions to help optimize your training, limit burnout, and avoid overdoing it.

- A 3-day Monday/Wednesday/Friday or Tuesday/Thursday/Saturday total-body routine lifting week can be supplemented as follows:

  » Monday: Total-body lift day + speed/agility and plyometrics

  » Tuesday: Speed/agility and conditioning

   » Wednesday: Total-body lift day

   » Thursday: Speed/agility and conditioning

   » Friday: Total-body lift day + speed/agility and plyometrics

- A 4-day Monday/Tuesday/Thursday/Friday split routine lifting week can be supplemented with the same four speed and agility sessions, two plyometric sessions, and two conditioning sessions as follows:

   » Monday: Lower-body lift day + speed/agility and conditioning

   » Tuesday: Upper-body lift day + speed/agility and plyometrics

   » Wednesday: Off

   » Thursday: Lower-body lift day + speed/agility and conditioning

   » Friday: Upper-body lift day + speed/agility and plyometrics

- A 3-day Monday/Tuesday/Thursday or Friday split routine lifting week could be supplemented in the following two ways:

   » Monday: Lower-body lift day + speed/agility and conditioning

   » Tuesday: Upper-body lift day + speed/agility and plyometrics

   » Wednesday: Off

   » Thursday: Speed/agility and plyometrics

   » Friday: Total-body lift day + speed/agility and conditioning

or

   » Monday: Lower-body lift day + speed/agility and conditioning

   » Tuesday: Upper-body lift day + speed/agility and plyometrics

   » Wednesday: Off

   » Thursday: Total-body lift day + speed/agility and plyometrics

   » Friday: Speed/agility and conditioning

- A 4-day Monday/Tuesday/Thursday/Friday total-body movement split training lifting week could be supplemented as follows:

   » Monday: Upper-body push/lower-body pull lift day + speed/agility and plyometrics

   » Tuesday: Upper-body pull/lower-body push + speed/agility and conditioning

   » Wednesday: Off

   » Thursday: Upper-body push/lower-body pull + speed/agility and plyometrics

   » Friday: Upper-body pull/lower-body push + speed/agility and conditioning

PRESEASON TRAINING

The preseason spans from the first day of organized practice to the first game of the regular season. The primary focus during this season will be the actual basketball practices; however, it's even more important for the players to maintain their lifting schedule of 3 or 4 days per week so as not to lose all the muscle size and strength gains accomplished during the off-season. After all, these are needed to meet the specific physical demands of basketball competition. The athletes will also do more speed and functional movement training during their lifts as the regular season approaches.

During the preseason phase, on-court sport-specific conditioning is emphasized, with much of it done through team practices and scrimmages. Weight room workouts maintain the muscle size and strength gained during the off-season while increasing sport-specific speed and movement training as part of the lifting. The lifting schedule during the preseason can stay the same as that of the off-season but with some decreases in volume or even lifting one day less per week if athletes are playing or scrimmaging more than 3 times per week. In the sample preseason program in table 12.3, you won't see the supplemental speed/agility, plyometric, and conditioning training sessions that appeared in the off-season programs. Instead, basketball practices and preseason games will train speed/agility, plyometrics, and conditioning.

Table 12.3 Sample Preseason Program: 3 Days per Week

Day 1: Total body		
Exercise	**Page #**	**Sets × reps or time**
1A. Trap bar deadlift	98	1 × 3 2 × 3 3 × 3 4 × 3
1B. Cable dead bug	161	1 × 8 2 × 8 3 × 8
2A. Dumbbell or barbell bench press	116-117	1 × 5 2 × 5 3 × 5
2B. Pull-up	122	1 × 5 2 × 5 3 × 5
3A. Single-arm dumbbell lateral lunge	90	1 × 5 each side 2 × 5 each side 3 × 5 each side
3B. Half-kneeling single-arm overhead press	109	1 × 5 each arm 2 × 5 each arm 3 × 5 each arm
4A. Copenhagen side plank	178	1 × 20 sec each side 2 × 20 sec each side

Exercise	Page #	Sets × reps or time
4B. Single-leg wall sit	99	1 × 20 sec each leg 2 × 20 sec each leg
4C. Single-leg stability ball leg curl	84	1 × 8 each leg 2 × 8 each leg
Day 2: Total body		
1A. Goblet squat	96	1 × 5 2 × 5 3 × 5
1B. Resisted lateral drive	92	1 × 4 each side 2 × 4 each side 3 × 4 each side
2A. Dumbbell alternating incline bench press	118	1 × 8 2 × 6 3 × 6
2B. Medicine ball rotational chest pass	181	1 × 5 each side 2 × 5 each side 3 × 5 each side
3A. Barbell hip thrust	102	1 × 6 2 × 6 3 × 6
3B. Bird dog row	121	1 × 8 2 × 6 3 × 6
4A. Weighted push-up	123	1 × 8 2 × 8
4B. Cable face pull	127	1 × 20 2 × 20
4C. Split stance Paloff press	175	1 × 8 2 × 8
Day 3: Total body		
1A. Trap bar clean pull	75	1 × 3 2 × 3 3 × 3
1B. Ab wheel rollout	173	1 × 6 2 × 6 3 × 6
2A. Rear foot elevated split squat	99	1 × 4 each leg 2 × 4 each leg 3 × 4 each leg
2B. Split stance cable single-arm low row	112	1 × 8 each arm 2 × 8 each arm 3 × 6 each arm
3A. Supported single-leg Romanian deadlift	88	1 × 5 each leg 2 × 5 each leg 3 × 5 each leg

(continued)

Table 12.3 *(continued)*

Exercise	Page #	Sets × reps or time
Day 3: Total body *(continued)*		
3B. Single-leg wall sit	99	1 × 20 sec each leg 2 × 20 sec each leg 3 × 20 sec each leg
4A. Stork press	127	1 × 10 each side 2 × 10 each side
4B. Weighted crunch with leg lift	159	1 × 10 each leg 2 × 10 each leg
4C. Front foot elevated dumbbell ankle pops	106	1 × 15 sec each leg 2 × 15 sec each leg

IN-SEASON TRAINING

In-season training entails all the regular season games and postseason tournament or playoff games. During this season the primary aim of training is to maintain all the physical gains players made during the off-season and preseason while getting proper nutrition and recovery between contests. This is the season we train for! This is the season when players demonstrate the performance benefits of all their hard work!

Training volume and frequency are decreased to 2 or 3 times per week, and the number of sets are decreased as well from the off-season and preseason routines. (See table 12.4 for an in-season sample week with 2 training days per week.) When we decrease the weightlifting and increase the conditioning and basketball playing, it is more difficult to maintain muscle mass and strength. This makes the type, amount, and intensity of in-season training extremely important. Coaches and trainers must be mindful of the "balancing act" of this season's workouts: pushing the athlete to train hard while limiting delayed-onset muscle soreness and minimizing injury risk. The exercise selections here are more focused to help limit soreness. Proper technique, appropriate loading and progressions, and time for recovery can ensure successful in-season training.

Table 12.4   Sample In-Season Program: 2 Days per Week

Day 1: Total body		
Exercise	**Page #**	**Sets × reps or time**
1A. Trap bar clean pull	75	1 × 3 2 × 3 3 × 3
1B. Medicine ball rips	180	1 × 8 each side 2 × 8 each side
2A. Rear foot elevated split squat	99	1 × 5 each leg 2 × 5 each leg 3 × 5 each leg
2B. Single-arm cable chest press	110	1 × 5 each arm 2 × 5 each arm 3 × 5 each arm

Exercise	Page #	Sets × reps or time
3A. Single-arm dumbbell row	121	1 × 6 each arm 2 × 6 each arm 3 × 6 each arm
3B. Single-leg long leg bridge iso	103	1 × 6 (3 sec iso) 2 × 6 (3 sec iso)
4A. Front plank with alternating shoulder taps	172	1 × 20 2 × 20
4B. Side plank (top leg in air)	177	1 × 20 sec each side 2 × 20 sec each side
4C. Leg press Achilles iso	107	1 × 5 (5 sec iso) each leg 2 × 5 (5 sec iso) each leg 3 × 5 (5 sec iso) each leg
Day 2: Total body		
1A. Dumbbell single-leg Snatch to Box	80	1 × 4 each leg 2 × 4 each leg 3 × 4 each leg
1B. Barbell hip thrust	102	1 × 5 2 × 5 3 × 5
2A. Weighted push-up	123	1 × 6 2 × 6 3 × 6
2B. Single-arm dumbbell lateral lunge	90	1 × 5 each side 2 × 5 each side
3A. Pull-up	122	1 × 6 2 × 6
3B. Dumbbell split stance curl and press	126	1 × 12 2 × 12
4A. Vertical core	174	1 × 10 2 × 10
4B. Blackburn isometric series	130	1 × 6 (10 sec iso) 2 × 6 (10 sec iso)
4C. Leg press Achilles iso	107	1 × 5 (5 sec iso) each leg 2 × 5 (5 sec iso) each leg 3 × 5 (5 sec iso) each leg

In-season training will vary from maintenance mode only for players who participate infrequently or get minimal minutes in games and those returning from injury. Those athletes should increase lifting to 3 or 4 times per week, with the volume of work (number of sets) slightly decreased but at a higher intensity (that is, heavier weights).

In-season lifting days can also be strategized for optimal recovery and best efforts. For example, when possible, lifting 2 days prior to a game or competition allows a longer recovery time. For example, if a high school team is playing on Tuesday and Friday, then the best lifting days would be Sunday and Wednesday. However, teams might have days off or have other scheduling conflicts that mean the only day available to lift might be the day before the game. This is acceptable if 2 days before doesn't work. For maximal recovery purposes, 2 days is best, but more important than lifting on a certain day is actually completing the lifts for the week.

In-season lifting is also customized for the individual athlete. Most players will just need to maintain strength and size in-season, so each lift should be a total-body exposure if they are lifting only 2 times per week. However, some athletes may still want to increase size and strength in-season, and for these athletes we'd recommend they lift 3 or 4 times per week. These workouts could be three total-body sessions or a split routine of two lifts (upper body and lower body), allowing for more volume, with the third being a total-body lift.

POSTSEASON TRAINING

Following the in-season is the postseason, the final phase of the mesocycle, which could last 2 to 4 weeks, depending on when the season or play-offs ends. The postseason is when athletes recover from all the physical, emotional, psychological, and social stresses accumulated throughout the season. Usually, the longer the in-season, the longer the postseason. Players need a longer recovery time to prepare for the vigorous off-season that lies ahead. For many, the postseason is when the athletes might take vacations, spend more time with family and friends, and enjoy participating in other activities, sports, or hobbies. This is the time to unwind, relax, and enjoy parts of life that take a back seat during the long in-season!

PROGRAM EVALUATION

After a player completes the full year-long macrocycle, the postseason recovery period is a good opportunity to assess the training experience and results. A short self-evaluation can be very useful in identifying areas in which the program can be improved for the next macrocycle. Ask players to answer the following questions:

1. Did I accomplish all I set out to do with my training? Did I reach my training goals (muscle gain, fat loss, increased speed, agility, and power, improved conditioning and strength, etc.)?
2. What areas of my athleticism did I improve? What areas stayed the same? What areas might not have received the needed attention, and which might I have worked a bit less?
3. How did I feel throughout each of the mesocycles? Did I feel energized? Did I feel overtrained? Did I feel I left more in the tank that I could have used?
4. How did I manage my nutrition? Did I eat healthily or persist in bad food choices?
5. Did I truly follow the program? Did I rest too much or not enough?

Once players have taken the time to recover and answer the questions, it's important to prepare for the next step: training again in the upcoming off-season. The tools and resources in this book will prepare you for any modifications you need to make for the next year of training. For example, if you lifted 3 times per week and didn't see the strength or muscle gains you wanted, the off-season is the time to start the 4-times-per-week program. This way you can increase your workload to achieve your goals. The off-season is also a good time to focus on your nutritional needs. If your training permitted you to excel in speed, power and explosiveness, and agility, it might be best to perform the agility and plyometric workouts only once per week while increasing your lifting to 3 to 4 times per week. Maybe an increase in muscle size isn't your focus. Instead of 4 weeks of hypertrophy, you can do only 3 weeks and increase the strength phase to 5 weeks.

Coaches can find self-evaluation responses very useful in modifying and maximizing training in the forthcoming macrocycle. It is essential that players, team coaches, and strength and conditioning coaches work together to achieve the best customized training plan for every athlete on the team while also having a common set of conditioning activities that they perform.

The information and programs in this book will take you a long way toward ensuring success in achieving your training goals. With sufficient effort and proper adjustments, you should see great benefits to your body and your game.

References

Chapter 1

Fox, J.L., A.T. Scanlan, and R. Stanton. 2017. "A Review of Player Monitoring Approaches in Basketball: Current Trends and Future Directions." *Journal of Strength and Conditioning Research* 31 (7): 2021-2029.

Chapter 5

Baechle, T. R., and R.W. Earle. 2016. *Essentials of Strength Training and Conditioning, 4ᵗʰ Edition*. Champaign, IL: Human Kinetics.

French, D., and L.R. Ronda. 2022. *NSCA'S Essentials of Sport Science*. Champaign, IL: Human Kinetics.

Schmolinsky, G. 1993. *Track & Field: The East German Textbook*. New York: Sport Books.

Weakley, J., B. Mann, H. Banyard, S. McLaren, T. Scott, and A. Garcia-Ramos. 2021. "Velocity-Based Training: From Theory to Application." *Strength and Conditioning Journal* 43 (2): 31-49. https://doi.org/10.1519/SSC.0000000000000560.

Zatsiorsky, V.M. 1995. *Science and Practice of Strength Training*. Champaign: Human Kinetics.

Chapter 6

Akuthota, V., A. Ferreiro, T. Moore, and M. Fredericson. 2008. "Core Stability Exercise Principles." *Current Sports Medicine Reports* 7(1): 39-44.

Bliven, K.H., and B.E. Anderson. 2013. "Core Stability Training for Injury Prevention." *Sports Health* 5(6): 514-522.

Chapter 7

Cross, M.R., M. Brughelli, P. Samozino, S.R. Brown, and J.-B. Morin. 2017. "Optimal Loading for Maximizing Power During Sled-Resisted Sprinting." *International Journal of Sports Physiology and Performance* 12 (8): 1069-1077.

Harris, G.R., M.H. Stone, H.S. O'Bryant, C.M. Proulx, and R.L. Johnson. 2000. "Short-Term Performance Effects of High Power, High Force, or Combined Weight Training Methods." *Journal of Strength and Conditioning Research* 14 (1): 14-20.

Jensen, R.L., and W.P. Ebben. 2005. "Ground and Knee Joint Reaction Forces During Variation of Plyometric Exercises." In *Proceedings of the XXIII International Symposium of the Society of Biomechanics in Sports*, edited by K.E. Gianikellis, 222-225. Beijing.

Knuttgen, H.G., and W.J. Kraemer. 1987. "Terminology and Measurement in Exercise Performance." *Journal of Strength and Conditioning Research* 1 (1): 1-10.

Kraemer, W.J., J.F. Patton, S.E. Gordon, E.A. Harman, M.R. Deschenes, K. Reynolds, R.U. Newton, N.T. Triplett, and J.E. Dziados. 1995. "Compatibility of High-Intensity Strength and Endurance Training on Hormonal and Skeletal Muscle Adaptations." *Journal of Applied Physiology* 78:976-989.

Newton, R.U., W.J. Kraemer, and K. Hakkinen. 1999. "Effects of Ballistic Training on Preseason Preparation of Elite Volleyball Players." *Medicine & Science in Sports & Exercise* 31(2): 323-330.

Turner, A.P., C.N. Unholz, N. Potts, and A. Coleman. 2012. "Peak Power, Force, and Velocity During Jump Squats in Professional Rugby Players." *Journal of Strength and Conditioning Research* 26 (6): 1594-1600.

Chapter 10

Sánchez-Ureña, B., K. Barrantes-Brais, P. Ureña-Bonilla, J. Calleja-González, and S. Ostojic. 2015. "Effect of Water Immersion on Recovery From Fatigue: A Meta-Analysis." *European Journal of Human Movement* 34: 1-14.

Chycki, J., T. Zając, A. Maszczyk, and A. Kurylas. 2017. "The Effect of Mineral-Based Alkaline Water on Hydration Status and the Metabolic Response to Short-Term Anaerobic Exercise." *Biology of Sport* 34 (3): 255.

Fullagar, H.H.K., S. Skorski, R. Duffield, D. Hammes, A.J. Coutts, and T. Meyer. 2015. "Sleep and Athletic Performance: The Effects of Sleep Loss on Exercise Performance, and Physiological and Cognitive Responses to Exercise." *Sports Medicine* 45:161-186.

Halson, S.L. 2014. "Sleep in Elite Athletes and Nutritional Interventions to Enhance Sleep." *Sports Medicine* 44 (1): 13-23.

Harris, P.R., D.A. Keen, E. Constantopoulos, S.N. Weninger, E. Hines, M.P. Koppinger, Z.I. Khalpey, and J.P. Konhilas. 2019. "Fluid Type Influences Acute Hydration and Muscle Performance Recovery in Human Subjects." *Journal of the International Society of Sports Nutrition* 16 (1): 1-12.

Hemmings, B., M. Smith, J. Graydon, and R. Dyson. 2000. "Effects of Massage on Physiological Restoration, Perceived Recovery, and Repeated Sports Performance." *British Journal of Sports Medicine* 34 (2): 109-114.

Kargarfard, M., E.T. Lam, A. Shariat, I. Shaw, B.S. Shaw, and S.B.M. Tamrin. 2016. "Efficacy of Massage on Muscle Soreness, Perceived Recovery, Physiological Restoration, and Physical Performance in Male Bodybuilders." *Journal of Sports Sciences* 34 (10): 959-965.

Machado, A.F., P.H. Ferreira, J.K. Micheletti, et al. 2016. "Can Water Temperature and Immersion Time Influence the Effect of Cold Water Immersion on Muscle Soreness? A Systematic Review and Meta-Analysis." *Sports Medicine* 46: 503-514.

Mah, C.D., K.E. Mah, E.J. Kezirian, and W.C. Dement. 2011. "The Effects of Sleep Extension on the Athletic Performance of Collegiate Basketball Players." *Sleep* 34 (7): 943-950.

Pearcey, G.E., D.J. Bradbury-Squires, J.E. Kawamoto, E.J. Drinkwater, D.G. Behm, and D.C. Button. 2015. "Foam Rolling for Delayed-Onset Muscle Soreness and Recovery of Dynamic Performance Measures." *Journal of Athletic Training* 50 (1): 5-13.

Pournot, H., F. Bieuzen, J. Louis, R. Mounier, J.-R. Fillard, E. Barbiche, and C. Hausswirth. 2011. "Time-Course of Changes in Inflammatory Response After Whole-Body Cryotherapy Multi Exposures Following Severe Exercise." *PloS One* 6 (7): e22748.

Vieira, A., M. Bottaro, J.B. Ferreira-Junior, C. Vieira, V.A. Cleto, E.L. Cadore, H.G. Simões, J. Do Carmo, and L.E. Brown. 2015. "Does Whole-Body Cryotherapy Improve Vertical Jump Recovery Following a High-Intensity Exercise Bout?" *Open Access Journal of Sports Medicine* 6:49-54.

Williamson, A.M., and A. Feyer. 2000. "Moderate Sleep Deprivation Produces Impairments in Cognitive and Motor Performance Equivalent to Legally Prescribed Levels of Alcohol Intoxication." *Occupational and Environmental Medicine* 57: 649-655.

Index

About the NBSCA

The **National Basketball Strength & Conditioning Association (NBSCA)** was formed in 2008 as a successor to the National Basketball Conditioning Coaches Association (NBCCA). Relaunched as a non-profit organization, the NBSCA seeks to continue the vision of the original NBCCA of continuing to grow the professional opportunities and enhance the knowledge, practices, and relationships for all strength and conditioning coaches within the NBA. The NBSCA supports its members by providing them the tools necessary to grow professionally and develop their skill set so that they may better serve the NBA, its organizations, and its players as leaders in the strength and conditioning industry.

About the Editor

Bill Foran, MS, CSCS, RSCC*E, has been with the Miami Heat since the organization was founded in 1988. In his first 29 seasons, Bill was the team's Head Strength & Conditioning Coach. After that he served as a Strength & Conditioning Consultant for the Heat as his son Eric assumed his previous role with the club. Bill was voted NBA Strength & Conditioning Coach of the Year in 2009. In 2014 he was inducted into the USA Strength & Conditioning Hall of Fame. In 2021 Bill was the first recipient of the Lifetime Achievement Award from the NBSCA and the award is named in his honor.

About the Contributors

Willie Cruz, MS, CSCS, RSCC, FAFS, is director of athletic performance for the Houston Rockets, a position he has held since 2020. Before joining the Rockets, Cruz was a strength and conditioning coach with the Oklahoma City Thunder, Fordham University, and his alma mater, Eastern Kentucky University.

Dwight Daub, MS, CSCS, RSCC*E, was head strength and conditioning coach for the Seattle Supersonics (which became the Oklahoma City Thunder) for 18 seasons. Before entering the league in 1997, he directed the strength program at the University of Utah for seven years and also worked at the University of Illinois and University of Arizona. Daub was voted NBA Strength & Conditioning Coach of the Year in 2009.

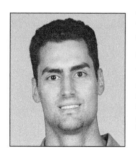

Felipe Eichenberger, MS, CSCS, RSCC*D, is director of performance and head strength and conditioning coach for the Denver Nuggets, having been promoted to that role starting with the 2016-2017 season after previously serving as the club's assistant strength and conditioning coach. Eichenberger was voted NBA Strength & Conditioning Coach of the Year in 2020.

Eric Foran, MS, CSCS, RSCC, has been part of the Miami Heat strength and conditioning staff since 2012. He became the head strength and conditioning coach in 2017. Foran was voted the NBA Strength & Conditioning Coach of the Year in 2024.

Todd Forcier, BS, LMT, CSCS, RSCC*E, was with the Portland Trail Blazers for 13 years, the last 11 of which he served as the team's head strength and conditioning coach. Forcier is currently head strength and conditioning coach at the University of Memphis and previously served in the same role at the University of Kentucky, Syracuse University, and the University of Dayton.

Hunter Glascock, BS, CSCS, RSCC, is assistant strength and conditioning coach for the Miami Heat. Glascock previously served as the strength and conditioning specialist for the Sioux Falls Skyforce.

Jeremy Holsopple, BS, CSCS, RSCC*D, CPSS, was the athletic performance director for the Dallas Mavericks for 11 seasons. Before joining the Mavericks, Holsopple worked as a performance-enhancing coach in the NFL, in MLS, and at the collegiate level. He was voted NBA Strength & Conditioning Coach of the Year in 2021.

Kevin Hyde, MS, CSCS, RSCC, has been an athletic performance coach for the Oklahoma City Thunder since 2016. He previously held strength and conditioning coach roles at Southwestern Oklahoma State University and the Memphis Redbirds, the Triple-A affiliate of the St. Louis Cardinals.

Michael Irr, DPT, CSCS, RSCC*D, was a head strength and conditioning coach in the NBA for 11 seasons with the Atlanta Hawks, Golden State Warriors, and Charlotte Bobcats after entering the league as assistant strength and conditioning coach for the Chicago Bulls.

Jonathan Lee, MS, CSCS, RSCC*D, is head strength and conditioning coach for the Toronto Raptors and has been with club since 2009. Lee's rise from ballboy with the Vancouver Grizzlies in 1999 to NBA Strength & Conditioning Coach of the Year in 2017 is one of the league's remarkable success stories.

Andrew Paul, DPT, CSCS, RSCC*D, is director of athletic performance and rehabilitation for the Oklahoma City Thunder. He previously worked with Exos and as assistant director of strength and conditioning at the University of Missouri. Paul was named NBA Strength & Conditioning Coach of the Year in 2023.

Daniel Shapiro, MS, CSCS, RSCC*E, is head performance coach and assistant director of performance for the Los Angeles Clippers. His previous NBA positions included eight seasons as head strength and conditioning coach with the Sacramento Kings and seven seasons as assistant strength and conditioning coach with the Seattle Supersonics. He also directed basketball conditioning at the University of Washington and University of Dayton earlier in his career. Shapiro was voted NBA Strength and Conditioning Coach of the Year in 2010 and 2022.

Shawn Windle, BS, ATC, CSCS, RSCC*E, was director of sport performance and assistant athletic trainer for the Indiana Pacers for 18 seasons after previously serving as the strength and conditioning coach at Rutgers University and the University of Connecticut. Windle was voted NBA Strength & Conditioning Coach of the Year in 2012.